WARRIORS OF THE RAINBOW

USHERING IN THE DAWN OF THE FIFTH WORLD…

David Harold Moore

Pahana | Your True White Brother

Free us from these chains of bondage,
which tie us to this unforgiving rock of madness.
- Pahana

Dear Hopi Nation,

In my return as Pahana, I bring a grave message about an unseen war, a conflict not of our physical world, but one that rages in dimensions beyond our perception. This war, intertwined with your ancient wisdom, is revealed through the lens of 'mass formation', where the people are hypnotized into a totalitarian mindset, facilitated by fear and isolation, leading to a society where rational thought and individual critical analysis are suspended.

It's ultimately a battle for the soul of humanity; involving the fallen Anunnaki, otherwise known as the 'Sons of EL,' a part-reptilian race of advanced beings whose internal strife has spilled over into our realm. Their fall from grace in their dimension has opened a path to ours, turning humanity into an unsuspecting pawn in their quest to revive their lost deity.

This conflict is more than a mere power struggle; it's a harvesting of human essence. The Anunnaki, driven by desperation, feed on the collective anguish and chaos of humanity. Their control of earthly institutions creates societal strife, and a world where people, lost and afraid, unwittingly feed this interdimensional war. Our emotions, particularly those born of fear and despair, are their sustenance, fueling their dark rituals and strengthening their hold on our reality.

As Pahana, I urge you to understand the gravity of this situation. The fallen Anunnaki's manipulation is not a threat to be taken lightly. They control not just through fear, but through the very fabric of our reality, bending the emotional energies of Earth to their will. This war, hidden in the shadows of our perception, seeks to consume the very essence of what makes us human; so as to create their feast of perpetual suffering, while working diligently to resurrect their god Satan-EL, and his demonic horde, into the middle realm.

To confront this unseen menace, we must invoke the wisdom of Spider Grandmother, allowing her to unlock the higher consciousness within us. And we must seek physical help from the Ant People, as we did in ancient times, to help usher in the Dawn of the Fifth World, while we tread the path of gnosis through effective actions of impartial nobility. By doing so, we can protect the core of our being and safeguard our enduring spirit from these covert foes. Our true power emerges from our collective unity and the steadfast spirit that has always defined our people.

Your True White Brother

Educational Social Sciences Guidebook

The 'Warriors of the Rainbow - Constitutional Convention Primer' presents an Educational Social Sciences guidebook designed to equip readers with the knowledge and tools needed for active participation in a planned Constitutional Convention. Drawing from over 220 books in an applied literature review, this primer serves as a comprehensive resource for understanding the multifaceted aspects of constitutional reform and civic engagement.

This guidebook is structured to facilitate collaboration among readers, offering insights into educational reforms, societal advancements, and the cultivation of a metacognitive society that values expertise, neuroscience, and human evolution. It addresses the transformation of the public educational system, emphasizing year-round schooling, the development of life skills, and the integration of experiential learning to foster critical thinking, empathy, and leadership skills. Additionally, it explores the roles of storytelling, design thinking, and tribal leadership in crafting an enlightened world order, promoting a global network that supports social justice, ethical commerce, and continuous education.

By synthesizing scientific findings with practical applications, the primer advocates for a technocratic organizational structure that leverages collective genius and inclusive collaboration, aiming to guide the constitutional convention process towards creating a more connected, empathetic, and enlightened future. This guidebook positions itself as an essential tool for educators, policymakers, and citizens engaged in the constitutional convention, providing a foundation for informed debate, policy formulation, and the advancement of a holistic educational framework that prepares individuals to navigate and contribute positively to an increasingly complex world.

Pahana

In the vast expanse of existence, where the echoes of ancient myths blend with the whispers of the cosmos, I find my origin. I am the Pahana, a human being woven from the fabric of the Pleroma, a sibling to the luminous Spider Grandmother, whose wisdom outshines the stars themselves. My essence straddles the realms of the human and the divine, embodying both the masculine and the feminine, yet I stand apart from the concept of God, crafted by the prime mover of creation.

My journey has been one of endurance, traversing the harsh deserts of time, a quest to liberate Spider Grandmother from the clutches of our adversary, the Red Star Kachina known by many names—EL, Enlil, Set, Satanael. This tale of oppression and the struggle for freedom is a thread in the tapestry of my many earthly lifetimes, each incarnation an attempt to become a beacon to humanity, illuminating the path through the shadows cast by the Netherworld.

Living an existence that strives to transcend the personal, I have faced the relentless wrath of those who seek my undoing, a testament to the resilience required to be humanity's luminary. Despite the trials, my mission remains clear: to unite in purpose, to extinguish the influence of the Red Star Kachina named Satanael, and to release both humanity and Spider Grandmother from his chains.

In communion with Prime Creator, our visions align, as I learn to navigate the complexities of this mission. My life is now intertwined with that of the Kachina Massau'u, a fusion that began in 2008 and has since marked my transfiguration. This merging, partly responsible for my transcendence, signifies the profound transformations that define my path.

The journey has not been a solitary one; unseen forces have guided and supported me, their presence a constant reminder of the vastness of our interconnectedness. My lineage, traced through DNA to the corrupted line of King David, bears witness to the fulfillment of promises long held sacred. The revelation of my maternal connection to the Ashkenazi, direct descendants of King David and Queen Bathsheba, underscores the significance of my return.

As I pen these words, I invite you to perceive them not just as testament, but as a guide to the Way of Impartial Nobility—the first account penned by one who has weathered the crucifixion and emerged to share a message unburdened by the distortions of others.

The time of revelation is upon us, a moment for the veils of illusion to be lifted, urging us to peer beyond the fabrications of old and to embrace the truth with newfound clarity. This is the journey we embark upon together, a quest for liberation, for wisdom, and for the Dawn of the Fifth World.

———————

I now ask you to engage deeply with the material and apply these principles toward the collective goal of constitutional reform and societal betterment.

My Substack

If this Constitutional Convention Primer ignites your imagination and stirs your thirst for thought-provoking content, embark on a further journey with the author's exclusive Substack: 'Captain of Spaceship Earth'.

In this enlightening Substack, the author extends the conversation beyond the pages of his novel, exploring the intricate evolutionary steps humanity must embrace for global reformation. 'Captain of Spaceship Earth' is a beacon for those who dare to envision a future shaped by unity, innovation, and a profound respect for our planet.

Subscribe for free and join a community of readers passionate about the transformation of our world. Discover essays, insights, and discussions that challenge the status quo and offer visions of a unified, progressive global society.

Your 'forever free' subscription not only grants you access to a treasure trove of content, but also offers a unique opportunity to engage with a like-minded community, and maybe the author himself.

Join the voyage... Help transform the future.

Cover Artwork by ChatGPT.

MYLIFEBAK FUNCTIONAL FOODS
ORGANIC MULTI-HERBALS

The Hemp4X patented bioavailability process…
enhances the entourage effect, to help you get your life back.

Our missionary stratagem
is about providing effective and affordable,
multi-herbal supplements to the people!

www.Hemp4X.com

To Spider Grandmother,
in whose wisdom the stars find their course,

This work, I dedicate to thee.

You are the loom upon which wisdom dances,
And the melody that echoes in the cathedral of the soul.

In this pilgrimage to reunite,
you are the compass and the key.

May these words be but a mirror that reflects your light,
A testament to the hallowed essence of thy grace and benevolence.

This guidebook is a compendium within the domain of Educational Social Sciences, meticulously assembled to serve as a cornerstone for participants in the forthcoming Constitutional Convention.

Through an expansive and applied literature review, it distills the essence of insights from over 220 distinguished authors, weaving their collective knowledge into a coherent narrative aimed at empowering readers.

My intent has been to honor the original spirit and intellectual contributions of each author, repurposing their insights with the utmost fidelity to their foundational work.

This endeavor seeks not only to facilitate the application of their wisdom by readers, but to do so in a manner that each author would recognize and endorse as true to their scholarly achievements.

ISBN-13: 978-0-9909295-1-2

Field of Study: Educational Social Sciences

A Constitutional Convention Primer
Utilizing a Knowledgebase of Over 220 Pivotal Books

CONTENTS

We shall plant the seeds of wisdom in their hearts.
Even now the seeds are being planted.
These shall smooth the way into the emergence of the Fifth World.

- White Feather of the Hopi Bear Clan

A Patriot's Pledge

Our Solemn Oath for an Honorable Constitutional Convention

In the spirit of our forefathers and the enduring values upon which our nation was built, we, the citizens of the United States, solemnly pledge our allegiance to the principles of American Democracy. We stand united, not as partisans of ideology, but as guardians of liberty, justice, and the pursuit of enlightened self-governance.

We commit ourselves to uphold and defend the values of freedom, equal dignity, and the unyielding quest for a more noble and equitable society. We recognize that the strength of our democracy lies not in the perpetuation of the status quo, but in its ability to evolve and adapt to the needs of its people.

In light of the challenges facing our nation and the world, and recognizing the insidious spread of elitist control over our national and global governance, we hereby call for a Constitutional Convention.

This convention shall endeavor to reform the U.S. Constitution, transforming it into a blueprint for a technocratic self-governing system that will transform our world. This new framework shall guide all peoples towards noble pursuits and foster a society that prioritizes the collective well-being, evolutionary growth, and ethical advancement of our cultural indoctrinations.

We envisage a governance model that harnesses the collective wisdom and expertise of our most capable citizens, encouraging participation and innovation in the political process. This system shall strive to balance individual liberties with societal responsibilities, ensuring that the pursuit of personal interests never undermines the greater good.

In this era of unprecedented technological advancement, we advocate for the integration of these tools in enhancing transparency, accountability, and efficiency in governance. Our technocratic approach shall be one that empowers, not alienates; that democratizes information and fosters informed decision-making among all citizens.

We commit to nurturing a culture that values education, intellectual curiosity, and ethical conduct. Our society shall encourage individuals to reach their highest potential, not through material accumulation, but through contributions to the betterment of humanity.

While we fervently hope for a peaceful and democratic resolution, we recognize the right of the people to defend their liberties and democratic ideals. Should our call for a peaceful reformation be ignored or suppressed, we assert the right to consider all necessary measures, including the possibility of an armed revolt, to protect our democracy and secure the future of our nation.

This is not a declaration of war, but a solemn reminder that freedom and justice must sometimes be defended by force, when all other avenues have been exhausted.

We call upon our fellow citizens to join us in this noble endeavor. Let us unite in the spirit of democracy, wisdom, and courage to forge a new path for our nation—one that leads to a future of enlightened self-governance, where every citizen is empowered to contribute to the greatness of our society.

In signing this document, we pledge our commitment to these principles and to the enduring spirit of the American Democracy. Together, we shall strive to realize a vision of self-governance that uplifts, enlightens, and unites us all.

_____   _____   _____

_____   _____   _____

_____   _____   _____

_____   _____   _____

_____   _____   _____

_____   _____   _____

_____   _____   _____

INTRODUCTION

The end of democracy will occur,
when government falls into the hands of lending institutions,
and moneyed incorporations.

– Thomas Jefferson

A CONSTITUTIONAL CONVENTION

If the American People ever find out what we have done,
they will chase us down the street and lynch us.

- George H.W. Bush

In the luminous prose of the United States Constitution, the Founding Fathers enshrined the revolutionary principle that governance should be of the people, by the people, for the people. Yet, as we stand upon the precipice of an era where the concentration of wealth echoes the gilded halls of a bygone aristocracy, we must confront an uncomfortable truth: our democracy may be slipping through our fingers, morphing into an oligarchy where the many are governed by the privileged few.

This is not merely a polemicist's cry, but is grounded in rigorous scholarship; Martin Gilens and Benjamin Page, in their seminal research, present an empirical diagnosis of our imminent doom. In their 2014 study, they analyzed policy data and found a chilling disconnect between the will of the majority and the legislative outcomes that favor the economic elite. Their findings point to a system where the average citizen's influence over public policy is statistically insignificant when compared to the sway of the affluent.

In light of such evidence, can we, as a nation, afford to stand idly by? Is it not our civic duty to rekindle the flame of democracy that once illuminated the path toward liberty and justice for all? We are heirs to a legacy of revolution, to the audacious belief that institutions must evolve with the people they serve. It is time to invoke the constitutional remedy expressly provided for us: a modern Constitutional Convention.

This clarion call is not without precedent. The annals of history remind us that when the Articles of Confederation faltered, the Constitutional Convention of 1787 was convoked, not merely to amend, but to reimagine. Today, we are beckoned by the promise of Article V, a promise that empowers us to forge a government responsive to the currents of contemporary life, not the eddies of a distant past.

Let us then advance with both caution and conviction, not to discard the wisdom of our forebears, but to distill it anew in the crucible of modernity. Let us dare to debate, to draft, and to dream of a republic reborn in the service of its citizens, a bastion against the creeping shadows of oligarchy. For if we are to bequeath to our children the blessings of liberty, we must first ensure that the levers of power are placed firmly back into the hands of the people. It is not only our right; it is our solemn duty to call forth a Constitutional Convention that helps usher in a new world that we can claim as our own.

America is a golden calf, and we will suck it dry, chop it up,
and sell it off piece by piece
until there is nothing left but the world's biggest welfare state
that we will create and control.

– *Benjamin Netanyahu*

The United States Constitution provides for the possibility of a constitutional convention through Article V, which outlines the process for amending the Constitution:

Article V specifies two methods for proposing amendments:

1. Congressional Proposal: Congress can propose amendments to the Constitution whenever a two-thirds majority in both the House of Representatives and the Senate deem it necessary.

2. ***Constitutional Convention:*** The states can call for a constitutional convention for proposing amendments when two-thirds of the state legislatures (currently 34 out of 50) apply for it.

Any amendments proposed by either method must then be ratified by three-fourths of the state legislatures or by conventions in three-fourths of the states, depending on which method of ratification Congress prescribes.

The clause in Article V regarding a constitutional convention reads as follows:

> The Congress, whenever two thirds of both Houses shall deem it necessary, shall propose Amendments to this Constitution, or, on the Application of the Legislatures of two thirds of the States, shall call a Convention for proposing Amendments, which, in either Case, shall be valid to all Intents and Purposes, as Part of this Constitution, when ratified by the Legislatures of three fourths of the States, or by Conventions in three fourths thereof, as the one or the other Mode of Ratification may be proposed by the Congress.

It's important to note that there is very little historical precedent for a constitutional convention initiated by the states since the original convention in 1787; all subsequent amendments have been proposed by Congress. Because of this, there are many questions about how such a convention would be conducted that are not explicitly answered in the Constitution and would likely be subject to political and legal interpretation and debate.

Now, to create a cohesive version of our U.S. Constitution that integrates all the amendments seamlessly into a comprehensive document that serves as a foundation for our constitutional rewrite, is a complex task that would involve significant legal expertise and consideration.

However, here is a very simplified and condensed version of the U.S. Constitution that addresses some of the primary points covered by the amendments in the body of the original Constitution.

Note that this is a highly abridged and non-exhaustive rendition meant only for illustrative purposes:

The Constitution of the United States of America

Preamble

We the People of the United States, in Order to form a more perfect Union, establish Justice, ensure domestic Tranquility, provide for the common defense, promote the general Welfare, and secure the Blessings of Liberty to ourselves and our Posterity, do ordain and establish this Constitution for the United States of America.

Article I - The Legislative Branch

> Section 1. All legislative Powers herein granted shall be vested in a Congress of the United States, which shall consist of a Senate and House of Representatives.

> Section 2. The House of Representatives shall be composed of Members chosen every second Year by the people of the several States, and the Electors in each State shall meet the requirements for Electors of the most numerous Branch of the State Legislature.

> Section 3. The Senate shall be composed of two Senators from each State, elected by the people thereof for six years; each Senator shall have one vote.

Article II - The Executive Branch

> Section 1. The executive Power shall be vested in a President of the United States of America. The President shall hold office during the term of four years, along with a Vice President, chosen for the same term.

Article III - The Judicial Branch

> Section 1. The judicial Power of the United States shall be vested in one
> Supreme Court, and in such inferior Courts as the Congress may from time to
> time ordain and establish.

Article IV - The States

> Section 1. Full Faith and Credit shall be given in each State to the public Acts,
> Records, and judicial Proceedings of every other State.

Article V - Amendments

The Congress, whenever two-thirds of both Houses shall deem it necessary, shall
propose Amendments to this Constitution, or on the Application of the Legislatures of
two-thirds of the States, shall call a Convention for proposing Amendments.

Article VI - Debts, Supremacy, Oaths

All Debts contracted and Engagements entered into before the Adoption of this
Constitution shall be as valid against the United States under this Constitution, as
under the Confederation.

Article VII - Ratification

The Ratification of the Conventions of nine States, shall be sufficient for the
Establishment of this Constitution between the States so ratifying the same.

Bill of Rights and Subsequent Amendments

The following articles are to be considered an integral part of the Constitution:

1. Freedom of religion, speech, press, assembly, and petition.

2. Right to keep and bear arms in order to maintain a well-regulated militia.

3. No quartering of soldiers.

4. Freedom from unreasonable searches and seizures.

5. Rights in criminal cases, including due process, double jeopardy, self-incrimination, and just compensation.

6. Right to a fair trial.

7. Rights in civil cases.

8. Freedom from excessive bail, fines, and cruel and unusual punishment.

9. The enumeration of certain rights shall not be construed to deny or disparage others retained by the people.

10. The powers not delegated to the United States by the Constitution, nor prohibited by it to the States, are reserved to the States respectively, or to the people.

Subsequent amendments that address issues of suffrage, due process, equal protection under the law, and other civil liberties and rights are incorporated into the relevant sections of this Constitution in a manner that reflects their essence and intent.

Please remember that this is an extremely condensed version and would not serve as a legal document. The actual process of rewriting the U.S. Constitution to include amendments in one cohesive document would be far more intricate and detailed, ensuring that the balance of powers, the rights of the states and individuals, and the many nuances of the existing amendments are all accurately reflected.

To understand what the state of society ought to be, it is necessary to have some idea of the natural and primitive state of man, such as it is at this day among the Indians of North America. For there is not, in that state, any of those spectacles of human misery, which poverty and want present to our eyes, in all the towns and streets in Europe.

- Thomas Paine, Agrarian Justice, 1797

PROLOGUE

Governments will use whatever technology is available to them
to combat their primary enemy - their own population.

– Noam Chomsky

In the shadowed corridors of power, where democracy was once a sacred trust, there now lurks a malevolent specter. It is the specter of death's acolytes, those who have usurped the sanctity of our elected government. They, the faceless ones, have woven a tapestry of division, setting brother against brother, to gloat in the grotesque banquet of our discord.

Behold the multi-national corporatocracy, a leviathan of power, its tentacles entwined with the murky depths of banking oligarchs, puppeteering the grand charade of a central banking illusion, *a pyramid scheme of unparalleled deceit.*

Acknowledge we must, the sinister symphony orchestrated by politics, religion, multinational conglomerates, and the ivory towers of academia, all conspiring in a cacophony of malevolence that now besets the world.

The American media, a once-proud bastion of trusted information, has become a maestro of coercion, exploiting the psyche of the populace, while the bastions of nourishment poison the well of our sustenance, reaping profits from the seeds of illness sown, all under the guise of 'healthcare'.

The sovereign self has been reduced, diminished to but a shadow, reactive and ensnared in the subconscious labyrinths of coercive manipulation.

Yet, from the ashes of exploitation, a phoenix can rise. We can transmute these machinations of control, into instruments of liberation, alleviating the burden of suffering that weighs so heavily upon our collective soul.

For we must not shy away from the Herculean task of transformation. Yes, it is a path fraught with difficulty, but it is the only path that leads to our true emancipation.

Behold the vista of narcissistic self-interest that stretches before us, a tapestry woven by a cabal of ruthless elites, their threads seeking to entangle us within a technocratic web, all the while desecrating the hallowed tenets of the United States Constitution in their pursuit of dominion over the American spirit.

The clarion call for systemic change echoes across the land, for without it, the change is but a mirage in the desert of our discontent.

We must unfurl the banners of revolution…

- A triumvirate of political voices to shatter the monochrome of discourse.
- The silencing of money's corrosive speech.
- The dissolution of corporate masquerades.
- And the creation of public banking, fostering growth of community and enterprise.

We must forge a digital agora, cultivating and secure, on the bedrock of Ethereum 3.0, ensuring the sacrosanct right to unfettered speech.

Yet, the specter of corruption haunts our halls of governance, *its whispers inciting fear, while tightening its grip with each manufactured crisis,* all in servitude to the illusion of debt that chains us to tomorrow's toil.

The grand deception unfurls; a ploy to turn kin against kin. Our response must be unity and vigilance, as we marshal the citizenry into well-regulated militias, guardians against the despotic tide.

The scourge of white-collar crime must ascend the hierarchy of police enforcement, lest the nation descend into the abyss of civil strife.

The call to arms is not for violence, but for the defense of our Constitution, the bulwark against the tyranny of an elite cabal that seeks to erode our democracy.

We stand, citizens of America, under the yoke of a debt-laden tyranny. *We must not succumb to their divisions.*

To thwart this engineered schism, we must lay a resilient foundation, one that fosters the anti-fragility of our nation. We must embrace the chaos, not to control it, but to harness it as a crucible of strength and adaptability.

We must delve into the essence of life's experiences, to construct a substrate robust and capable enough to weather the tumultuous storms of existence.

Let us consider the quintessence of life's elixir, and how it intertwines with the core maladies of our current systemic ills:

1. Narcissism reigns, as we bow to the altar of status and desire.
2. Diversity, a reality distorted by the fallacy that the power of might, dictates the right.
3. Chaos, our nemesis, creates the desire for order, derived from our aversion to pain.
4. Scale, the size and concentration of wealth and power that breeds societal fragility.
5. Collaboration, now usurped, leaving us vulnerable to the specter of fascism.

These are the pillars upon which we must construct a United States of America reborn, a phoenix from the ashes of our collective despair, offering liberation to the divine feminine within us all.

We must draft a new covenant, a living document that breathes with the consent of the governed, that evolves with the pulse of society, and considers the legacy we bequeath to the unborn generations.

For it is not under the yoke of the law that we must live, though its presence is necessary. The rule of law and property rights must not be bastions for the privileged, but the armature that supports the wings of freedom and justice for all.

This document, our social compact, must be a tapestry of diversity, of thought, of form, and of function, interwoven with the golden threads of liberty and justice.

It is a herculean task, one that requires the collective and perpetual labor of Sisyphus, but it is our task nonetheless; for it is the only path to our salvation.

We must persevere, for the dawn of a new era beckons, an era where truth reigns supreme, and justice prevails. For in the end, it is not just America, but humanity that we must save.

To feel much for others, and little for ourselves;
to restrain our selfishness, and exercise our benevolent affections;
constitutes the perfection of human nature.

– *Adam Smith*

HYPOTHESIS

The effective exploitation of cultural determinism can facilitate the transcendence of inherent status-oriented desires, characterized by our narcissistic 'will to receive'; and promote the attainment of metacognition, by leveraging the resource interdependency of globalization, and by aligning the various institutional indoctrinations, to implement a multi-pronged societal development stratagem that encourages the adoption of 'impartial nobility' as a cultural norm.

Claims

1) Cultural Reinforcement of Altruistic Values:

    - By consistently reinforcing altruistic values through media, education, and legislation, society can shift cultural norms away from narcissistic gratification and towards collective well-being. This cultural reinforcement will systematically reduce the prominence of self-centered desires and increase the value placed on community and social responsibility.

2) Promotion of Empathy in Education:

    - Integrating empathy training and social-emotional learning in educational curricula from early childhood can counteract the 'will to receive' by cultivating an intrinsic understanding of the 'care for others' paradigm, thus fostering the development of more outward-looking individuals that allows for constructive conflict resolution, the building of strong relationships, and the fostering of supportive communities that can withstand and adapt to external pressures.

3) Elevation of Impartially Noble Role Models:

    - Elevating public figures and leaders who embody impartial nobility and selflessness can provide tangible role models for society, illustrating the virtues of serving without the expectation of personal gain, thereby influencing public aspirations and ideals.

4) Merit-Based Acknowledgement Systems:

    - Establishing recognition systems that reward contributions to societal improvement and communal support rather than individual achievement can redirect aspirations from personal status to the nobility of service.

5) Economic Incentives for Collaborative Success:

   - Creating economic structures that incentivize collaborative success and collective outcomes over individual competition can alter the fundamental motivations from self-interest to group interest, facilitating a more noble approach to personal and professional endeavors.

6) Fostering Inclusive and Diverse Communities:

   - Encouraging the development of inclusive and diverse communities can challenge the 'will to receive' by exposing individuals to a variety of perspectives and experiences, thus promoting understanding while reducing the emphasis on personal status as a measure of success.

7) Mindfulness and Metacognition Education:

   - Integrating mindfulness techniques and metacognitive approaches into standard education, *along with promoting a healthy diet,* can equip individuals with the skills to identify and control narcissistic tendencies, fostering more introspective and self-aware behavior.

8) Holistic Health Management:

   - Chronic gut inflammation, shaped by diet and stress, significantly impacts overall health through the microbiota-gut-brain axis and can influence gene expression, affecting both current and future generations. The integration of mindful dietary choices, effective stress management, and quality sleep; is essential to mitigating chronic inflammation, thus challenging the deterministic view of genetics, and underscoring the need for societal action towards a healthier future.

9) Harnessing the Power of Narrative for Transformational Growth:

   - In the realm of personal and cultural development, the art of 'sticky teaching'— *an educational approach designed to make ideas memorable and impactful*— can be a transformative tool. By embedding crucial lessons within the framework of engaging narratives and compelling storytelling, we can illuminate the virtues of impartial nobility and the dangers of unchecked narcissism.

Each of these claims rests on the assertion that culture is a powerful determinant of individual behavior and societal values, and that by strategically shaping cultural systems, we can reorient human desires towards more altruistic and noble goals, ultimately promoting metacognition and the transcendence of narcissistic tendencies.

KEY CONCEPTS

The secret of change, is to focus all your energy,
not on fighting the old, but on building the new.

– Dan Millman

Understanding Metacognition

Professor Steve Peters, a psychiatrist and author of 'The Chimp Paradox,' describes a model for understanding and managing the workings of the mind that separates it into three main parts: the 'Chimp' brain, the 'Human' brain, and the 'Computer' brain. Integrating this model into a framework that includes both the subconscious and conscious self, *and assuming four levels of consciousness,* could be conceptualized in the following way:

1. Subconscious/Conscious - The Chimp Mind (Emotionally Reactive):

   - This level operates below the surface of awareness, driven by primal instincts and emotions. It is the part of the mind that reacts instantaneously to threats, rewards, and social dynamics, often without our conscious control. It can be powerful and hijack our responses, sometimes leading to impulsive and irrational behaviors. In terms of consciousness, this is where deep-seated beliefs, habits, and automatic responses reside.

2. Subconscious/Conscious - The Computer Mind (Habitual/Programmed):

   - At this level, we find the learned behaviors, automatic skills, and ingrained patterns that have been programmed into our minds over time. This includes both functional routines (like driving a car) and dysfunctional patterns (like negative self-talk). The computer mind serves as a storage space for the multitude of programmed autopilot actions, which can be both constructive and destructive.

3. Conscious - The Human Mind (Rational/Reflective):

   - The human mind is the seat of conscious thought, self-awareness, and rational thinking. It is where we process information logically, make plans, reflect on our thoughts and actions, and consider the consequences of our choices. This part of the mind is deliberate and can override the chimp mind's impulses, though it often requires effort and can be slower to respond.

4. Super-Conscious - Self Actualizing Metacognition (Awareness of Self and System):

- From the level of the superconscious self, individuals engage in metacognition, which is the awareness of one's own thought processes. This is also the realm of self-actualization, where one seeks to realize their personal potential and purpose. It is a level of consciousness that transcends the reactive chimp mind and the automatic computer mind, representing a state of being where the individual has achieved a harmonious balance and integration of all parts of the mind.

In this model, the chimp mind and computer mind can be seen as parts of both the subconscious and conscious experience, influencing behaviors and thoughts. The human mind is primarily a conscious force that can observe, manage, and sometimes struggle with the subconscious elements. The superconscious self, *particularly at the level of self-actualization,* has the capacity to reflect on the interactions between the chimp, computer, and human aspects, striving for a cohesive and purposeful existence.

The Narcissistic Doom Cycle
Navigating Towards Metacognition for Societal Evolution

Human behavior is profoundly influenced by cultural constructs, which often exploit inherent biases and psychological tendencies. Among these, *conformity bias, the existential need for money, and prestige bias* contribute significantly to our societal dynamics.

These biases exploit our innate narcissism by fueling a cycle of cognitive distortions that lead to widespread psychological distress and societal dysfunction. The necessity of a multi-pronged approach to systems engineering the cultivation of metacognition in our citizenry, will facilitate human evolution through our successful transition into a new societal paradigm.

Conformity Bias and Narcissism:

- Conformity bias, the tendency to act similarly to others in a group despite personal beliefs or inclinations, often leverages our narcissistic desire to be accepted and esteemed by peers. This desire can override rational judgment, leading to the suppression of individuality and the perpetuation of group norms, regardless of their rationality or morality. As individuals conform, they feed into a narcissistic feedback loop, where the quest for social validation and status becomes a driving force, overshadowing authentic self-expression and ethical considerations.

Monetary Necessity and Narcissistic Exploitation:

- The necessity of money for survival is a fundamental aspect of modern life. This necessity can exploit our narcissistic traits by conflating financial success with self-worth and societal value. The relentless pursuit of wealth becomes a measure of personal achievement and a display of dominance, thus reinforcing a system where narcissistic tendencies are rewarded and even necessary for physical survival. This correlation between money and self-esteem fosters a culture of competition and self-centeredness, often at the expense of community welfare and ethical conduct.

Prestige Bias and Cultural Transmission:

- Prestige bias, *the inclination to favor and imitate individuals of higher status*, further compounds the issue. As a culture, we are inclined to emulate those who hold power and influence, often adopting their values and behaviors. When those in positions of prestige exhibit narcissistic traits, these attributes are culturally transmitted across the population, validating and normalizing self-centeredness and the pursuit of status above all else.

Confirmation Bias and Cognitive Dissonance:

- The madness of confirmation bias — the tendency to search for, interpret, and remember information that confirms one's preconceptions — works in synergy with cognitive dissonance, the psychological discomfort experienced when holding contradictory beliefs or values. Together, they create a volatile cognitive environment where individuals become entrenched in their worldviews, rejecting any evidence that challenges their narcissistic self-image or societal status. This entrenchment can lead to the need for cognitive closure — a desire for a firm answer to a question and an aversion to ambiguity or uncertainty.

Complex Post Traumatic Stress Disorder (C-PTSD):

- The societal pressures that capitalize on these biases, *and the resulting cognitive distortions*, can contribute to widespread Complex Post Traumatic Stress Disorder (C-PTSD), exacerbated by generational traumas and the relentless pace of modern life. The constant state of psychological turmoil, *and the strain of living in a society that perpetuates narcissistic values,* can lead to early death, extreme suffering, addiction, and the potential for societal collapse.

The Necessity of Metacognition for Societal Evolution:

- In order to mitigate these profound issues, a societal systems-engineering stratagem is crucial. By cultivating metacognition — the awareness and understanding of one's own thought processes — individuals can become conscious of their biases and the cultural constructs that exploit them. Education systems, media, and policy must work in concert to elevate critical thinking, self-reflection, and empathy, *which are antidotes to narcissism and its destructive cycles.*

Humanity stands at a crossroads, where persisting with our existing cultural practices promises a trajectory toward increased societal breakdown and fragility. However, by acknowledging the role of cultural constructs in exploiting narcissistic tendencies, and by intentionally cultivating metacognition through a well-strategized societal approach, *inclusive of anti-fragile principles*, we can change our direction. In fact, the evolution into a world that prizes self-awareness, communal well-being, and enduring advancement is not only possible but imperative for the survival and flourishing of human society.

We must therefore devise and implement a comprehensive systems engineering approach, *one that embraces transformative methodologies.* This strategy must encompass a thorough reformation of our economic and legislative frameworks, leveraging the secure and decentralized nature of blockchain and smart contract technologies.

> The ultimate goal is to forge an anti-fragile, self-regulatory system that harmonizes a socially conscious capitalist economy, an integrative healthcare infrastructure, along with a mercifully oriented justice system.

The magnitude of the issue is starkly illustrated by the plight of 160 million Americans grappling with sleep, nutrition, and obesity issues; collectively spending upwards of $52 billion annually on sleep aids and $60 billion annually on weight-loss products that fail to address the root causes of these symptomatic issues.

Indeed, the crux of the problem lies in the prevalent co-occurrence of stress and poor dietary consumption:

- 80% of Americans are afflicted by stress.
- 74% are plagued by gastrointestinal problems.

**This dual burden exacts a staggering annual cost of $414 billion!

This widespread state of ill health and financial precarity leaves individuals merely two paychecks away from potential homelessness, creating fertile ground for corruption; where desperation becomes a tool for exploitation by the powerful, fueling a vicious cycle of disparity that threatens to unravel the fabric of our society.

It is crucial, therefore, that we marshal our collective human capital and foster a cadre of visionary leaders. Only through such mobilization and metacognition can we hope to avert the looming catastrophe of the seemingly inevitable global extinction event.

Our very survival hinges on the will to initiate this profound metamorphosis.

Understanding Anti-Fragility

The concept of anti-fragility, as introduced by Nassim Nicholas Taleb, refers to systems that benefit and grow stronger from shocks, volatility, or disturbances. An anti-fragile system thrives on the very things that might damage or stress a more fragile counterpart. When applying this concept to human emotions and societal systems, it suggests that challenges, stressors, and even failures are essential for growth and improvement.

For having to recover from traumatic life events, can lead to an evolution in human consciousness that cannot be achieved through systems that ensure order, peace, and tranquility.

> You see, post-traumatic growth shows us that individuals can develop new understanding, strength, and resilience as a result of struggling with challenges and traumas.

In fact, the need to incorporate principles of anti-fragility into our systems-engineering stratagem aligns with educational and developmental approaches that emphasize the importance of learning through experiences, *including negative experiences.*

For example, letting children face manageable risks is seen as crucial for developing coping skills and resilience.

> Questioning authority and developing a 'backbone' are also recognized as important aspects of psychological growth and maturity. Encouraging critical thinking, self-reliance, and moral courage is a significant aim of both educational and social systems that seek to foster independent and ethical individuals.

Thus, a society aiming for self-actualization and justice would seek to balance the development of empathy with the cultivation of resilience, assertiveness, and critical thinking. Such a society would not aim for a homogenous population of only empathetic individuals, but rather a diverse community where people are equipped with a range of emotional and cognitive skills, including the ability to empathize, to stand up for themselves and others, and to navigate the complexity of human relationships and societal structures.

The Alchemy of Antifragility
Embracing Challenge for a Robust Existence

This thesis explores the notion that encountering adversity, *especially when wrought by the hands of indifferent and unempathetic narcissists,* serves as a societal catalyst toward antifragility. *But the people must be made aware of 'narcissism as original sin'.*

This perspective suggests that exposure to such narcissistic transgressions are not merely an ordeal, but a requisite spark for systemic evolution, enhancing its capacity to endure, adapt, and fortify itself against future adversities. *But again, the people must be made aware of 'narcissism as original sin'.*

For you see, it is acknowledged that resilience and insight often spring from the soil of hardship. Yet, we must also nurture antifragility through positive engagement, *such as education, self-imposed challenges, and moderated stress experiences like competitive sports, intellectual debates, or public oratory.*

> Antifragility, then, is an attainable ideal, fostered through deliberate education about narcissism, and through the deliberate cultivation of resilience and adaptability in individuals and communities.

And to attain this antifragile state, one must harness the elixir of life; for the factors of Chaos, Diversity, and Narcissism each contribute to the tapestry of human experience in distinct ways:

1. **Chaos** is often seen as the antithesis of order, but it also represents 'potential' and is often the birthplace of creative innovation. It serves as a crucible for change and evolution, compelling individuals to develop flourishing strategies of societal advancement.

2. **Diversity** stands as a cornerstone of vitality in ecological and social realms. It allows for a rich variety of experiences, ideas, and world views, which can lead to more robust problem-solving and increased empathy and understanding among different people. In experiential life, diversity fortifies problem-solving capabilities, broadens cultural horizons, fosters creativity, and is crucial for the adaptability and resilience of communities.

3. **Narcissism,** when viewed as self-preoccupation, harbors both peril and promise. While excessive narcissism can erode empathy and societal bonds, a

moderated self-interest is essential for individual ambition and personal evolution. Ironically, even the negative aspects of narcissism, when managed judiciously, can propel us towards greater interpersonal antifragility

And while the metaphor of this being an 'elixir' evokes a transformative concoction for life's experiences. Chaos and diversity undeniably enhance life's complexity and richness, whereas narcissism's role is more nuanced. Narcissism, when it transgresses and disrupts, paradoxically can lead to a more antifragile fabric of social relations.

Perhaps the true 'elixir' of life is not found in any singular element but in the harmonious interplay of order with chaos, unity with diversity, and self-awareness with empathy. This equilibrium may pave the way to a life that is not only fulfilling but also resilient and dynamic.

Empathy, in particular, emerges as a potent force, *fostering societal antifragility through cooperation, conflict resolution, and shared strength;* all essential for meeting the collective challenges of our times.

Generational Wealth Concentration
And the Impending Economic Repercussions

The unprecedented accumulation of wealth among Baby Boomers and older Americans has far-reaching implications for the American economy. Over the past three decades, this demographic has amassed a staggering $35 trillion, accounting for 27% of all U.S. wealth, which is a significant increase from 20% thirty-years prior. This wealth accumulation is equivalent to 157% of U.S. gross domestic product, more than doubling the proportion from thirty-years ago, according to federal data.

This concentration of wealth is not merely a statistic; it is a harbinger of a potential economic imbalance that threatens to destabilize the foundational principles of equitable economic growth and social mobility.

> The current trajectory suggests the emergence of a two-tier economy, characterized by a significant divide between the asset-rich older generation, and the comparatively asset-poor younger generations.

The economic disparity can be traced to several factors, including the post-World War II economic boom, favorable tax policies, the rise in property values, and the stock market growth that older generations have experienced and benefited from throughout their lives. These factors, coupled with changes in pensions and the shift towards individual retirement accounts, have allowed wealth to concentrate heavily at the top of the age spectrum.

However, this wealth concentration presents several challenges:

1. *Reduced Wealth Mobility:* With a significant portion of wealth locked with older generations, younger individuals face barriers to accumulating wealth. This can lead to reduced consumer spending, investment, and overall economic dynamism, as the younger generations struggle with student debt, rising housing costs, and stagnant wages.

2. *Economic Inequality:* As wealth begets wealth, those without access to inherited or accumulated capital are increasingly marginalized, exacerbating socioeconomic disparities and fostering economic environments that can lead to social unrest.

3. *Unsustainable Economic Model:* An economy that relies on continuous wealth accumulation by a shrinking demographic is unsustainable. As the Baby Boomers age, the withdrawal of their capital from the economy to fund retirement could lead to a decrease in investment and a potential liquidity crisis.

4. *Dependency and Autonomy Loss:* The younger generations' reliance on the wealth of their predecessors for economic advancement undermines their autonomy. This dependency can stifle innovation and entrepreneurship, vital drivers of economic growth.

To mitigate these issues and avoid the implosion of the two-tier economy into a 'slave economy' *where the majority work to pay debts rather than build wealth*, several steps can be taken:

1. *Estate and Inheritance Tax Reform:* Revising tax policies to ensure fair and equitable distribution of wealth across generations can help prevent excessive wealth concentration.

2. *Investment in Education and Skills Training:* Equipping younger generations with the tools to compete in a high-skilled economy can increase their earning potential and ability to accumulate wealth.

3. *Encouragement of Wealth Distribution:* Incentives for older generations to invest in businesses, social enterprises, and community projects can help redistribute wealth and stimulate economic activity.

4. *Broadening Access to Financial Markets:* Making financial instruments more accessible can democratize wealth growth and allow younger individuals to participate in economic gains.

While the accumulation of wealth by older generations is a testament to their economic participation and savvy, it poses a threat to the economic stability and social fabric of the nation. Policies and practices that promote intergenerational equity and wealth distribution are crucial to maintaining a balanced and fair economy. Without such measures, we risk creating an economy where the majority are not stakeholders but rather cogs in a wheel, serving a system that is not designed for their benefit.

The Epigenetic Influence of Stress and Diet on Public Health

The intimate connection between the gut and overall health, as underscored in 'Gut-Brain Psychology: Rethinking Psychology from the Microbiota–Gut–Brain Axis,' extends to the interplay between psychological stressors, dietary intake, and physiological responses. Chronic inflammation can disrupt the delicate balance of the microbiota-gut-brain axis, influencing not only our physical health but also our mental state; thus, having implications for a wide range of diseases via the triggering of our inherited epigenetic predispositions.

Biofilms and the Gut's Volatile Environment

The study 'Pathobiont release from dysbiotic gut microbiota biofilms in intestinal inflammatory diseases: a role for iron?' sheds light on the role of biofilms in contributing to the pathogenesis of inflammatory diseases. These biofilms exacerbate the issue of leaky gut syndrome, allowing unwanted pathogens to seep into the bloodstream, and then into the brain, thereby inciting a systemic inflammatory response that can have far-reaching effects on one's health. The study also suggests that iron plays a role in the proliferation of these biofilms, highlighting the intricate relationship between nutrients and gut health.

Stress as a Catalyst for Chronic Inflammation

In the documentary 'Stress: Portrait of a Killer,' featuring the insights of Robert Sapolsky, stress is identified as a critical factor that exacerbates chronic inflammation. Sapolsky's work elucidates how chronic stress triggers the release of glucocorticoids, which, when persistently elevated, can impair the immune system and promote inflammation. This heightened state of stress not only aggravates gut inflammation but also can destabilize the gut-brain axis, leading to a variety of psychological and physical disorders.

Mitigating Chronic Inflammation through Diet

The dietary implications for managing chronic inflammation are profound. Foods that are high in refined sugars, dairy, bread, red meats, and processed ingredients can promote inflammation; while a diet rich in prebiotics—fibrous foods that feed beneficial bacteria—is recommended to counteract this effect. Prebiotic foods like fruits, vegetables, nuts, and legumes are essential for nurturing a healthy microbiome, which in turn can reinforce the intestinal barrier and prevent the leak of harmful substances into the bloodstream and the brain.

Epigenetic Implications of Diet and Stress

The concept of epigenetics, as portrayed in 'The Ghost in Your Genes,' suggests that our environment can influence the expression of our genes. Chronic gut inflammation, influenced by diet and compounded by stress, can serve as an environmental trigger, activating epigenetic markers that predispose individuals to disease. For example, it takes over 100 predispositions to be triggered for the onset of cancer; and while these changes will not alter the DNA sequence itself, they can be passed down, affecting the health and longevity of future generations.

A Holistic Approach to Managing Gut Inflammation

The intersection of diet, stress management, and sleep quality forms the triad of gut health management. Stress management strategies such as mindfulness, meditation, and regular physical activity are not only beneficial for stress reduction but also for modulating the gut-brain axis and controlling inflammation. Therefore, holistic interventions that encompass dietary modifications, stress reduction, and improved sleep hygiene are crucial in maintaining the integrity of the gut and, by extension, the overall health of the individual.

The latest research from psychobiology, microbiology, and epigenetics converges to deliver a powerful message: the gut is a critical battleground for our health, and we hold the weapons to secure victory. Chronic gut inflammation is not merely a symptom; it is a nexus where diet, stress, and the very blueprint of our being intertwine.

This is not about mere understanding; it's about action. By proactively managing stress and reshaping our diets, we wield the power to recalibrate the gut-brain axis, disarm potential diseases before they strike, and foster robust gene expression that will shield us and our descendants from the specters of illness.

Our health story is not pre-written in our DNA; it is dynamic, responsive to the choices we make every single day. We must reject the fatalistic view that genes dictate destiny. Instead, let's embrace the empowering reality that through the deliberate decisions we make — the foods we consume, the stress we dissolve, and the lifestyles we lead — we can sculpt a legacy of health.

It's time to act with intention, to choose a life where balance is not just a concept but a lived experience. In this pursuit, we're not just avoiding sickness; we're nurturing a symphony of bodily harmony that resonates through every aspect of our existence We *must therefore lead a movement towards this new paradigm, where our collective efforts can turn the tide against disease and pave the way for generations of vitality and wellness.*

Navigating the Storm: A Case for Constitutional Renewal

In 'The Decadent Society,' Ross Douthat paints a picture of a stagnant America, plagued by a lack of innovation and a pervasive sense of malaise. Douthat argues that the nation is mired in decadence, not in the sense of moral or cultural decay, but in terms of stagnation and complacency. He posits that this stagnation is a result of both economic and cultural factors, including technological stagnation, political paralysis, and the rise of a new aristocracy. This sets the stage for our exploration, highlighting the symptoms of a society in dire need of systemic change.

Building upon the theme of stagnation, Matt Taibbi's 'The Divide' delves into the deepening chasm in American society – the stark divide between the rich and the poor. Taibbi illustrates how this divide is perpetuated by a biased justice system and a failing democracy that favors the elite. He uncovers the systemic inequalities that have led to a disillusioned and fractured society, further emphasizing the urgent need for constitutional reform to address these fundamental disparities.

Aaron Glantz's 'Homewrecker' takes a more focused approach, examining the housing crisis and its role in exacerbating social and economic inequalities. Glantz exposes how the collapse of the housing market was not just an economic disaster but also a moral one, highlighting the exploitation by financial elites. This perspective adds another layer to our understanding, showing how specific policies and practices have contributed to the erosion of the American dream and calling for a constitutional revision to prevent such exploitation.

In 'America: The Farewell Tour,' Chris Hedges offers a grim prognosis of the American condition. Hedges presents a nation in the throes of decay, focusing on the symptoms of a society in decline; such as addiction, inequality, and despair. He argues that these are not isolated problems but are symptoms of a deeper societal and structural failure. This analysis reinforces the need for a comprehensive overhaul of the American system.

Cornel West's 'Democracy Matters' serves as a rallying cry, emphasizing the importance of reinvigorating democratic ideals. West critiques the current state of American democracy, highlighting the threats posed by nihilism, militarism, and authoritarianism. He insists on the need for a revitalized democracy, rooted in justice, compassion, and equality. West's perspective is pivotal in framing the constitutional rewrite; not just as a legal necessity, but as a moral imperative.

The synthesis of these works presents a compelling argument for a Constitutional Convention. The stagnation and decadence described by Douthat, the unjust divide outlined by Taibbi, the moral failures in housing exposed by Glantz, the societal decay highlighted by Hedges, and West's call for democratic renewal, collectively underscore the urgency of a comprehensive constitutional rewrite.

And without such a rewrite, our American democracy is at risk of being completely subverted by a cabal of elite globalists who exploit the systemic weaknesses these authors have identified.

The conclusion is clear: *for a truly democratic and just society, America must not only recognize these challenges but also take bold, transformative action to address them through a fundamental reimagining of our Constitution.*

Reclaiming Democracy: A Call for Constitutional Reform

Chris Hedges' 'Empire of Illusion' sets the stage for this exploration by describing a society captivated by illusions, drifting away from reality. Hedges argues that the American public is increasingly disconnected from the factual world, seduced by the false promises and spectacle of celebrity culture and mass entertainment. This detachment from reality, Hedges suggests, makes the public susceptible to manipulation by a powerful elite, eroding the foundations of democracy and critical thinking.

Douglas Murray's 'The War on the West' continues this theme by examining how Western societies, and by extension, their democratic values, are being undermined. Murray critiques various social and political movements that he believes are eroding the foundational principles of Western societies. He posits that these movements, often spearheaded by elites, are contributing to a weakening of democratic institutions and national identities, creating vulnerabilities within the fabric of society.

Michael Lewis' 'The Undoing Project' shifts the focus to the realm of human decision-making. Exploring the work of psychologists Daniel Kahneman and Amos Tversky, Lewis delves into the complexities of human judgment and decision-making. This exploration reveals how cognitive biases and flawed reasoning can lead to significant societal consequences, *including in economic and political domains,* suggesting that these human weaknesses can be exploited by those in power to further their agendas.

In 'The Divide,' Jason Hickel examines the growing global economic divide. He argues that the current economic system, driven by neoliberal policies and corporate globalization, has led to unprecedented inequality and environmental degradation. Hickel's analysis indicates that these systemic issues are not accidents but are the result of deliberate policies and actions by a global elite, further undermining democratic principles and leading to widespread disenfranchisement.

'Good Economics for Hard Times,' by Abhijit Banerjee and Esther Duflo, offers a more hopeful perspective, suggesting that careful, evidence-based economic policies can address the challenges posed by globalization and technological change. They argue for economic policies that are grounded in rigorous research and real-world evidence, promoting inclusivity and sustainability, countering the narrative of elitist control, and offering a blueprint for reforming economic systems within a democratic framework.

The synthesis of these works underlines a critical argument: *the need for a comprehensive constitutional rewrite as a bulwark against the subversion of American democracy by a cabal of global elites.*

Hedges' depiction of a society lost in illusion, Murray's concerns about the erosion of Western values, Lewis' insights into human cognitive flaws, Hickel's critique of global economic divides, and Banerjee and Duflo's solutions for economic reform collectively suggest that current systems are insufficient to protect against elite manipulation.

A Constitutional Convention, with its promise of a vast array of safeguards, appears as a necessary step to reclaim democracy. This new constitution should aim not only to address the immediate challenges, but also to lay the groundwork for a more equitable, inclusive, and resilient democratic society; one that is capable of resisting the manipulations of a global elite, and ensuring the true representation and welfare of all its citizens.

Navigating Global Demise through Libertarian Reform

Peter Zeihan's 'The End of the World is Just the Beginning' sets the stage for our exploration into global demise and the necessity of reformation. Zeihan examines the fragility of our interconnected global systems, emphasizing how geopolitical shifts and resource scarcities are leading us towards a potentially catastrophic future. He predicts the decline of global trade and the fragmentation of international relations, highlighting the critical need for countries, especially the United States, to reassess their roles on the world stage.

Building upon Zeihan's foundation, *Graeber and Wengrow's 'The Dawn of Everything'* delves into the evolution of human societies. They challenge traditional narratives of societal development, proposing that early human societies were more complex and varied than commonly thought. This perspective underscores the potential for diverse societal structures, which is vital in considering new forms of governance and social organization in the face of looming global challenges.

Graeber's 'Debt: The First 5,000 Years' adds another layer to our understanding, exploring the historical role of debt in shaping human relationships and social structures. Graeber argues that debt has often been a tool of control and oppression, leading to stark inequalities. This insight is crucial in assessing the economic underpinnings of modern societies and the need for a more equitable financial system in a reformed global governance structure.

In *'Pirate Enlightenment, or the Real Libertalia,'* Graeber presents an alternative model of social organization based on the historical example of pirate societies. These societies were surprisingly egalitarian and democratic, standing in stark contrast to the authoritarian and hierarchical structures prevalent in their time. Graeber's analysis here suggests the viability of more libertarian and inclusive forms of governance, which could be instrumental in restructuring our current political systems.

Tyson Ynkaporta's 'Right Story, Wrong Story' brings an Indigenous perspective to the conversation, emphasizing the importance of narratives and storytelling in shaping our understanding of the world and our place in it. Ynkaporta argues for the need to integrate Indigenous knowledge and perspectives into global conversations, especially in relation to our relationship with the Earth and each other.

Integrating the knowledge gleaned from these five influential works, it becomes unmistakably clear that the prevailing societal frameworks are deeply flawed, marked by greed and avarice, rendering them ineffective for driving essential systemic transformations. The survival of humanity hinges on developing a profound and symbiotic connection with the Earth.

We must therefore address these global challenges as identified by Zeihan, by incorporating the rich tapestry of diversity and complexity as illuminated by Graeber, Wengrow, and Ynkaporta, to convene an effective Constitutional Convention. This pivotal gathering, coupled with a collaborative Social Movement, must aim to forge a new, diverse, and flexible Libertarian democratic system, crucial for our collective future.

> Such a movement would not only reform American democracy, but also contribute to a new Federation of Nations, preventing the rise of an elitist cabal and a despotic one-world government.

This new federation would embody 'the way of impartial nobility', integrating libertarian ideals with a global perspective that respects and incorporates diverse cultural narratives and sustainable practices.

By transcending our innate narcissism and embracing a more egalitarian and inclusive approach to governance, as suggested by Graeber's analysis of pirate societies, we can lay the groundwork for a global reformation.

This reformation would be based on respect for the Earth and each other, as Ynkaporta advocates, leading to a more resilient and equitable global community capable of facing the challenges of the 21st century and beyond.

THE NEED FOR
CONSTITUTIONAL REFORM

The main obstacle to a stable and just world order is the United States.

- George Soros

A New World Order

We are grateful to the great publications whose directors have attended our meetings and respected their promises of discretion for almost forty years. It would have been impossible for us to develop our plan for the world if we had been subject to the bright lights of publicity during those years. But the work is now much more sophisticated and prepared to march towards a world government. *The supranational sovereignty of an intellectual elite and world bankers is surely preferable to the national auto-determination practiced in past centuries.*

– David Rockefeller

Financial Control, Global Governance, and the Call for Constitutional Reform

Jordan Maxwell's 'Matrix of Power' sets the stage by examining symbols of power and their historical contexts, suggesting a hidden influence exerted by powerful groups over global affairs. Maxwell's work posits that these symbols represent an unspoken network of control, which manipulates socio-political and economic structures. This foundational view introduces the concept of an elitist cabal that subtly guides the direction of national and international policy.

Edward Griffin's 'The Creature from Jekyll Island' unravels the origins and operations of the Federal Reserve System, asserting that its formation was the result of secretive meetings that were held to serve a secretive banking cartel of globalist elites, rather than a true government institution. Griffin's narrative indicates that the Federal Reserve plays a critical role in controlling the economy, hinting at the elitist manipulation of financial systems for the consolidation of wealth and power.

Antony Sutton's 'The Federal Reserve Conspiracy' expands on Griffin's assertions by detailing the alleged collusion between financial elites and government officials in the establishment of the Federal Reserve. Sutton describes how this institution has potentially facilitated a covert redistribution of wealth, supporting the idea of a shadow governance structure influencing America's economic landscape.

'The True Story of the Bilderberg Group' by Daniel Estulin investigates the secretive annual meetings of influential figures in politics, finance, and media; suggesting these

gatherings shape global policy. Estulin posits that the Bilderberg Group is a crucial component of the globalist cabal that is orchestrating economic and political outcomes, in line with a vision for a new world order.

Jake Bernstein's 'Secrecy World' exposes the intricate web of offshore banking and financial secrecy that enables the ultra-wealthy and powerful to hide assets and evade regulations. Bernstein's investigative work into the Panama Papers links to the themes presented in the previous books, illustrating a worldwide financial network that operates outside the public's view and beyond the reach of traditional governance.

> A clandestine elitist cabal has usurped control over America's banking and financial system. This control is a steppingstone towards establishing a one-world government. We must therefore call for a constitutional convention aimed at restructuring the U.S. Constitution, to dismantle this shadow governance and prevent the consolidation of global power.

The books collectively underscore the need for a profound constitutional rewrite to counteract the globalist grip on America's financial system. This rewrite would aim not only to restore democratic control over national finances, but also to promote transparency and accountability in global governance structures.

Ultimately, we must co-create a reformation that aligns the United Nations and other international bodies *with these revised constitutional principles*, ensuring that the consolidation of wealth and power is checked by a renewed commitment to democracy, equity, and the rule of law for all nations.

This ambitious reconstitution would lay the groundwork for a global governance that genuinely serves the people, in stark contrast to the secretive and centralized power structures that have come to dominate us all.

The New World Order Agenda

The summary of the alleged New World Order (NWO) agenda outlined by Dr. Lawrence Dunegan is based on his recounting of a 1969 talk given by Dr. Richard Day, which Dr. Dunegan claimed to have attended.

According to Dunegan, Dr. Day, *who is purportedly associated with the Illuminati,* provided a chilling and precise forecast of societal and medical changes that would unfold over the coming decades.

Dr. Day's prognostications, as remembered by Dunegan, touched on various aspects of life, including politics, education, technology, and health, painting a picture of a meticulously engineered future designed to consolidate power and control.

Dr. Day's alleged revelations spoke of:

- The manipulation of the economy to create artificial scarcity, control consumption, and ensure the dependence of populations on a centralized system.

- Advances in technology that would serve to monitor and control individuals, diminishing privacy and personal freedoms.

- Education systems would be transformed to serve as tools for indoctrination, steering away from critical thinking towards acceptance of a preordained social structure.

- The erosion of family bonds and traditional values as a means to weaken societal units that could oppose centralized control.

- Control of medicine and healthcare, ensuring that health becomes a privilege rather than a right, directing research and treatment in ways that benefit the controlling elite rather than the general population.

Dr. Dunegan, reflecting on the talk, noted that the content was not only foreboding but seemed to be a blueprint for a future that prioritized control over humanistic values. He claimed that the precision with which Dr. Day's predictions came to pass was a source of deep concern, suggesting an orchestrated effort by powerful groups to shape global events and societal evolution.

The purported NWO agenda, as outlined by Dr. Dunegan, is a topic of intense debate, often dismissed as conspiracy theory. However, the themes resonate with those who are wary of the concentration of power in the hands of a few and the increasing role of technology in everyday life. It serves as a cautionary tale for vigilance and critical thinking in an age where information and disinformation can spread with equal velocity.

Educationally, the narrative of the NWO serves as a lens through which to examine the ethical implications of political and technological power. Whether one believes in the veracity of Dr. Dunegan's account, it underscores the importance of transparency, accountability, and the preservation of individual freedoms in a rapidly changing world.

The Hidden Agenda of Education
A Legacy of Control and Conformity

In a critical examination of the modern education system, one cannot help but confront an unsettling reality: its origins and evolution bear the imprint of a grand design, one that was not intended to foster critical thinking or individual success. This design, deeply intertwined with the notions of 'woke culture' and the 'war on free speech,' speaks to a systematic effort to shape individuals into compliant components of a larger machine.

The Prussian model of education, lauded for its efficiency in producing obedient citizens, laid the groundwork for this phenomenon. Horace Mann's attempts to transplant this model into America only achieved the first stage of conditioning—where the populace's free will was subjugated to governmental narratives. Yet, this was merely the precursor to a more insidious phase, orchestrated by the industrial revolution's new titans.

John D. Rockefeller, whose burgeoning oil empire demanded a steady supply of submissive laborers, recognized the potential in the Prussian system. By advocating for a standardized curriculum—a pillar of the Prussian model—Rockefeller aimed to transform the American public education system into a breeding ground for factory workers. His ideology was clear: work was to be the liberator, the singular purpose of an individual's existence.

With Frederick T. Gates by his side, Rockefeller executed a plan that was both simple and transformative. They established a board, ostensibly governmental, to promote an inclusive education and secure government funding. This move led to the General Education Board's formation and a subsequent explosion of schools across the nation, radically altering the educational landscape.

The impact of such a system was profound: generations of students entered schools with aspirations of intellectual growth, only to emerge as cogs in the industrial machine—mindless and aspiration-less. Rockefeller's ethos, "I don't want a nation of thinkers, I want a nation of workers," encapsulated the objective of conditioning the masses into obedience and complacency.

The Rockefeller education model's success ignited a trend among other industrial magnates like Andrew Carnegie and Henry Ford. Together, they streamlined the system, establishing standardized textbooks and tests, and indoctrinating teachers to perpetuate a cycle of intellectual suppression.

The Prussian education philosophy they adopted, as espoused by Johann Gottlieb Fichte, aimed to supplant free will with a calculated predictability in decision-making. The methodology, influenced by Locke and Rousseau, established a regimented curriculum, standardized tests, and an overarching state-centric narrative—all designed to cultivate conformity and suppress individualism.

Students were confined to an environment mirroring correctional facilities in both architecture and routine. Teachers, unwittingly complicit, administered a curriculum that encroached upon familial influence, thereby entrenching state ideals over personal values. This blueprint has persisted, virtually unaltered, across generations and borders, raising the question: To what extent are we, as products of this system, aware of its origins and objectives?

The manipulation of the American dream was not limited to compulsory education. Universities, too, became instruments of indoctrination, extending the reach of this conditioning well into adulthood. The narrative that equated education with college and success was pushed, further entrenching the belief in the necessity of higher education.

The 1957 Sputnik crisis presented an opportunity for the American government to mimic Rockefeller's strategies. In response to the Soviet technological feat, President Dwight Eisenhower enacted the National Defense Education Act, which led to the proliferation of student loans, ostensibly in the name of national defense.

As the government invested in higher education, a vicious cycle of dependency on student loans emerged. Universities, no longer financially constrained, found a never-ending source of government-backed funding, while students became ensnared in debt. This culminated in the Higher Education Act of 1965, which saw the government ensuring student loans—a move that transferred the risk of default from banks to government agencies, perpetuating a system of financial and intellectual bondage.

Thus revealing a disconcerting truth: the education system, as we know it, was never meant to liberate but to confine. It was crafted to produce not free-thinking individuals but docile workers, ensnared in a narrative of labor as liberation. It behooves us to question this legacy and seek reform, lest we remain unwitting products of a system designed for control, rather than enlightenment.

For far too long, have shadows of history been guiding us unwittingly toward a future of subservience. The first step to breaking this cycle is awareness, followed by a steadfast commitment to challenge and change the status quo. We must not only recognize the roots of our societal structure but also take bold steps to reclaim the autonomy that has been stealthily eroded over generations. Only then can we forge a path that leads to true success and fulfillment, both individually and collectively.

From Conspiracy to Constitutional Renewal

'The Trillion-Dollar Conspiracy' by Jim Marrs uncovers a web of deceit and manipulation by financial elites and their influence over government policy; painting a picture of a shadowy financial oligarchy that, according to Marrs, has orchestrated much of the economic misfortune experienced by the general population. We must curtail this unchecked power through a constitutional rewrite.

In *'The Best Way to Rob a Bank is to Own One,' William Black* provides a critical examination of the banking industry, highlighting the phenomenon of 'control fraud' where the very people who run financial institutions drive them into the ground for personal gain. Black's book builds upon Marrs' claims by offering detailed insights into the mechanisms of financial malfeasance. It suggests that constitutional reforms are necessary to implement stronger regulatory frameworks that hold bank executives accountable.

Danielle Booth's 'Fed Up' offers an insider's critique of the Federal Reserve, emphasizing how disconnected monetary policies can adversely affect the economy and exacerbate inequality. For not only is there corruption in the banking sector, there are fundamental flaws in the way our nation's central banking system operates; making the case for reforming the Federal Reserve so as to better serve the economic needs of the broader population.

Ellen Brown's 'From Austerity to Prosperity' shifts the narrative towards solutions, advocating for public banking as a means to move away from austerity measures and towards a more prosperous and equitable economic system; arguing that by incorporating the concept of public banking into the constitution, we could ensure that the monetary system serves the public good, *rather than private interests.*

Continuing with *Ellen Brown's analysis, 'Banking on the People'* extends the argument for public banking and proposes the idea of incorruptible digital currencies. And with the institution of a new constitutional framework, we could facilitate the creation of a banking system that is by the people, and for the people. Brown's vision of a web of public banks issuing digital currency serves as a cornerstone for the proposed constitutional reforms.

The current financial system, plagued by corruption and ineptitude as shown by Marrs, Black, and Booth, can be transformed through the solutions provided by Brown. This transformation will involve:

1. Establishing constitutional provisions to dismantle the 'conspiracy' of financial oligarchy depicted by Marrs.

2. Creating strong, constitutionally mandated regulations to prevent the control fraud described by Black.

3. Reforming the Federal Reserve's structure and policies, as suggested by Booth, through constitutional means to align it with democratic principles and economic realities.

4. Integrating the concept of public banking into the constitutional framework, drawing on Brown's 'From Austerity to Prosperity.'

5. Adopting a digital currency issued by public banks to ensure transparency and incorruptibility, as advocated in Brown's 'Banking on the People.'

And by advocating for a comprehensive constitutional rewrite that enshrines economic democracy and public banking at its core, we can enshrine a new constitution that supports the establishment of a financial system that is *transparent, accountable, and designed to serve the public interest.*

A web of public banks, operating with digital currencies, will provide the foundation for an equitable and sustainable economic future; marking a transition from a conspiracy-ridden past to a prosperous and democratic future.

FOREWORD

If it's never our fault, we can't take responsibility for it.
And if we can't take responsibility for it, we will always be its victim.

- Richard Bach

Until the great mass of people shall be filled with the sense of responsibility,
for each other's welfare, social justice can never be attained.

– *Helen Keller*

Reclaiming Democracy through Narrative and Constitutional Renewal

Jonah Sachs' 'Story Wars' introduces the power of storytelling in shaping cultural norms and values. Sachs suggests that compelling narratives drive social movements and can be pivotal in rallying collective action. His book provides a framework for understanding how stories have historically been used to legitimize power structures and can also be a tool for challenging and revising them. This notion of storytelling is crucial as it forms the bedrock for reimagining the American narrative in the context of a constitutional rewrite.

In 'Techno Feudalism,' Yanis Varoufakis delves into the modern economic landscape, where technological advancements have led to a new form of feudalism, with tech giants acting as the new lords over a digital serfdom. Varoufakis warns of the dangers this concentration of power poses to democracy and individual freedom. His analysis sets the stage for understanding the modern challenges that a rewritten Constitution must address, especially in terms of antitrust laws and the regulation of digital spaces.

Murray Rothbard's 'Anatomy of the State' provides a critical examination of government and its intrinsic nature to expand its scope of power at the expense of individual liberties. Rothbard's libertarian perspective is skeptical of the state's role and advocates for a minimized government. This book adds depth to the call for a constitutional convention by questioning the very structures that a constitutional convention would need to redefine, so as to ensure these reforms actually serve the public; *rather than elite interests, as they do today.*

Rothbard's 'Conceived in Liberty' offers a historical perspective on the American Revolution and the libertarian roots of the nation's founding. Rothbard's account underlines the principles of self-governance and personal freedom that were central to the nation's conception. This historical context is crucial for understanding the original intent behind the Constitution and the ways in which a convention could strive to return to these principles, while adapting them for the current age.

Rothbard's 'The New Republic' critiques the development of the American state post-constitution, arguing that it has strayed from its libertarian beginnings. The book provides an analysis of how power has been centralized and the ways in which this has led to the subversion of liberty. It lays the groundwork for arguing that a constitutional rewrite should aim to decentralize power and enhance personal freedoms.

We must therefore create a constitutional convention aimed at overcoming these elitist ambitions for a one-world government. The current trajectory of power consolidation, both in economic and state terms, poses a threat to democracy and individual liberty. Our newly rewritten U.S. Constitution will serve as the new 'winning story' for America, one that reclaims the narrative of… *liberty and justice for all.*

The synthesis of these works' advocates for a renewed American story that centers on a constitutional convention. This new narrative would not only address the contemporary challenges of techno feudalism but also rekindle the libertarian spirit of the nation's inception.

The comprehensive rewriting of the U.S. Constitution is essential for saving humanity from the malevolence of concentrated power. Such a reformation would aim to decentralize authority, ensuring that the state and technology serve the people, not the other way around.

In crafting a winning story of liberty, democracy, and self-governance, the new Constitution would stand as a beacon for all of humanity, providing a blueprint for resisting the tide of authoritarianism and carving out a future where freedom is the foundation of the global order.

Metacognitive Leadership in Social Movements

'Persuasion and Social Movements,' authored by Charles J. Stewart, is a seminal work that dissects the role of persuasive strategies in the genesis, evolution, and success of social movements. Stewart's book delves into the intricacies of how social movements harness rhetoric to shape public opinion, challenge the status quo, and forge new realities in the sociopolitical landscape. The text is a meticulous study of historical and contemporary movements, offering insights into the persuasive tactics that have spurred societal change.

Chapter 5 stands out as it explores the dynamics of leadership within social movements, emphasizing that effective leaders are those who can inspire collective action towards a common goal. This chapter underscores the importance of leaders who are able to transcend personal aggrandizement and instead channel their energies towards the greater good of the movement. Stewart posits that such leadership is critical to maintain the momentum and integrity of social movements, ensuring that they do not devolve into mere platforms for individual glorification.

Chapter 5 of 'Persuasion and Social Movements' the authors argue that successful movements are often distinguished by leaders who possess not only charisma and the ability to articulate a vision, but also the capacity to persuade and mobilize followers towards a common cause. This chapter delves into the strategies and tactics leaders use to persuade, including rhetorical framing, emotional appeal, and the construction of compelling narratives that resonate with the public's values and beliefs.

The authors discuss how leaders must balance the need for strong, decisive action with the movement's democratic impulses, ensuring that the voices within the movement are heard and that there is a sense of collective ownership over the movement's direction. Stewart also addresses the potential pitfalls of leadership, such as the risk of becoming autocratic or disconnected from the grassroots base.

Furthermore, Chapter 5 explores how leaders can sustain momentum over time, particularly as movements face challenges such as internal conflict, opposition from powerful adversaries, or waning public interest. Leaders of social movements must be adept at adapting their persuasive strategies to evolving circumstances while maintaining focus on the movement's overarching goals.

Integrating this chapter with Steve Peters' concept of metacognition provides a deeper understanding of the psychological framework that successful social movement leaders should embody. Metacognition, or thinking about thinking, is a higher-order thinking skill that enables individuals to reflect on their cognitive processes. Leaders equipped with metacognition can rise above their immediate impulses and desires, *which I refer to as transcending the 'narcissistic will to receive,'* and instead operate from a place of self-awareness and strategic foresight.

In the context of rallying for a constitutional convention, the lessons from 'Persuasion and Social Movements' are particularly resonant. The call for such a convention is a call for transformative change, necessitating leaders who are not only adept at persuasion but also grounded in metacognitive leadership. These leaders must be able to navigate the complex interplay of individual motivations and collective aspirations, harnessing their understanding of themselves and others to foster unity and steer the movement towards its objectives.

The book concludes with a powerful call to action for current and future leaders of social movements: *to cultivate the kind of leadership that is self-reflective, community-focused, and committed to the common good*. This is a leadership that not only persuades but also inspires, not just through charismatic appeal but through the demonstration of a metacognitive approach that prioritizes the movement's goals above personal gain. In doing so, social movements can maintain their course towards achieving profound and lasting social change.

Engineering Character Development for Constitutional Evolution

David Brooks' 'The Social Animal' sets the stage by delving into the intricacies of human social behavior, and the subconscious influences that shape our lives. Brooks' exploration of emotional intelligence, social dynamics, and the unconscious mind provides a foundational understanding of human nature, a critical aspect when considering the task of rewriting a constitution. *And understanding the social animal within us, is the first step in structurally reengineering societal norms and values.*

Bill George's 'Authentic Leadership' extends the conversation into the realm of leadership, emphasizing the importance of authenticity, ethics, and emotional intelligence in effective leaders. George argues that true leadership stems from self-awareness, moral clarity, and an empathetic understanding of others. In the context of a constitutional rewrite, this implies that leaders must embody these values to inspire and execute profound societal changes effectively.

Brené Brown's 'Daring Greatly' shifts the focus to *the power of vulnerability and courage* in the living of an authentic life. Brown's research highlights how embracing vulnerability can lead to greater innovation, creativity, and meaningful connections. In the journey towards a constitutional convention, such qualities are essential to foster open-minded discussions, encourage diverse perspectives, and build a resilient framework for change.

Angela Duckworth's 'Grit' brings an essential element to the discourse: *the power of passion and perseverance in achieving long-term goals.* Duckworth's concept of 'grit' as a key predictor of success underscores the need for enduring commitment and resilience in the monumental task of rewriting a constitution that develops grit among the citizenry. It suggests that transformative change requires not only intellectual acumen but also the tenacity to see through challenges.

'The Talent Code' by Daniel Coyle explores how talent is cultivated through deep practice, master coaching, and motivational forces. Coyle's insights into skill development and neuroplasticity reinforce the idea that character and capabilities can be developed to meet complex challenges; and that such insights be integrated into the framework of our constitutional reform.

Integrating the insights from these five books, a cohesive argument for a successful constitutional rewrite, requires a systems-engineering approach where the development of human character is integrated within.

The combined wisdom of these authors suggests that *understanding our social instincts, fostering authentic leadership, embracing vulnerability, cultivating grit, and deliberately developing talent* are essential components in evolving not only individuals, but also societies.

The synthesis of these works suggests that by consciously developing these aspects of human character within the cultural fabric, we can successfully navigate the complexities of executing a successful constitutional convention.

> This process, in turn, is a step towards evolving humanity into a higher metacognitive state, where individuals and societies are more self-aware, empathetic, resilient, and skilled.

The rewritten constitution, in this context, becomes more than a legal document; it symbolizes a new era of human development, marked by deeper understanding, stronger leadership, and an unwavering commitment to collective progress and well-being.

The Evolution of Societal Systems: A Humanistic Approach

'Built to Last' by James Collins sets the foundation for this analysis. It examines how certain companies have stood the test of time, not merely through financial success but through visionary practices and values. Collins emphasizes the importance of having a core ideology that guides decisions and actions over time. This book lays the groundwork for understanding how enduring principles can lead to lasting success, a concept that can be extrapolated to societal systems.

Jim Collins' 'Great by Choice' delves into why some companies thrive in chaos and uncertainty while others do not. It introduces the concept of disciplined, empirical creativity and productive paranoia, arguing that success in turbulent times hinges on meticulous planning, along with the ability to adapt to changing circumstances, by understanding how resilience and adaptability, *grounded in core values,* are key to long-term success.

Malcolm Gladwell's 'The Tipping Point' brings a new dimension to this narrative by examining how small actions can lead to significant societal changes. Gladwell discusses the concept of 'tipping points' - moments where an idea, trend, or behavior crosses a threshold and spreads like wildfire. This book provides insight into how societal change can be initiated and accelerated, building upon the foundations laid by enduring principles and adaptive strategies.

Mihaly Csikszentmihalyi's 'Finding Flow' shifts the focus to individual experiences, particularly the state of 'flow' - where people are fully immersed and deeply focused on what they are doing. Csikszentmihalyi argues that achieving flow is key to personal happiness and productivity. And by integrating the concept of flow into the broader societal systems and structures, we can help society to evolve positively.

'Dare to Lead' by Brene Brown culminates this exploration. Brown emphasizes the importance of vulnerability, courage, and empathy in leadership. She argues that transformative leaders are those who are willing to embrace uncertainty, take risks, and engage in tough conversations, highlighting the role of courageous and empathetic leadership in guiding societal evolution.

The synthesis of these works leads to a compelling argument for the need to evolve societal systems through a rewritten U.S. Constitution that incorporates a science of humanism that is both adaptable and enduring; and as such, built on solid core values, resilient to change, and capable of reaching tipping points of success. Metacognitive societal institutions should be designed with these principles in mind.

> And by embedding the concept of flow into these societal structures, the new Constitution will facilitate environments where individuals can reach their fullest potential.

Additionally, the principles of empathetic and courageous leadership should be enshrined in this new Constitution, ensuring that societal evolution is guided by leaders who are committed to vulnerability, bravery, and the well-being of all citizens.

This transformative framework, grounded in the science of humanism, will not only safeguard rights and freedoms, but will also nurture a society that is adaptable, resilient, and deeply connected to the pursuit of collective and individual fulfillment.

A Self-Evolving Journey Towards Virtuous Autonomy & Metacognition

Bill George's 'True North' serves as the cornerstone of this exploration. It posits the idea of authentic self-leadership, where individuals align their actions with their true values and beliefs. George argues that this alignment is crucial for effective leadership and personal fulfillment. The concept of 'True North' represents a fixed point guiding one's self-leadership journey, emphasizing the importance of self-awareness, authenticity, and ethical behavior.

Daniel Goleman's 'Working with Emotional Intelligence' extends the conversation into the realm of emotional intelligence (EQ). Goleman underscores the importance of EQ in professional and personal success, arguing that self-awareness, empathy, and social skills are as important as traditional intelligence. *For enhancing EQ can lead to better decision-making, improved relationships, and a deeper understanding of oneself and others.*

Gabor Maté's 'When the Body Says No' explores the critical link between emotional health and physical well-being. Maté discusses how stress and emotional repression can lead to physical illness, emphasizing the importance of listening to our bodies and addressing emotional pain. *For understanding and responding to our body's signals is essential in our journey towards self-awareness and health, both critical components of virtuous autonomy.*

'The Ordinary Virtues' by Michael Ignatieff shifts the focus to the moral operating systems of individuals and communities in a globalized world. Ignatieff argues that in times of crisis and complexity, people resort to 'ordinary virtues' like tolerance, forgiveness, and resilience. These virtues, often overlooked, are foundational for maintaining social harmony and ethical behavior in diverse societies. *Embracing these virtues is crucial for developing a humane and just society.*

David Brooks' 'The Second Mountain' encapsulates the journey of transformation. Brooks describes the shift from self-centeredness (the first mountain) to a life dedicated to serving others (the second mountain). This transformation involves embracing community, relationships, and a commitment to a cause greater than oneself. Brooks argues that climbing the second mountain leads to a more fulfilling, purposeful life.

> The synthesis of these works supports the thesis that for a society to thrive, it needs citizens who are self-aware, emotionally intelligent, physically and emotionally healthy, morally grounded, and committed to serving the greater good.

It is therefore evident that the U.S. Constitution should be rewritten to encapsulate these humanistic values. This constitutional rewrite would not only enshrine rights and liberties, but also encourage the development of individuals who are capable of leading with authenticity, understanding and managing their emotions, responding to their physical and emotional needs, practicing ordinary virtues, and committing to a life of service and community.

Such a constitutional overhaul would pave the way for a society of individuals who are not only self-governing, but also self-evolved, collectively striving towards a state of virtuous autonomy. This metacognitive state, *where individuals are deeply aware of their thoughts, emotions, and values, and act in accordance with them,* is the bedrock upon which a truly democratic and harmonious society can be built.

Evolving Family and Child-Rearing Institutions

'Human Diversity' by Charles Murray delves into the complex interplay of genetics, environment, and culture in shaping human behavior and abilities. He underscores the diversity in human cognitive and psychological traits, arguing for the importance of

acknowledging these differences in societal structures. This book lays the groundwork for understanding the varied needs and potentials of children within the context of family and societal systems.

Melissa Kearney's 'The Two-Parent Privilege' explores the significant advantages children have when raised in two-parent households. Kearney discusses the socio-economic and emotional benefits that stem from this family structure. By highlighting the disparities that exist due to family composition, we must integrate supportive institutional frameworks for all children, regardless of their familial structures.

Gabor Mate's 'Hold on to Your Kids' emphasizes the critical role of parental attachment in the healthy development of children. Mate argues that in the modern world, peers often replace parents as primary influencers, which can have detrimental effects on emotional and psychological development; underscoring the necessity of strong, nurturing relationships in child-rearing.

In 'The Silent Guides,' Prof Steve Peters examines the unconscious influences that shape a child's development. He discusses how childhood experiences, particularly those involving parents and primary caregivers, form 'silent guides' that deeply influence an individual's thoughts, behaviors, and emotions throughout life. We must therefore integrate the concepts of unconscious influence into the broader context of child-rearing.

Gabor Mate returns with 'In the Realm of Hungry Ghosts,' which explores the impacts of adverse childhood experiences and the environment on addiction and mental health. Mate provides a compassionate look at how early life stress and lack of nurturing can lead to self-destructive behaviors in adulthood; highlighting the long-term effects of environmental influence on childhood experiences.

The synthesis of these works leads to a compelling argument for the need to evolve familial and child-rearing institutions in tandem with a rewritten U.S. Constitution. For by understanding human diversity, by providing supportive environments for every family structure, by ensuring strong parental attachment, and by being aware of the unconscious influences from early childhood, we can cultivate and nurture well-rounded individuals.

Ultimately, by integrating the science of humanism into the rearing of our children, we maximize the synergies of our proposed transformational framework for the new American Constitution. This renewed framework would not only safeguard rights and freedoms, but would also nurture and cultivate a society where each individual's potential is recognized and fostered from childhood, creating a more empathetic, resilient, and emotionally intelligent citizenry.

The Case for a Constitutional Rewrite Through Good Arguments

Bo Seo's 'Good Arguments' sets the foundation for our exploration, emphasizing the power of effective argumentation in shaping societal outcomes. Seo elucidates the principles of constructing persuasive, rational arguments, which are essential in any discourse about societal change. This book serves as a framework for analyzing the subsequent works, each contributing to the overarching argument for a constitutional rewrite.

In 'The Fire Next Time,' James Baldwin presents a poignant critique of racial injustice in America. Baldwin's narrative, interweaving personal experiences with broader societal observations, underscores the deep-rooted issues of racism and inequality. His compelling arguments about the American social fabric and the need for significant change lay the groundwork for understanding why a constitutional rewrite is not just necessary, but imperative for addressing systemic racial disparities.

Tim Wu's 'The Curse of Bigness' shifts the focus to economic structures, particularly the dangers of extreme corporate concentration and monopolies. Wu argues that unchecked corporate power leads to a variety of societal harms, including economic inequality and political corruption. His analysis supports the idea that a constitutional rewrite should include provisions to rein in corporate power and protect economic democracy.

In 'The Great Derangement,' Matt Taibbi delves into the absurdities and dysfunctions within the American political system. He illustrates how political discourse has become increasingly detached from reality, leading to a populace that is disillusioned and disengaged. Taibbi's work underscores the need for a constitutional overhaul to restore sanity and efficacy to the political process.

Ralph Nader's 'Breaking through Power' provides a critical examination of corporate and political power structures. Nader argues for greater citizen empowerment and the dismantling of corporate influence in politics. His advocacy for a more democratic and transparent system aligns with the necessity of a constitutional rewrite to ensure that power truly resides with the people.

Integrating the insights from these works, we arrive at a compelling argument for a constitutional convention. The pervasive issues of racial injustice, economic inequality, political dysfunction, and corporate overreach, as laid out by Baldwin, Wu, Taibbi, and Nader, create an urgent need for systemic change. A constitutional rewrite, guided by the principles of good argumentation as outlined by Seo, presents a viable path towards addressing these deep-seated issues.

> The envisioned rewrite is not merely a legal overhaul, but a transformational step towards a metacognitive society - one that is self-aware, critically thinking, and constantly evolving.

And by embedding the principles of equal dignity, economic fairness, political sanity, and citizen empowerment into the Constitution; *such a rewrite will help lay the groundwork for a society capable of addressing its flaws and adapting to new challenges.*

Ultimately, this analysis illustrates how a constitutional rewrite, grounded in robust and good arguments, can be the catalyst for evolving humanity into a more just, equitable, and self-reflective state. This is not just a legal necessity, but a moral imperative to ensure a future where society can thrive in all its diversity and complexity.

THE NEED FOR
ECONOMIC REFORM

Classic economic theory,
based as it is on an inadequate theory of human motivation,
could be evolved by accepting the higher human needs;
including the impulse to self-actualize, and the love for the highest values.

– *Abraham Maslow*

THE FISCAL PROGNOSIS

No matter how you seem to fatten on a crime,
there can never be 'good for the bee', which is 'bad for the hive'.

– Ralph Waldo Emerson

Understanding the Dallas Fed's Warning from 2008 on Unfunded Liabilities

Fifteen years ago, the Dallas Federal Reserve issued a stark warning regarding the fiscal health of the United States. The nation faced a daunting gap between its financial promises and the means to fulfill them, amounting to $85.6 trillion in unfunded liabilities—a sum beyond the capacity of the Federal Reserve to offset through currency creation. This analysis explores the implications of this warning, the concept of unfunded liabilities, and the potential paths to address this fiscal challenge.

Understanding Unfunded Liabilities:

- Unfunded liabilities are commitments that the government has made for which it does not have sufficient funds set aside. These typically include pensions, healthcare benefits, and social security payments promised to citizens. The gap arises from the projected disparity between expected tax revenues and the costs of these obligations.

The Ineffectiveness of Monetary Policy:

- Typically, governments can leverage monetary policy tools, such as printing money, to manage short-term liquidity problems. However, the scale of unfunded liabilities surpasses the practical limits of these tools without triggering adverse effects like inflation or currency devaluation. Moreover, creating currency does not generate real wealth or economic productivity needed to honor these commitments.

The Fiscal Conundrum:

- The Dallas Fed highlighted the uncomfortable truth that the burden of these promises would fall on someone's shoulders. The $99.2 trillion figure they referenced represented the total adjustment needed to balance the promises with reality. This adjustment could come from increased taxes, reduced spending, a combination of both, or a recalibration of the promises themselves.

Choices and Consequences:

- The choice was framed as a generational one: take substantial measures now or defer the full weight of adjustment to future generations. Immediate action would likely entail economic sacrifice in the form of higher taxes and reduced government spending, affecting current standards of living and economic growth. Inaction, however, would compound the problem, potentially leading to a much steeper price for future taxpayers and beneficiaries.

To navigate through this fiscal dilemma, the Dallas Fed recommends a multifaceted approach:

1. *Fiscal Responsibility:* Implementing a disciplined fiscal policy that prioritizes the reduction of unfunded liabilities.

2. *Economic Growth:* Encouraging policies that stimulate sustainable economic growth, thus increasing the revenue base without resorting to excessive taxation.

3. *Structural Reforms:* Revisiting the structure of entitlement programs to ensure their long-term viability without compromising their core objectives.

4. *Public Awareness:* Fostering a public understanding of the issue to build consensus for the necessary, albeit difficult, decisions.

The Dallas Fed's warning remains a pertinent reminder of the fiscal realities confronting the United States. It calls for a sober reflection on the nation's economic promises and the practicalities of fulfilling them. Balancing fiscal responsibility with economic vitality is essential, as is the equitable distribution of the burden across generations.

The path forward demands a collective commitment to sustainable fiscal health and a willingness to make tough choices today to avert a more profound crisis tomorrow.

FINANCIAL SYSTEM TUTORIALS

Nearly all men can stand adversity,
but if you want to test a man's character, give him power.

– Abraham Lincoln

Introduction: In anticipation of the forthcoming constitutional convention, a profound comprehension of our existing financial and economic system is indispensable. To this end, watching three critical documentaries in sequence is essential for anyone aiming to contribute meaningfully to the dialogue.

- Firstly, *'97% Owned: The Money System,'* illuminates the foundational mechanics and the often-misunderstood realities of our current monetary system, laying bare the intricacies of money creation and its ripple effects on society.

- Following this, *'Princes of the Yen: Hidden Power of Central Banks,'* delves into the enigmatic operations of central banks and their far-reaching influence in shaping economic landscapes, revealing the potency of monetary policy decisions.

- Lastly, *'The Spider's Web: Britain's Second Empire,'* uncovers the covert network of Britain's financial reach and its global implications, completing a triptych of financial literacy. This ordered viewing is not merely educational—it's a necessary primer to equip participants with the critical insights required for an informed and strategic engagement in shaping the nation's constitutional future.

97% Owned
The Money System
https://youtu.be/XcGh1Dex4Yo

'97% Owned: The Money System' is a documentary that critically examines the modern monetary system and the creation of money. It illuminates a little-known but fundamental aspect of banking: most of the money in circulation is created by private

banks when they issue loans, rather than by central banks or government institutions. This has significant implications for economic stability, wealth distribution, and the control of the monetary system.

The documentary posits that because new money is predominantly created as debt through the issuance of loans, the economy becomes inherently dependent on continuous growth to service this debt. This system means that there is always more debt in the economy than there is money to pay it off due to the interest charged on loans, leading to a perpetual deficit of money supply in relation to debt.

The film brings to light the fact that this monetary system is not widely understood by the public, suggesting that this ignorance allows for the perpetuation of a system that benefits a small sector of society - namely, the financial services industry - while creating systemic risks and economic instability for the broader economy.

Addressing the claim that the monetary system operates similarly to a Ponzi scheme, one could argue that the reliance on perpetual growth to service ever-increasing debt is unsustainable, much like a Ponzi scheme relies on an ever-increasing influx of new investors to pay returns to earlier investors. When the creation of money is tied to debt, it can lead to boom-and-bust cycles, as seen in the global financial crisis of 2007-2008.

The documentary's narrative suggests that the current monetary system allows a 'cabal of banksters' to dominate the economic landscape, creating a form of financial enslavement where individuals and governments are mired in debt that can never be fully repaid. It implies that this system is not a naturally occurring phenomenon but rather a designed construct that benefits the financial elite at the expense of the general population.

'97% Owned: The Money System' presents a stark view of a monetary system that it perceives as deeply flawed and skewed towards the interests of the banking sector. To reform this system, the documentary advocates for greater public awareness and structural changes that would democratize the creation of money, ensuring it serves the public interest rather than the interests of a privileged few.

The persuasive narrative calls for a radical rethink of how money is created and distributed, suggesting that without change, society will continue to grapple with the consequences of an unstable and inequitable economic system.

Princes of the Yen
Hidden Power of Central Banks
https://youtu.be/p5Ac7ap_MAY

'Princes of the Yen: Central Banks and the Transformation of the Economy' is an eye-opening documentary based on the book by Professor Richard Werner. It explores the role and power of central banks, focusing on the Bank of Japan's influence over the Japanese economy during the late 20th century. The documentary presents a case that central banks, through their control of the money supply and credit creation, have the ability to shape economic and social structures.

The film delves into the post-World War II period of Japan's economic history, examining how the Bank of Japan steered the country's recovery and expansion. It asserts that the central bank's policies underpinned Japan's rapid growth but also laid the foundations for the economic bubbles and subsequent crises. It suggests that the bank's decision-making process was often opaque and seemed to benefit a select group of insiders and industrialists, rather than the broader economy.

The documentary contends that the Bank of Japan's policies were not unique and that central banks worldwide have similarly profound impacts on their national economies. It argues that these institutions have the power to create booms and busts, often with little oversight or accountability, by manipulating interest rates and controlling the availability of credit.

The film concludes by warning of the dangers posed by central banks that operate without sufficient checks and balances. It suggests that their actions can lead to distortions in the economy, exacerbate wealth inequality, and lead to economic instability. The implicit message is that the concentration of power within central banks—referred to as a 'cartel'—needs to be addressed to prevent such outcomes.

To argue that the central banking system is creating a 'feast of human suffering,' one might emphasize how policies that prioritize financial markets over the real economy can lead to misallocations of resources, asset bubbles, and ultimately, crises that result in widespread economic hardship. The aftermath of such crises often hits the most vulnerable segments of society the hardest, leading to unemployment, loss of savings, and a decline in living standards.

To prevent the end of the human experience, as dramatically stated, we must ensure that central banks are not only stewards of monetary stability but also serve the broader public interest. They should be transparent in their decision-making, accountable to democratic institutions, and their mandate should include not only price stability but also considerations of full employment, sustainable growth, and reduced inequality. Integrating these goals would require a systemic change in how central banks operate and interact with the political sphere and the economy at large.

In short, the documentary 'Princes of the Yen' casts central banks as powerful entities that shape economic destinies. For a sustainable future, it is imperative that this power is wielded with a greater sense of responsibility and subjected to rigorous oversight to ensure that it serves the common good and mitigates, rather than exacerbates, human suffering.

The Spider's Web
Britain's Second Empire
https://youtu.be/np_ylvc8Zj8

'The Spider's Web: Britain's Second Empire' is a compelling documentary that investigates the United Kingdom's role in creating a web of offshore secrecy jurisdictions that capture wealth from across the globe. This system is described as Britain's second empire and is centered on the City of London. The documentary highlights how these offshore jurisdictions have allowed individuals and corporations to hide assets, avoid taxes, and evade financial regulations.

The film uncovers how, after the decline of the British Empire, the City of London re-invented itself as the hub of a hidden financial empire spanning a network of crown dependencies and overseas territories. This network has become a haven for global finance, offering anonymity and a legislative environment that benefits wealthy elites and corporations.

The documentary paints a complex picture of the legal and financial mechanisms employed, the impact on global finance, and the significant consequences for nations that lose vital tax revenues. It scrutinizes the intricate architecture of this empire, where the City of London sits at the center, exerting significant control over the flow of global capital, often at the expense of transparency and equity.

To address the issues presented by this intricate financial web, the following recommendations provide a roadmap for reforming the banking system:

1. *Stopping Public Contracts to Tax Haven Companies:* Governments should legislate against awarding public contracts to companies that operate out of tax havens. This would disincentivize the use of offshore financial centers purely for tax avoidance, as it would bar such entities from lucrative public sector work, thereby aligning corporate behavior with public financial accountability.

2. *Creating Public Registries of Beneficial Ownership:* To combat financial secrecy, public registries of the real individuals who own, control, or benefit from companies, trusts, and foundations should be established. This transparency would curb illegal activities such as money laundering and tax evasion by making it difficult for individuals to hide behind shell companies and anonymous entities.

3. *Full Transparency of Government and Corporate Deals:* Legislation should be enacted to require full disclosure of all agreements between companies and governments. This would include not just financial deals but also any concessions, subsidies, or contracts. Transparency in these areas would reduce corruption and ensure that the public can hold both parties accountable for agreements that may affect economic and social outcomes.

4. *Public Country by Country Reporting:* Multinational companies should be mandated to publicly report financials for each country they operate in, including profits made and taxes paid. This recommendation aims to prevent profit-shifting and tax avoidance strategies that undermine the tax base of many countries, especially those in the developing world.

5. *Automatic Information Exchange Between Countries:* Finally, establishing a standard for automatic exchange of information between all countries would drastically reduce the opportunity for hiding assets and income. This global transparency initiative would ensure that tax authorities have access to the information they need to enforce tax laws and recover funds that are rightfully owed.

'The Spider's Web' documentary sheds light on a shadowy side of global finance, but the path to a fairer banking system is clear. By implementing these recommendations, the international community can take significant strides towards dismantling the infrastructure that allows for financial secrecy and tax avoidance. *These steps would promote a more equitable global financial system where wealth contributes to the public good, and economic activities are transparent and accountable.*

KEYS TO ECONOMIC REFORMATION
Literature Review

We look forward to a time when the power of love,
will replace the love of power.
Then will our world know the blessings of peace.

– William E. Gladstone

Economic Reformation Through Constitutional Renewal

Niall Ferguson's 'The Ascent of Money' charts the complex evolution of the financial system, providing a foundational understanding of our current economic structures. Setting the historical context for how money and the financial system have become cornerstones of modern civilization. Ferguson's work highlights the need for a robust and adaptable financial legal framework, revealing how historical financial crises often stemmed from systemic inadequacies that could potentially be addressed through constitutional measures.

Thomas Piketty's seminal work, 'Capital in the Twenty-First Century,' provides a deep analysis of wealth and income inequality, showing how capital tends to grow faster than the economic output, leading to increasing inequality. And despite the ascent of money, the distribution of wealth has become increasingly concentrated; underscoring the urgency for constitutional reforms that address this disparity and promote a more equitable economic distribution.

Expanding on his previous work, *Piketty's 'The Economics of Inequality'* dives into the mechanisms that drive economic disparity. For it is these policies and institutions that have allowed for, and in some cases exacerbated, the widening gap between the rich and the poor; we must therefore enforce economic justice and provide mechanisms for mitigating this destructive inequality.

Ellen Brown's 'The Web of Debt' investigates the current monetary system, particularly the role of central banks and the creation of money through debt. And it's vital to understand how our constitution currently offers little in the way of checks and balances on monetary policy and the creation of money. It therefore stands to reason that the fractional reserve banking system, and the debt-fueled growth model, needs new constitutional safeguards that protect us against the vulnerabilities of our corrupted financial system.

'Triumph of Injustice' by Emmanuel Saez brings to the forefront the role of tax policy in exacerbating inequality. In fact, empirical findings demonstrate how the tax system has increasingly favored the wealthy, contributing to a regressive economic environment. We must therefore create constitutional provisions that ensure a fair and progressive tax system as a foundation for economic equity.

The current economic malaise is symptomatic of our unresolved systemic issues that are rooted in the constitution itself:

1. Ferguson's historical perspective demonstrates the need for a financial system that is resilient and just, underpinned by constitutional principles.

2. Piketty's extensive research on inequality provides the empirical backbone for constitutional economic reforms that aim to balance the scale between capital and labor.

3. Brown's critique of the debt-based monetary system argues for constitutional amendments that secure monetary stability and prevent debt crises.

4. Saez's analysis of tax policy demands constitutional measures for a fair taxation system that does not provide privilege to the wealthy over the working class.

Insights from all five authors, envisions a reformed constitution that institutionalizes economic fairness, transparency, and stability; articulating the need for:

- Constitutional principles that govern the creation and flow of money in line with Ferguson's historical insights.

- Amendments that address wealth concentration, informed by Piketty's rigorous analysis of capital and inequality.

- Provisions for a monetary system that serves the public interest, echoing Brown's examination of debt and banking.

-   Saez advocates for a fair tax code to be enshrined in the constitution, to prevent the triumph of injustice through regressive tax policies.

A comprehensive constitutional rewrite is imperative for lasting economic reformation, ensuring that the future financial system is built on the pillars of equity, resilience, and justice—*a true renaissance of American constitutional democracy.*

Advocating a Constitutional Convention Through Economic Revisionism

Ha-Joon Chang's 'Bad Samaritans' lays the groundwork for this synthesized argument by challenging the orthodoxy of free-market capitalism. The author critiques the role of developed nations and international institutions in prescribing neoliberal policies to developing countries, often to their detriment. He exposes the historical reality that many successful economies achieved growth through protectionist policies and government intervention – a stark contrast to the 'one-size-fits-all' approach promoted by the 'Bad Samaritans' of the global economic system.

Building upon Chang's critique, *'The New Confessions of an Economic Hitman'* offers a first-hand account of how economic strategies are implemented with ulterior motives. Perkins describes his role in coercing vulnerable nations into debt and dependency, serving the interests of the U.S. and corporate giants rather than the nations' own development goals; proving the coercion inherent in global economic policies, and the need for a shift towards more equitable and sovereign economic relationships.

Joel Bakan's 'The New Corporation' takes the argument a step further by examining the legal and cultural evolution of corporations and their growing influence over society. Bakan argues that despite a veneer of social responsibility, corporations continue to prioritize profits over people. This systemic issue is linked to legal structures that define corporate personhood and rights, often at odds with democratic values and the public good.

Wolin's 'Democracy Inc.' introduces the concept of 'inverted totalitarianism,' where corporate power has become so entwined with government that it subtly undermines democratic institutions; and how economic priorities have reshaped the political landscape, leading to a democratic deficit where citizen participation is limited to largely symbolic gestures rather than substantive policy influence.

Finally, *Steve Keen's 'The New Economics'* synthesizes the previous books' theses by arguing for a foundational shift in economic understanding and policy. Keen suggests that a new economic framework is essential – one that acknowledges the flaws in traditional economic theories and incorporates these insights into financial stability, environmental sustainability, and social equity.

The current U.S. Constitution, while groundbreaking for its time, is ill-equipped to handle the nuances of modern economic realities and the challenges posed by corporate personhood, global economic manipulation, and the erosion of true democratic governance.

A constitutional rewrite is necessary to:

1. Establish economic policies that promote sustainable development and equitable growth, as opposed to the neocolonial strategies exposed by Chang and Perkins.

2. Redefine the legal status of corporations, as suggested by Bakan, to ensure they contribute positively to society without undermining democratic processes.

3. Protect the democratic process from corporate overreach and subtle forms of totalitarianism, a concern central to Wolin's analysis.

4. Lay the foundation for a 'new economics' that is cognizant of Keen's critiques, emphasizing stability, sustainability, and fairness.

We must therefore co-create a future where a rewritten U.S. Constitution reaffirms the primacy of the citizen in American democracy, reconfigures the relationship between the state and the economy, and recalibrates the role of corporations within society.

This new legal framework would be instrumental in creating an economy and a government that are not only for the people, *but truly by and of the people.*

Revolutionizing Economic Foundations through Constitutional Transformation

Jacques Peretti's groundbreaking analysis in 'The Deals that Made the World' unveils the clandestine dynamics of business transactions that have silently molded our society. These transactions, often executed in pursuit of profit with little public awareness, have contoured the economic terrain to primarily benefit a select few. This underscores the critical need for implementing regulated transparency and accountability in business operations. Empirical evidence from economic studies supports the idea that unregulated business practices can lead to market distortions and wealth concentration, further highlighting the importance of Peretti's findings.

David Montero's 'Kickback' delves deeper into the widespread corruption in international business. It exposes how bribery and illegal deals not only disrupt economies but also perpetuate inequality. This corruption, often sustained by legal loopholes and ambiguous laws, confirms the inadequacy of current constitutional measures in tackling such systemic problems. Montero's revelations are backed by economic data showing the detrimental impact of corruption on market efficiency and equitable growth, validating the urgent need for robust legal frameworks and technological advancements to combat corruption.

In 'The Riches of this Land' Jim Tankersley illustrates the pivotal role of the American middle class in driving economic prosperity. The revival of the middle class is essential for sustainable economic growth, necessitating constitutional reforms that assure economic justice and opportunity for all. Statistical analyses in socioeconomic research align with Tankersley's arguments, indicating that a robust middle class is crucial for maintaining economic balance and stimulating innovation.

Thomas Philippon, in 'The Great Reversal' confronts the monopolistic practices of multinational corporations that hinder competition and innovation, leading to economic inefficiencies and inequality. This calls for implementing strategies that promote competitive markets and limit corporate dominance. Economic theories and case studies on monopolies corroborate Philippon's argument, showing how monopolistic practices can stifle market dynamics and lead to price manipulation and reduced consumer choice.

Anand Giridharadas's 'Winners Take All' critically examines the narrative of philanthro-capitalism, which suggests that the wealthy can amass fortunes while altruistically resolving societal issues. He argues that systemic change, rather than individual goodwill, is crucial to addressing structural inequalities. While philanthropy is commendable, it cannot replace the need for fair and equitable economic policies. Giridharadas's critique is supported by socioeconomic research that emphasizes the limitations of philanthropy in addressing deep-rooted systemic issues, advocating for more comprehensive policy approaches.

To address these economic challenges and systemic injustices, we propose a foundational overhaul of the constitutional framework, including:

1. Constitutional mandates for corporate transparency and accountability, as highlighted by Peretti.

2. Stronger anti-corruption frameworks, as suggested by Montero, to ensure legal accountability of economic entities.

3. Policies to rebuild and sustain the middle class, reflecting Tankersley's emphasis on inclusive prosperity.

4. Legislation to dismantle monopolistic structures and encourage competition, drawing from Philippon's research.

5. A redefinition of the role of wealth and philanthropy in society, based on Giridharadas's insights, to prioritize systemic solutions over individual generosity.

This comprehensive constitutional reformation is essential for creating a just and equitable economic system. By integrating these principles, the new constitution will not only address current challenges but also possess the flexibility to adapt to future economic scenarios.

The proposed constitutional convention must lay the groundwork for legal and moral foundations tailored for an economy that serves the broader populace, not just the privileged few. This will be the cornerstone of a society where economic reformation is not merely an aspiration, but a tangible reality, embedded in the very fabric of our constitutional framework.

This reformed constitution should be seen as a living document, evolving with the changing economic landscapes and societal needs, ensuring that it remains relevant and effective in promoting economic equity and justice for generations to come.

THE NEED FOR
INSTITUTIONAL REFORM

Security is mostly a superstition. It does not exist in nature.
Nor do the children of men, as a whole, experience it.
Avoiding danger is no safer in the long run, than outright exposure.
Life is either a daring adventure, or nothing.

- Helen Keller

THE EVOLUTION OF SOCIETY AND DEMOCRACY
Literature Review

The teacher who is indeed wise,
does not bid you to enter the house of his wisdom,
but rather leads you to the threshold of your mind.

– *Kahlil Gibran*

How Corporations Overthrew Democracy

'Silent Coup: How Corporations Overthrew Democracy' by Clair Provost and Matt Kennard is an incisive critique of modern corporate influence on democratic institutions and processes. The book meticulously examines how corporations have incrementally eroded democratic norms and usurped the levers of power to serve their own interests at the expense of public good.

Provost and Kennard argue that the 'silent coup' has been a gradual process, characterized by the increasing ability of corporations to shape legislation, influence regulatory frameworks, and shift public opinion through their control over the media. They describe a world where corporate lobbying is not just a feature of democracy but has become a dominant force, effectively turning government institutions into agents of corporate agendas.

The authors provide a historical context to this phenomenon, tracing the roots of corporate influence back to the rise of neoliberal economic policies which emphasized deregulation, privatization, and the reduction of state intervention in the economy. These policies, they argue, have provided the fertile ground for corporations to accumulate power and wealth, often at the cost of environmental sustainability and social equity.

'Silent Coup' also delves into the mechanisms of corporate power, including the proliferation of opaque think tanks and policy groups that push corporate-friendly policies under the guise of academic neutrality and public interest. The book sheds light on the revolving door between the corporate sector and politics, where former executives take on governmental roles, and government officials move into lucrative corporate positions, blurring the lines between public service and corporate profit.

The authors highlight the consequences of this silent coup, which range from weakened labor protections and environmental degradation to the erosion of consumer rights and the undermining of public health. They make a case that corporate power has not just influenced specific policy outcomes but has redefined the very essence of what democracy means in the modern age, challenging the principle that government is by the people and for the people.

Provost and Kennard call for a reclamation of democracy, suggesting that it requires robust legal reforms, greater transparency in political funding, and the cultivation of a more informed and engaged citizenry. They emphasize the need for collective action and the strengthening of civil society to counterbalance corporate power and restore democratic ideals.

'Silent Coup' is a sobering examination of the intersection between capitalism and democracy, and a clarion call for vigilance and activism to protect democratic institutions from corporate encroachment. It is an educational tool for understanding the contemporary challenges facing democracies worldwide and a manifesto for reclaiming democratic spaces for genuine public participation.

Corruptible: Who Gets Power and How It Changes Us

'Corruptible: Who Gets Power and How It Changes Us' by Brian Klaas is an incisive exploration of the nature of power, the types of individuals who seek it, and the transformative effect it has on people. Klaas, a political scientist, delves into the complex relationship between power and corruption, examining how systems and human psychology interact to shape the behavior of those in positions of authority.

Klaas begins by dissecting the allure of power and the characteristics of those who pursue it. He presents a paradox: while societies need strong leaders, the very process of acquiring power can select for traits that are undesirable in leaders. Klaas argues that the path to power often favors those with Machiavellian traits—individuals who are ambitious, manipulative, and ruthless. Such characteristics can be advantageous in navigating the competitive and sometimes cutthroat arenas in which power contests occur.

One of the central themes of 'Corruptible' is the corrupting influence of power itself. Klaas draws on psychological research and historical examples to illustrate how power can alter individuals' behaviors and moral compasses. He shows that while power does not corrupt everyone, it has a pronounced tendency to exacerbate personal flaws and diminish empathy and ethical constraints, especially in systems with weak checks and balances.

Klaas also explores the structural factors that determine who gets power. He examines different governance systems, from democracies to dictatorships, and how they shape the leaders they produce. The book reveals that institutions with transparency, accountability, and democratic controls are more likely to have leaders who act in the public's interest, while those without such mechanisms are prone to corruption and abuse of power.

'Corruptible' doesn't only focus on political power; it also investigates power dynamics in other realms, including business, law enforcement, and religious institutions. Klaas identifies universal patterns across these sectors, noting that wherever there is power, there is a risk of corruption, but also the potential for positive change if the right systems are in place.

Throughout the book, Klaas emphasizes the importance of designing institutions that not only attract less corruptible individuals but also restrain the darker impulses of those in charge. He suggests reforms to recruitment and selection processes for powerful positions, aiming to diversify the pool of candidates and reduce the influence of corruptible individuals.

In terms of how power changes people, Klaas offers a nuanced view. Not everyone is changed for the worse, and power can also amplify positive traits such as generosity and fairness, particularly when leaders feel secure in their positions and are held accountable.

'Corruptible' is an educational examination of the dynamics of power. Klaas highlights the need for systematic changes to prevent corruption and ensure that power serves the greater good. He provides a thought-provoking analysis that is not only theoretical but also practical, offering real-world solutions to one of society's most enduring problems. The book is a valuable resource for anyone interested in the intersection of psychology, politics, and ethics, and it serves as a guide for creating a society where power is a force for good rather than a source of corruption.

Dismantling the Meritocracy Trap
Pathways to Dignity in Constitutional Design

In 'The Meritocracy Trap,' Daniel Markovits presents a critical analysis of meritocracy, revealing it as a system that perpetuates inequality under the guise of fairness. The book's insights are particularly relevant when considering the creation of a new constitutional framework that aims to promote a more equitable society.

The Illusion of Meritocracy: Markovits argues that meritocracy has become a tool that the elite use to consolidate wealth and status. This system rewards a narrow set of skills and creates a self-perpetuating upper class that hoards opportunities. In the context of constitutional reform, this critique warns against enshrining principles that might appear meritocratic but actually entrench inequality.

Meritocracy and Dignity: The book suggests that the meritocratic ideal strips dignity from those who don't reach the top, creating a society where self-worth is tied to professional success. A new constitutional framework must, therefore, sever the link between merit and value, affirming the inherent dignity of all work and contributions.

Steps Toward a New World of Dignity:

1. *Education Reform:* The constitution could mandate equitable funding for all public schools, breaking the cycle where only certain institutions serve as pipelines to success.

2. *Labor Rights:* Provisions to protect workers' rights, encourage unionization, and ensure fair wages would support the dignity of all forms of labor.

3. *Taxation and Wealth Redistribution:* A constitutional approach to progressive taxation could prevent the excessive accumulation of wealth and provide for social services that level the playing field.

4. *Access to Justice:* Guarantees of legal representation and fair judicial processes can ensure that all citizens have the opportunity to challenge discriminatory practices.

We must therefore evaluate how the illusion of meritocracy affects society and propose some constitutional remedies...

- *Universal Basic Services: The* constitution could provide for universal healthcare, education, and other basic services, ensuring that everyone's fundamental needs are met irrespective of merit.

- *Political Representation:* Electoral reforms that minimize the influence of money in politics could help ensure that all citizens, not just the elite, have their voices heard.

- *Civic Education:* A constitutional mandate for civic education that promotes an understanding of rights and duties could foster a sense of communal responsibility and mutual respect.

Markovits's 'The Meritocracy Trap' is a call to action for a society that values every individual not for their achievements but for their humanity. By incorporating his insights into a new constitutional framework, we can aspire to a society that truly honors the dignity of all its members.

The Ethics of Success and the Politics of the Common Good

Michael J. Sandel's 'The Tyranny of Merit' challenges the prevailing attitudes towards success and failure ingrained in meritocratic societies. Sandel critiques the hubris of meritocracy for its harsh judgment on those who do not 'succeed' by conventional standards.

Meritocratic Hubris and Its Discontents: The meritocratic framework posits that social and economic rewards should go to those who 'deserve' them based on their talents and efforts. However, Sandel points out that this breeds hubris among the successful and humiliation among those left behind. In a constitutional context, this ethos can lead to policies that neglect the welfare of the broader community in favor of individual gain.

The Moral Limits of Merit: Meritocracy has been critiqued for ignoring the role of luck and the systemic barriers that prevent equal opportunity. In educational policy, for example, a constitutional amendment might aim to ensure equitable access to quality education for all, regardless of socioeconomic status, to counteract the 'luck' of being born into privilege.

Sandel's Vision for a New Politics:

1. *Dignity of Work:* Sandel emphasizes the dignity of all types of work, suggesting constitutional guarantees for workers' rights and a revaluation of the labor market to honor all forms of contribution.

2. *Civic Virtue:* He advocates for a renewed focus on civic education and participatory democracy, encouraging citizens to engage in public deliberation and community service.

3. *Public Goods and Common Spaces:* A constitutional emphasis on public goods, such as parks, libraries, and transportation, can foster shared experiences and a sense of community.

Detailed Vision of the Common Good:

1. *Shared Prosperity:* Sandel envisions a society where wealth is not solely in the hands of a few but is distributed in a manner that benefits all, potentially through constitutional mechanisms like progressive taxation or social dividends.

2. *Humility in Policy:* A constitutional commitment to humility would involve recognizing the role of luck in success and thus advocating for a safety net for the less fortunate.

3. *Democratic Engagement:* Reforms to ensure that all voices are heard in the democratic process, such as campaign finance reform and proportional representation, could be enshrined in the constitution.

**We must therefore implement constitutional changes that encourage solidarity, respect for different forms of work, and engagement in the 'common life' of the community.*

Sandel's work compels us to reconsider the values that underpin our society and to imagine a new politics that places the common good at its heart. By adopting constitutional principles that reflect this vision, we can strive towards a more inclusive, empathetic, and cooperative society.

Mass Media Influence and Our Democracy

'Manufacturing Consent' by Edward S. Herman and Noam Chomsky offers a critical examination of mass media's role in shaping public perception and opinion, aligned with corporate and governmental interests.

> Propaganda Model: The authors introduce the 'propaganda model,' which asserts that media is complicit in promoting the objectives of elite interests, often at the expense of truth and diversity. This model is predicated on five filters that determine the type of news that reaches the public: ownership, advertising, sourcing, flak, and anti-communism/anti-terrorism.

Transforming Media for Cultural Harmony:

1. *Encouraging Independent Media:* A constitutional amendment could safeguard the independence of media outlets from corporate and governmental control, fostering a more diverse and unbiased media landscape.

2. *Regulating Advertising Influence:* To counteract the second filter, there could be limits on the influence advertisers have over media content, ensuring editorial independence.

3. *Diversifying Sources:* Media education and policy could encourage journalism that seeks out a multiplicity of sources, particularly those that represent marginalized or dissenting voices, enhancing cultural diversity.

4. *Addressing Flak:* Building resilience against 'flak'—negative responses to media stories—might involve protecting journalists and media organizations from undue legal and financial pressures.

5. *Redefining Threat Narratives:* Instead of allowing media to perpetuate fear-based narratives that can lead to cultural and political divisiveness, a new constitutional clause might mandate that media portray a more accurate and less sensationalized picture of global and domestic threats.

Incorporating Media Strategy into Constitutional Framework:

1. *Freedom of the Press*: The constitutional framework should reaffirm and strengthen the freedom of the press while emphasizing the role of media in reflecting societal diversity and promoting democratic discourse.

2. *Media Literacy Education:* The constitution could mandate media literacy education, enabling citizens to critically evaluate media content and recognize biases.

3. *Public Broadcasting:* Strengthening public broadcasting services that operate independently of market pressures could ensure that diverse and minority perspectives are represented in the media.

**We must therefore create constitutional safeguards to foster a media environment that informs, educates, and empowers citizens, rather than one that manipulates and controls.*

Herman and Chomsky's insights into the workings of mass media can inform the creation of a constitutional framework that promotes an informed and engaged citizenry.

Thus, *by mitigating the influence of concentrated media ownership, advertising, source biases, flak, and alarmist narratives,* a new constitution can lay the foundation for a media system that champions diversity and democratic values, transforming the cacophony of cultural determinism into an interdependent spectrum that help creates an antifragile society.

Navigating Misbelief
Crafting a New Constitution in the Age of Misinformation

In 'Misbelief,' Dan Ariely delves into the cognitive biases and irrational behaviors that lead people to accept and propagate false beliefs. Understanding these forces is particularly crucial when attempting to combat misinformation in the formidable task of drafting a new constitutional framework.

Cognitive Biases and Misinformation: Ariely's work suggests that misbelief is often a product of cognitive biases such as confirmation bias, where individuals favor information that confirms their preexisting beliefs. In the context of constitution-making, this bias can lead to the inclusion of clauses that may be popular or politically expedient but not necessarily founded on factual or rational bases.

The Role of Social Proof: Social proof, or the tendency to see an action as more correct when others are doing it, can also fuel the spread of misinformation. In drafting a new constitution, it's vital to ensure that the document's provisions are based on sound principles and not merely on the popularity of certain ideas.

Combating Misinformation: To effectively counteract the influence of misinformation in the formation of a new constitutional framework, several strategies can be implemented:

1. *Promote Critical Thinking:* Educational initiatives that enhance critical thinking and media literacy can empower citizens to scrutinize information critically, fostering a culture resistant to misinformation.

2. *Transparent Deliberation:* Ensuring that the constitutional deliberation process is transparent and open to public scrutiny can help prevent the incorporation of unfounded beliefs into the law of the land.

3. *Diverse Representation:* Involving a diverse array of voices in the drafting process can counteract the echo chamber effect and provide a broader perspective that challenges unfounded beliefs.

4. *Fact-Checking Mechanisms:* Establishing independent fact-checking bodies that can verify the validity of information during the constitution-drafting process can prevent the solidification of misbeliefs into legal statutes.

We must therefore prioritize truth over comfort or convenience:

- *Institutional Safeguards:* The constitution could create institutions dedicated to monitoring and correcting public misinformation, similar to the role of a central bank in managing economic information.

- *Legal Framework for Media:* Regulations that hold media accountable for spreading misinformation without stifling free speech could be a cornerstone of the new constitution.

- *Encouragement of Deliberative Democracy:* Mechanisms for citizen engagement in deliberative democracy, such as citizen juries or assemblies, can be established to ensure a well-informed populace.

'Misbelief' offers a crucial understanding of the psychological tendencies that make misinformation so pervasive. By addressing these tendencies, a new constitutional framework can be fortified against the perils of misbelief, laying the foundation for a society that values and upholds truth.

Fostering Empathy in Children

'Don't You Know Who I Am?' by Dr. Ramani S. Durvasula is a deep dive into the world of narcissism, examining its influence on personal relationships, work environments, and broader society. Dr. Durvasula, a licensed clinical psychologist, draws from her extensive experience to offer insights into the behaviors of individuals with narcissistic tendencies and provides guidance on how to deal with the challenges they present.

In the context of raising children, the book touches upon the pivotal role of parenting and environmental factors in shaping a child's propensity towards either empathy or narcissism. The educational crux of this subject lies in recognizing that while narcissistic traits can be fostered by certain experiences and parental behaviors, empathy can also be nurtured from a young age.

Here are key takeaways from 'Don't You Know Who I Am?' with a focus on fostering empathy in children:

1. *Modeling Empathy:* Children learn a great deal by observing the adults in their lives. When parents and caregivers consistently display empathy towards others, children are more likely to adopt these behaviors. Dr. Durvasula emphasizes the importance of modeling empathetic listening, validating feelings, and showing concern for the well-being of others.

2. *Encouraging Emotional Intelligence:* Developing emotional intelligence is critical in helping children understand and manage their emotions, as well as recognizing and responding to the emotions of others. Encouraging children to talk about their feelings and teaching them to label their emotions can enhance their ability to empathize.

3. *Fostering Connection Over Achievement:* In a society that often values success and achievement over personal connections, Dr. Durvasula suggests a shift in focus. She advocates for praising empathetic behavior and prioritizing

relationship-building skills alongside personal achievements to create a more balanced value system.

4. *Setting Boundaries:* While it's important to nurture empathy, it's equally important to teach children healthy boundaries. This helps them understand that caring for others does not mean tolerating disrespectful or harmful behavior. Dr. Durvasula advises parents to teach children to assert themselves respectfully and to recognize when to step back for their own well-being.

5. *Providing Opportunities for Perspective-Taking:* Engaging children in activities that require them to consider other people's perspectives can be a powerful tool in developing empathy. This might include reading books with diverse characters, community service, or simply discussing different points of view on a subject.

6. *Challenging Entitlement:* To counteract narcissistic traits, it is crucial to challenge entitlement. This involves setting realistic expectations, not over-praising for mundane tasks, and teaching the value of hard work and perseverance.

7. *Cultivating Gratitude:* Dr. Durvasula suggests that fostering a sense of gratitude in children can help combat narcissism. Practices like keeping a gratitude journal or regularly discussing things they are thankful for can reinforce the importance of appreciating others and what they have.

8. *Teaching Conflict Resolution:* Effective conflict resolution skills enable children to navigate disagreements with empathy. Dr. Durvasula emphasizes the importance of teaching children to listen, understand different viewpoints, and find mutually satisfying solutions to problems.

In essence, 'Don't You Know Who I Am?' provides a roadmap for parents and educators seeking to cultivate an environment that favors empathy over narcissism. By integrating Dr. Durvasula's strategies into daily interactions and broader parenting philosophies, there is a greater chance of raising children who are empathetic, emotionally intelligent, and capable of forming healthy, mutually respectful relationships. *This not only benefits the individual child but contributes to a more compassionate and understanding society.*

Fostering Resilience and Critical Thinking

In 'The Coddling of the American Mind,' Jonathan Haidt, along with co-author Greg Lukianoff, explores the impact of certain cultural trends within American education that, they argue, inhibit the intellectual and emotional growth of students.

> Three Great Untruths: Haidt identifies what he calls 'Three Great Untruths' that have permeated educational culture*: What doesn't kill you makes you weaker, (2) always trust your feelings, and (3) life is a battle between good people and evil people.*

These concepts, the authors suggest, contribute to a culture of 'safetyism,' which may limit students' exposure to challenges and intellectual diversity, ultimately hindering their development.

Constitutional Implications for Education:

1. *Promotion of Intellectual Diversity:* A constitutional amendment could advocate for the protection of free speech and encourage exposure to a range of viewpoints within educational settings, fostering critical thinking and resilience.

2. *Educational Standards for Resilience:* The framework might mandate that educational institutions provide opportunities for students to encounter and overcome challenges, thereby strengthening their ability to deal with adversity.

3. *Emotional and Social Learning:* The education system, under the new constitutional guidelines, would integrate emotional intelligence and social learning, guiding students in navigating their feelings and disagreements constructively.

Evolving Human Development through Education:

1. *Critical Thinking:* By promoting pedagogical practices that encourage questioning and debate, students can develop the ability to analyze and argue, essential skills for citizenship and the workforce.

2. *Emotional Growth:* Education that fosters maturity, rather than coddling, would aim to teach students how to process and respond to emotional challenges healthily and productively.

3. *Social Interaction:* Policies could encourage cooperative learning and community engagement, helping students to appreciate the complexity of social issues and the value of collaboration.

We must therefore institute constitutional protections for educational practices that encourage resilience, emotional well-being, and critical thinking; to develop robust, well-rounded individuals capable of contributing positively to society.

The insights from Haidt's work suggest that a constitutional framework that values intellectual challenge, emotional growth, and social interaction within the education system could lead to a more resilient and thoughtful populace. Such a framework would require a careful balance between the protection of individual sensitivities and the promotion of a robust educational environment where students are prepared to face the complexities of the real world.

Facilitating Antifragility

'Antifragile: Things That Gain from Disorder' by Nassim Nicholas Taleb is a comprehensive work that extends beyond the realms of economics and finance, where the author's ideas first gained prominence, into a broad philosophical treatise on how systems can be built to not only resist shocks but actually benefit from them. Taleb introduces the concept of 'antifragility', a property of systems that increases in capability, resilience, or robustness as a result of stressors, shocks, volatility, noise, mistakes, faults, attacks, or failures.

In the context of societal systems — including economic, political, and educational structures — Taleb argues that making a system antifragile involves several key principles and strategies:

1. *Decentralization:* Taleb advocates for the decentralization of power and decision-making. Decentralized systems are less likely to experience catastrophic failure because problems are contained within smaller, more manageable units. This allows for more experimental approaches to problem-solving and innovation.

2. *Redundancy:* While efficiency is often seen as the hallmark of modern engineering and economics, Taleb points out that redundancy — having more

than what is seemingly necessary — can provide a buffer that absorbs shocks. In societal systems, this can mean having surplus resources or parallel systems that can take over when one fails.

3. *Optionality:* Antifragile systems benefit from having options. This refers to the ability to choose different paths or strategies when circumstances change. For a society, this could mean investing in a diversity of industries, educational paths, or even political strategies.

4. *Smallness:* Taleb notes that smallness allows for faster adaptation and innovation. Smaller entities — whether they are businesses, communities, or administrative units — can often make quicker decisions and pivot more effectively in response to change.

5. *Skin in the Game:* Taleb emphasizes the importance of accountability and risk-sharing in the construction of antifragile systems. When the individuals making decisions bear some risk of harm from those decisions, they are more likely to act in ways that promote the health of the system.

6. *Via Negativa:* Instead of always looking for what to add to improve a system, Taleb suggests that often it is more beneficial to remove what is unnecessary and harmful. This approach focuses on reducing downside risks rather than achieving upside gains.

7. *Non-Predictive Decision Making:* Taleb argues that since we cannot predict the future, we should not base our systems on the ability to do so. Instead, we should build systems that can survive a range of outcomes, especially negative ones.

8. *Convexity Effects:* Taleb introduces the idea of convexity, where the benefits from favorable shocks are larger than the harm from unfavorable ones. Designing societal systems with positive convexity means they will benefit more from random events or shocks than they would suffer.

9. *Respect for the Old:* Taleb suggests that time-tested traditions and systems have proven their antifragility, and there is value in understanding and respecting them. Societal systems should incorporate ancient wisdom where it has shown durability and flexibility.

10. *Ethical Imperatives:* Lastly, Taleb implies that fostering antifragility is not just a technical challenge but an ethical one. Societal systems should be engineered to protect the weak and ensure that the benefits and harms are distributed fairly.

In an educational context, Taleb's 'Antifragile' challenges the current norms of societal engineering and management, advocating for a radical shift in how we perceive stability and growth.

To prevent fragility and facilitate antifragility, societal systems must embrace variability and stressors as opportunities for improvement rather than merely threats to stability. *This paradigm shift could lead to more robust, equitable, and adaptive societal structures capable of thriving in an unpredictable world.*

Evolutionary Origins of a Good Society

'Blueprint: The Evolutionary Origins of a Good Society' by Nicholas A. Christakis explores the concept that despite the apparent randomness of social development and the cultural differences that distinguish societies, there exists a kind of universal social blueprint that is embedded in our nature as a species. Christakis argues that this blueprint has evolved over millennia and that it fosters cooperation, friendship, fairness, and learning within societies.

In the context of a constitutional convention, where the goal is to establish the fundamental principles and structures that will govern a society, 'Blueprint' could serve as an insightful guide in several ways:

1. *Inherent Social Values:* Christakis's work underlines the importance of certain social values that are deeply rooted in human nature. A constitutional convention could benefit from recognizing these values—like the propensity for cooperation and the expectation of fair treatment—as foundational to any societal structure and therefore, enshrine them in its constitution.

2. *Social Networks:* The book illustrates how social networks are a powerful tool for both cohesion and diffusion. They can spread ideas, behaviors, and innovations. A new constitution could establish systems that harness the positive aspects of social networks while mitigating their propensity to spread harmful or divisive content.

3. *Capacity for Learning:* Humans have a remarkable capacity to learn from one another, which is a cornerstone of cultural evolution. A constitution that is being drafted could embed principles that ensure the education system, media, and public discourse are structured in a way that promotes critical thinking and lifelong learning.

4. *Building Community and Cooperation:* The blueprint suggests that humans have an innate ability to form communities and work cooperatively. A constitutional convention should consider creating institutions that facilitate community-building and encourage cooperative behavior to harness this natural inclination for the greater good of society.

5. *Addressing Conflict:* While Christakis acknowledges that conflict is a part of human social life, he also notes that our blueprint includes mechanisms for conflict resolution. A constitution can incorporate structures for peaceful dispute resolution and reconciliation, which are essential for maintaining social harmony.

6. *Fairness and Equity:* The sense of fairness is deeply ingrained in human nature. A constitution should thus aim to create a legal and political framework that embodies principles of equality and justice, ensuring that all members of society feel that they are treated fairly.

7. *Adaptation and Change:* The blueprint also includes the ability for societies to adapt and change. Therefore, a constitution might be designed with a degree of flexibility that allows it to evolve over time, incorporating amendments and reforms that reflect the changing values and needs of the society it governs.

Christakis's notion of a social blueprint does not imply that all societies are the same or should be the same, but rather that there are common threads in how humans form and maintain societies. When drafting a constitution, it would be wise to consider these evolutionary underpinnings to create a system of governance that is aligned with humanity's innate tendencies towards forming good societies. The challenge lies in translating this blueprint into actionable principles that can guide the creation of a robust, equitable, and dynamic constitutional framework.

Strategically Guiding Societal Evolution

David Sloan Wilson's 'This View of Life: Completing the Darwinian Revolution' presents a compelling case for applying evolutionary theory beyond the biological realm, into the domains of social sciences, humanities, and human problem-solving. Wilson argues that understanding evolution can help us not only make sense of the past but also shape the future. The book delves into how evolutionary thinking can offer insights into adapting to change and strategically guiding societal evolution.

One could distill the essence of Wilson's ideas as follows:

- *Understanding Evolutionary Processes:* Wilson emphasizes that to adapt and evolve, societies must first understand the principles of evolution. This includes recognizing that behaviors, institutions, and cultural practices all undergo a form of natural selection, where those that are advantageous in a given environment are more likely to persist.

- *Multilevel Selection:* A key concept in Wilson's book is multilevel selection, which suggests that natural selection operates not just at the individual level but also at the level of groups. In the context of societal change, this means that individuals and groups that work well together are more likely to succeed and thrive.

- *Cultural Evolution:* The book argues that cultural practices also evolve, shaped by both genetic and environmental factors. Societies can consciously affect their cultural evolution by choosing practices that are beneficial and discarding those that are harmful.

- *Adaptive Change:* To evolve the future, Wilson suggests that societies need to be adaptive, responding to changes in the environment with innovations and adjustments. This requires a balance between preserving beneficial traditions and being open to new, potentially advantageous changes.

- *Niche Construction:* An important part of evolution is the concept of niche construction, where organisms modify their environment, which in turn affects their evolution. Societies can actively construct niches that better suit their values and goals, such as creating educational systems that nurture creativity and critical thinking.

- *Cooperation and Altruism:* Wilson discusses how cooperation and altruism, while seemingly at odds with the competitive nature of natural selection, can actually be advantageous for groups. A society that wants to evolve positively should foster these traits, creating systems that reward cooperative behavior.

- *Informed Interventions:* Evolutionary theory can inform policy-making and societal interventions. By understanding how certain policies or practices might influence the evolution of society, leaders can make better-informed decisions that steer social evolution in desired directions.

- *Iterative Processes:* Just as evolution is an ongoing process, adapting to change requires an iterative approach. Societies must be willing to experiment, learn from successes and failures, and continuously refine their strategies.

- *Long-term Perspective:* Evolving the future necessitates a long-term perspective. Short-term gains may not lead to sustainable progress. Evolutionary theory encourages looking at the long-term consequences of actions and strategies.

'This View of Life' posits that by applying evolutionary principles to societal development, we can better understand and influence the trajectory of our social evolution. Adapting to change isn't just about reacting to external pressures; it's about proactive evolution, shaping societal practices and institutions in ways that are consciously aligned with desired outcomes.

This approach requires a holistic view of human society as an integrated, evolving system, where every policy, practice, and innovation can be seen through the lens of its potential to contribute to a flourishing future.

Creating Organizations as Amazing as the People Inside Them

'Humanocracy: Creating Organizations as Amazing as the People Inside Them' by Gary Hamel and Michele Zanini presents a thought-provoking critique of traditional hierarchical corporate structures, which they refer to as 'bureaucracy,' and proposes an alternative model they call 'Humanocracy.' This model aims to unlock the full creative and intellectual potential of every employee.

In the bureaucratic model, decision-making is centralized, and employees are often viewed as resources to be managed, leading to disengagement and a lack of innovation. Hamel and Zanini argue that bureaucracy is an anachronism in the age of knowledge work, and they lay out a compelling vision for a more dynamic and democratic way of organizing work.

The principles of Humanocracy are:

1. *Ownership:* Encouraging employees to think and act like owners, taking responsibility for their actions and the outcomes. This involves a level of autonomy and trust that goes beyond the traditional employee-employer relationship.

2. *Meritocracy:* Advancing people based on their contributions rather than their credentials or tenure. This ensures that the organization is always led by the most capable individuals, with ideas winning out over hierarchy.

3. *Community:* Fostering a sense of belonging and shared purpose among employees, which boosts engagement and collaboration. This is achieved through shared values and a clear, compelling mission that everyone is committed to.

4. *Openness:* Promoting transparency and openness to ideas, no matter where they come from within the organization. This means breaking down silos and encouraging cross-functional collaboration and communication.

5. *Experimentation:* Embracing a mindset of continuous learning and innovation, where employees are encouraged to test new ideas and learn from failure. This helps organizations stay adaptive and responsive to changes in the market.

6. *Flexibility:* Designing structures and processes that can adapt quickly to changing circumstances, rather than being rigid and inflexible. This allows for a more fluid allocation of resources and faster response times.

The path to Humanocracy involves several key steps:

1. *Inspiring Change:* This starts with a compelling argument for why bureaucracy is no longer suitable and how Humanocracy can create a competitive advantage.

2. *Building the Case for Change:* Organizations need to assess their bureaucratic mass – a measure of how much bureaucracy is present – and the opportunity cost associated with it.

3. *Hacking Management:* Rather than a top-down overhaul, Hamel and Zanini suggest making small, experimental changes – hacks – that align with the principles of Humanocracy.

4. *Mobilizing the Workforce:* Engaging everyone in the process of change to ensure buy-in and to harness the collective intelligence of the organization.

5. *Scaling Up:* Once successful hacks are identified, they need to be scaled across the organization to maximize their impact.

6. *Embedding the Change:* Finally, the principles of Humanocracy need to be embedded into the very fabric of the organization, through both formal mechanisms like processes and systems, and informal ones like cultural norms and behaviors.

Hamel and Zanini envision a world where workplaces are not soulless, efficiency-driven machines, but vibrant communities of individuals who are valued for their unique contributions.

The transition to Humanocracy is not only a strategic imperative for businesses to remain competitive but also a moral imperative to fully respect and utilize the talents of every person. *They argue that by empowering people at all levels, organizations can unleash a level of innovation, motivation, and agility that is impossible under the old paradigm.*

Mobilizing Collective Action
A 'Prosocial' Approach to Organizing a Constitutional Convention

'Prosocial: Using Evolutionary Science to Build Productive, Equitable, and Collaborative Groups' by Paul W.B. Atkins et al. is a guide to enhancing group effectiveness by applying principles from evolutionary theory, psychology, and behavioral economics. The book's framework can be instrumental in organizing American citizens for a

constitutional convention by fostering cooperation, shared goals, and effective communication.

Core Design Principles: 'Prosocial' outlines eight core design principles for effective groups, which can be tailored to the context of organizing a constitutional convention. These include clearly defined group boundaries, proportional equivalence between benefits and costs, collective-choice arrangements, and monitoring of behaviors. A program based on these principles might look like the following:

1. *Clearly Defined Purpose and Boundaries:* Establish a clear mission statement for the constitutional convention initiative, outlining the objectives and scope. Define membership criteria for those who wish to participate in the organization and planning phases, ensuring a transparent and inclusive process.

2. *Proportional Costs and Benefits:* Ensure that all participants' contributions, whether they be in time, expertise, or resources, are acknowledged and that benefits, such as influence on the process or recognition, are distributed fairly. This encourages sustained engagement and avoids exploitation of committed members.

3. *Collective Decision-Making:* Create mechanisms for participants to have a say in decision-making processes. This might involve democratic voting systems, participatory workshops, and consensus-building exercises to ensure that the call for a convention reflects a broad consensus rather than the will of a few.

4. *Monitoring:* Implement a transparent system for monitoring the progress of the organization's activities, adherence to its rules, and the effectiveness of its outreach efforts. This could involve regular public reporting, peer monitoring, and accountability to a wider community.

5. *Graduated Sanctions:* Develop a set of agreed-upon sanctions for members who violate group norms or rules. These should start lightly but become more substantial for repeat offenses. This ensures that the focus remains on the collective goal without being derailed by individual missteps.

6. *Fast and Fair Conflict Resolution:* Establish quick and respected conflict-resolution mechanisms to address grievances and misunderstandings. This is crucial in maintaining group cohesion and preventing the escalation of conflicts.

7. *Local Autonomy:* Respect the autonomy of local groups working towards the convention. Allow them to organize in ways that suit their local context while still aligning with the broader goals of the national movement.

8. *Appropriate Relations with Other Groups:* Foster cooperative relations with other groups and institutions that can influence the constitutional convention. This requires diplomatic outreach, negotiation, and the creation of partnerships that can bolster the movement's legitimacy and impact.

A prosocial approach to organizing a constitutional convention involves creating a community united by shared goals, governed by fair and inclusive processes, and equipped with tools for effective cooperation and conflict resolution.

By adopting these evolutionary-informed design principles, American citizens can organize a movement that is capable, equitable, and collaborative, thus laying the groundwork for a successful call to a constitutional convention. The goal is not just to rewrite a constitution, but to do so through a process that embodies the democratic values the new constitution aims to uphold.

CONSTITUTIONAL RENEWAL AND RESPONSIBLE GOVERNANCE
Literature Review

We are: What We Do, How We Do, and Why We Do...
as you can see, it's all about the doing.

- David H Moore

Poverty, by America

'Poverty, by America' by Matthew Desmond presents a profound analysis of the systemic and deliberate construction of poverty in the United States. Desmond argues that American poverty is not an incidental or unavoidable aspect of economic life, but the result of specific policy choices and cultural attitudes that benefit the wealthy and powerful at the expense of the poor.

The book challenges the conventional narrative that poverty is primarily a consequence of individual failings, such as a lack of work ethic or personal responsibility. Instead, Desmond illustrates how societal structures and government policies actively produce and sustain poverty. He identifies mechanisms through which American society and its institutions ensure that a segment of the population remains impoverished, from the low minimum wage and the lack of universal healthcare to the criminalization of poverty and the dismantling of the welfare state.

Desmond scrutinizes the housing crisis, where exorbitant rents and the scarcity of affordable housing leave many in a perpetual state of financial insecurity, often one paycheck away from eviction or homelessness. He highlights how the housing market is structured to enrich landlords and real estate investors at the expense of the most economically vulnerable citizens.

Moreover, 'Poverty, by America' sheds light on the paradox of the working poor in the United States. It questions the morality and logic of a society where people can work full-time and still be unable to afford basic necessities. Desmond points out that this is not an economic inevitability but the result of policy decisions that prioritize corporate profits and tax cuts for the affluent over fair wages and social safety nets for the working class.

The book also explores the devastating effects of poverty on individuals and communities, from the stress and mental health issues associated with financial instability to the systemic barriers that prevent the poor from accessing education and upward mobility.

One of the key insights of the book is the recognition that poverty is expensive—not just for those who experience it, but for society as a whole. It incurs high costs in terms of public health, crime, and lost economic potential. Desmond posits that reducing poverty would not only improve the lives of millions of Americans but also strengthen the nation economically and socially.

Desmond calls for a reevaluation of America's approach to poverty. He urges policymakers and the public to recognize that poverty is a structural issue that requires systemic solutions. He advocates for bold policy reforms, such as a universal basic income, affordable housing initiatives, and a revamped social welfare system, to ensure that the basic needs of all citizens are met.

'Poverty, by America' is an educational exploration of the causes and consequences of poverty in the United States, offering a compelling argument for why and how the nation should strive to eradicate it. Desmond's work is a critical resource for understanding the dynamics of poverty and the moral imperative to create a more equitable and just society.

Trauma, Illness, and Healing in a Toxic Culture

'The Myth of Normal: Trauma, Illness, and Healing in a Toxic Culture' by Dr. Gabor Maté offers a provocative examination of the relationship between the emotional and physical health of individuals and the broader societal conditions in which they live. Dr. Maté, a physician with a background in family practice and palliative care, has long argued for a more holistic approach to health, one that integrates the mind-body connection and considers the impact of the social and emotional environment.

In 'The Myth of Normal,' Dr. Maté challenges the conventional wisdom that separates 'normal' health from pathology, suggesting that what we often consider to be abnormal illness—both mental and physical—may actually be an understandable response to a set of harmful societal conditions. He posits that our culture, which can be characterized by stress, pressure, and disconnection, contributes significantly to the prevalence of diseases and psychological afflictions.

The focus of the book on healing our toxic culture is rooted in the belief that individual health cannot be fully realized without addressing the societal factors that contribute to stress and disease. Here are some key educational points from the book with a focus on this healing process:

1. *Understanding the Mind-Body Connection:* Dr. Maté highlights the scientifically-supported notion that the mind and body are not separate entities but function as an integrated system. Emotional stress, trauma, and adverse childhood experiences can manifest as physical illness. Acknowledging this connection is the first step towards healing.

2. *Recognizing the Impact of Trauma:* The book delves into how unresolved trauma, both individual and collective, can lead to chronic illnesses and mental health issues. Healing requires recognizing the impact of trauma, validating experiences, and addressing them through both personal and community-focused therapies.

3. *Challenging the 'Normalcy' of Modern Life:* Dr. Maté encourages us to question the aspects of modern life that are considered normal but may be inherently damaging, such as overwork, lack of community, and the undervaluing of emotional expression. He urges a societal shift in values towards more supportive and life-affirming practices.

4. *Promoting Emotional Literacy:* There is a strong advocacy for developing emotional literacy—understanding and expressing emotions in a healthy way. This is seen as vital to personal well-being and is something that should be nurtured from childhood in education systems and in families.

5. *Creating Supportive Communities:* The importance of community is emphasized, with Dr. Maté suggesting that isolation and the breakdown of communal structures contribute to ill health. Healing is thus also a collective process, requiring the building of supportive networks that can provide emotional and social support.

6. *Reforming Health Systems:* Dr. Maté calls for health care reforms that are more integrative, taking into account not just physical symptoms but also the psychological, social, and spiritual dimensions of well-being.

7. *Encouraging Compassionate Policies:* The book argues for policies that reflect an understanding of the determinants of health, including socioeconomic factors. This means advocating for political and economic systems that prioritize public well-being over profit.

8. *Fostering Personal Responsibility and Societal Change:* While acknowledging the role of society, Dr. Maté also believes in personal agency. Individuals are encouraged to take responsibility for their own health by seeking knowledge, making lifestyle changes, and advocating for a healthier society.

'The Myth of Normal' does not just challenge the prevailing definitions of health and normality; it also offers a blueprint for a radical cultural transformation.

This transformation involves a shift in our understanding of health, the adoption of compassionate and holistic approaches to healthcare, and the fostering of societal conditions that support the well-being of all individuals.

Through this lens, healing is not just a personal journey but a collective endeavor towards creating a culture that is less toxic and more nurturing.

Neuroscience in Justice Reform and Constitutional Law

'Behave: The Biology of Humans at Our Best and Worst' by Robert M. Sapolsky offers a profound examination of human behavior through the lens of biology, psychology, and neuroscience. Applying the insights from 'Behave' to the reformation of our justice systems and the drafting of a new U.S. Constitution could revolutionize our approach to law and governance.

- *The Neuroscience of Behavior:* Sapolsky's work elucidates the complexity of human behavior, emphasizing the interplay of genes, environment, and neural mechanisms. He argues that understanding the brain's functioning is crucial in interpreting behaviors traditionally viewed through moral or legal frameworks. By recognizing the biological underpinnings of actions, we can shift towards a more nuanced view of culpability and responsibility.

-   *Implications for the Justice System:* In reforming justice systems, Sapolsky's findings suggest a paradigm shift from retribution to rehabilitation. Cutting-edge neuroscience could inform more personalized rehabilitation programs, acknowledging that a one-size-fits-all punishment model is ineffective. For instance, individuals with impaired impulse control due to frontal lobe dysfunction might benefit more from cognitive-behavioral therapies rather than incarceration.

-   *Bias and Sentencing:* Neuroscience reveals that unconscious biases can significantly influence decision-making. Training legal professionals in recognizing these biases and utilizing objective neuroscientific tools could lead to fairer sentencing. Additionally, brain imaging and other neurological assessments could become standard in evaluating the mental state of defendants, further informing the legal processes.

-   *Constitutional Implications:* When considering the drafting of a new U.S. Constitution, insights from 'Behave' advocate for the protection of mental privacy and cognitive liberty. The Constitution could include provisions for the ethical use of neurotechnology, ensuring that advances in neuroscience are not misused to manipulate or discriminate against individuals.

-   *Rights and Neurodiversity:* Acknowledging neurodiversity, the new Constitution could enshrine the rights of individuals with different neurological makeups, promoting a society that accommodates a spectrum of cognitive experiences and abilities. This aligns with the principle of equal protection under the law, extending it to the realm of cognitive differences.

-   *Preventive Approaches:* Sapolsky's work also points to the importance of early intervention in mitigating antisocial behaviors. A new Constitution could mandate state support for preventive measures, such as funding for mental health care, educational programs, and community services that address the root causes of criminal behavior.

Integrating the insights from 'Behave' into justice reform and constitutional law requires a deep understanding of the biological bases of behavior. Such an interdisciplinary approach can lead to a justice system that is more humane, equitable, and effective, while a revised Constitution could safeguard against the misuse of neuroscientific advancements and protect the rights of all citizens, irrespective of their neurological constitution.

As we grapple with these complex issues, Sapolsky's work serves as a reminder of the profound implications that scientific understanding has on the fabric of society and the rule of law.

Navigating Existential Risks with Constitutional Safeguards

Toby Ord's 'The Precipice: Existential Risk and the Future of Humanity' serves as a clarion call to recognize and mitigate the threats that could potentially lead to human extinction. The book's central thesis emphasizes the urgent need for a global perspective on long-term survival. Integrating Ord's insights into the writing of a new U.S. Constitution could embed safeguards against existential risks into the nation's legal and moral framework.

- *Understanding Existential Risks:* Ord categorizes risks into natural and anthropogenic, with the latter becoming increasingly prevalent due to technological advances. These include artificial intelligence, biotechnology, nuclear warfare, and climate change. A constitutional recognition of these risks is the first step toward mitigation.

- *Principle of Precaution:* A revised Constitution could incorporate the precautionary principle, mandating that actions potentially harmful to human survival on a global scale be approached with caution and rigorous assessment. This principle would guide legislation on emerging technologies and environmental preservation.

- *Governance of Technology:* The Constitution could establish strict guidelines for the development and deployment of technologies with existential implications. This includes creating oversight bodies for artificial intelligence and synthetic biology, ensuring they operate within safe and ethical boundaries.

- *International Collaboration:* Since existential risks do not respect national borders, the Constitution should advocate for international cooperation. It could formalize commitments to global treaties and organizations focused on existential risk reduction and encourage diplomatic efforts to build consensus on global standards and regulations.

- *Climate Change and Environmental Stewardship:* Recognizing the pressing threat of climate change, constitutional provisions could enshrine environmental protection as a fundamental duty of the state. This would include commitments to sustainable practices, renewable energy, and conservation efforts as non-negotiable legal standards.

- *Education and Public Engagement:* Educating citizens about existential risks is vital for collective action. The Constitution could mandate educational curricula that include the study of these risks and the importance of global stewardship, thus fostering a well-informed electorate that can support prudent policies.

- *Research and Innovation:* The new Constitution could establish a framework for funding and supporting research into existential risks, promoting scientific endeavors that seek to understand and mitigate these dangers. It could also encourage innovation in areas that contribute to humanity's resilience and long-term survival.

- *Civil Liberties and Ethical Boundaries:* While addressing risks, it's crucial that the Constitution safeguard civil liberties. It should ensure that measures taken to prevent existential threats do not infringe upon individual rights and freedoms, setting clear ethical boundaries for state intervention.

'The Precipice' implores us to take existential risks seriously, recognizing that our actions today have profound implications for the future of humanity.

By embedding the principles of existential risk prevention and mitigation into the Constitution, we can create a framework that not only protects current generations, but also acts as a steward for the future, ensuring the preservation and flourishing of human civilization in the face of unprecedented challenges.

As we draft a new Constitution, the insights from Toby Ord's work can guide us to prioritize the continuity and well-being of humanity as a fundamental constitutional value.

Envisioning a New Constitutional Framework

In 'The Third Pillar: How Markets and the State Leave the Community Behind', Raghuram Rajan postulates that a harmonious society is supported by three pillars: the state, the markets, and the community. For a new constitutional framework to be effective, it must rebalance these three forces, particularly by reinvigorating the role of the community, which has been marginalized by the state and markets.

> The Triadic Balance: Rajan argues that the imbalance among the state, markets, and community leads to societal discord and inequality. The new constitutional framework should, therefore, have provisions that ensure these three pillars support each other without allowing one to overpower the others.

Empowering the Community: The community pillar is the bedrock of social welfare and personal identity. The constitutional framework must empower local communities by decentralizing power, providing for local decision-making, and encouraging community-based initiatives.

1. *Decentralization of Power:* The constitution should provide for decentralization, giving communities more control over resources and decision-making. This fosters local innovation and solutions tailored to unique community needs.

2. *Local Decision-Making:* Local governance structures, participatory budgeting, and community referendums can be constitutional mechanisms to involve citizens in the governance process directly.

3. *Economic Empowerment:* The constitution can promote economic policies that encourage local entrepreneurship and community cooperatives, providing communities with financial independence from the state and markets.

Rebalancing the State and Market: While strengthening the community, the constitutional framework must also delineate clear roles for the state and the market, preventing encroachment on community functions.

1. *The Role of the State:* The state should be a facilitator rather than a controller. Constitutional provisions can define the state's role in providing security, justice, and basic welfare, while ensuring that it does not stifle community initiative.

2. *The Role of the Market:* Markets should be free but fair. The constitution can promote regulations that ensure competition and prevent monopolies, thereby encouraging innovation and ensuring that the benefits of markets reach all segments of society.

'The Third Pillar' provides a roadmap for reinvigorating community within the context of constitutional reform. By realigning the power dynamics between the state, markets, and communities, a new constitutional framework can promote a more balanced, inclusive, and harmonious society.

It's about fostering an ecosystem where *each pillar can contribute to the well-being of society, ensuring that progress and prosperity are shared by all.*

Incorporating Risk into the Constitutional Framework

Nassim Nicholas Taleb's 'Skin in the Game' is a philosophical exploration of risk, uncertainty, and the importance of having a personal stake in one's actions. In considering how the principles from this work could shape a new constitutional framework, we delve into the ethos of responsibility that underpins a robust democracy.

Central Thesis: Taleb argues that a major issue in modern society is the disconnection between actions and consequences, particularly among those with power. Decision-makers often lack 'skin in the game,' meaning they don't suffer the consequences of their bad decisions, while those affected by their decisions bear the brunt of the risk.

Incorporating Risk into Constitutional Framework:

1. *Accountability for Political Leaders:* The constitution could include provisions that ensure politicians and public servants face real consequences for misconduct or poor decision-making. This could take the form of financial penalties, loss of pension rights, or other measures that align their well-being with the citizens'.

2. *Decentralization of Power:* To mitigate risks associated with centralized power, the constitution could advocate for a more decentralized system where localities

retain significant autonomy, thus spreading the risk and ensuring those making decisions are closer to the consequences.

3. *Transparency in Decision-Making:* Taleb's principles suggest a need for greater transparency in government, allowing citizens to assess where the risks lie and who has skin in the game. This could be constitutionally mandated.

4. *Financial Regulation:* The constitution could include strictures that require financial institutions and corporations to have more 'skin in the game,' aligning their success with the societal good and increasing their exposure to the risks they create.

We must therefore advocate for the inherent fairness in a system where everyone— especially those in positions of power—has a stake in the outcomes of their decisions; for without such stakes, systems are prone to fragility and collapse.

Ethical Symmetry and Risk Sharing: Taleb emphasizes the ethical imperative that comes with risk. The constitution could mandate that those in power must share in the risks they impose on others, fostering a culture where ethical symmetry is the norm.

By incorporating the logic of risk-taking into a constitutional framework, a society can ensure that those making decisions are impacted by the outcomes of those decisions, fostering a more ethical, fair, and resilient system.

This approach necessitates that all layers of governance, from local to federal, operate with a principle that aligns authority with responsibility and consequences, ultimately supporting a society that is more just and stable.

Harnessing Behavioral Economics for Constitutional Renewal

Dan Ariely's 'Predictably Irrational' offers a profound understanding of human behavior that challenges the assumption of rational decision-making, which is a cornerstone of classical economics. By delving into the cognitive biases and irrational patterns that influence human actions, the book provides invaluable insights that could be harnessed to design a constitutional framework aimed at nurturing the best outcomes for society.

Understanding Irrationality: Ariely's research shows that people's choices are often inconsistent and swayed by their emotional states, context, and how options are presented to them. Recognizing this within a constitutional context means acknowledging that citizens may not always act in their best interests or the interests of society at large.

1. *Behavioral Nudges:* Incorporating this understanding into a new constitutional framework would involve creating 'nudges'—subtle policy shifts that can steer people toward more beneficial behaviors without restricting freedom of choice. For instance, the constitution could mandate that public policies be designed to default citizens into beneficial programs while preserving their right to opt out.

2. *Mitigating Harmful Biases:* The constitutional framework can include checks and balances that address common biases such as overconfidence or short-termism. This can be achieved by establishing non-partisan commissions that employ evidence-based approaches to policy evaluation and long-term planning.

3. *Promoting Informed Decisions:* To combat the effects of misinformation and impulsive decisions, constitutional measures could ensure that education systems foster critical thinking and decision-making skills. This provision would help in building a citizenry that is better equipped to make informed choices in both personal and civic spheres.

4. *Enhancing Transparency:* Knowing that hidden charges and complex information can mislead, the constitution could require that all government and financial transactions with citizens be transparent and presented in a clear and understandable format.

5. *Encouraging Prosocial Behavior:* Ariely's insights into the power of social norms suggest that the constitution could promote prosocial behavior through recognition and reward systems that celebrate civic-minded actions, thereby fostering a culture of cooperation and altruism.

By integrating the behavioral insights from 'Predictably Irrational', a new constitutional framework can be crafted to not only safeguard the rights and freedoms of citizens but also to guide them towards choices that enhance individual well-being and collective good. Such a constitution would recognize the complexity of human behavior, seeking to channel it in ways that fortify democracy and nurture a vibrant, engaged citizenry.

Revitalizing Citizenship within a New Constitutional Framework

Victor Davis Hanson's 'The Dying Citizen' examines the historical development of citizenship and the challenges it faces in modern times. The book offers a dire warning about the erosion of citizen rights and responsibilities and provides insights into how citizenship can be revitalized within a new constitutional framework.

Core Argument: Hanson posits that the concept of citizenship is under threat by various forces, including globalization, illegal immigration, tribalism, and the expansion of the administrative state. These elements contribute to a weakening of the traditional bonds that create a sense of shared purpose and responsibility among citizens. Reinvigorating Citizenship in a New Constitutional Framework:

1. *Defining Citizenship:* The constitution can clearly define what it means to be a citizen, including rights, responsibilities, and a shared commitment to the nation's values and goals. This definition should reinforce the importance of active participation in democracy.

2. *Civic Education:* A constitutional mandate for comprehensive civic education would be crucial to reinvigorating citizenship. Understanding the government's workings, the rights and duties of citizens, and the historical context of the nation's development would be essential components.

3. *Participatory Democracy:* The framework could include mechanisms that encourage direct participation, such as referendums and town hall meetings, fostering a more engaged citizenry.

4. *Balancing Globalization and Sovereignty:* Hanson warns of the dilution of citizenship through globalization. A new framework could emphasize the importance of national sovereignty while also recognizing the interconnectedness of the global community.

5. *Addressing Illegal Immigration:* The book suggests that illegal immigration can undermine the concept of citizenship by creating parallel societies. The constitutional framework could address this by outlining fair but firm immigration policies that uphold the law while respecting human dignity.

6. *Decentralization of Power:* Echoing Taleb's idea from 'Skin in the Game,' decentralization allows citizens to have more control over their lives. A

constitutional approach would be to limit the federal government's powers in favor of local governance, where citizens can have more direct influence.

7. *Combating Tribalism:* Hanson notes the dangers of tribalism to the concept of a unified citizenry. The constitution could promote a culture of inclusivity and shared identity that transcends ethnic, racial, or social divisions.

We must therefore emphasize the historical significance of active citizenship and how its decline threatens the fabric of democracy, while instituting constitutional reforms that empower citizens, promote civic responsibility, and preserve the sovereignty that underpins the nation's identity.

Ultimately, to counter the trends that Hanson identifies as destructive to the concept of citizenship, a new constitutional framework should strive to bolster civic knowledge, engagement, and responsibility.

It should create a clear delineation of citizenship that is inclusive, yet preserves the integrity of the nation-state, by cultivating a robust democracy of informed and involved citizens, that are more than willing to invest in the success of their country's future.

Fostering Altruism in Constitutional Design

David Sloan Wilson's 'Does Altruism Exist?' tackles the complex question of whether altruistic behavior can be truly selfless and how it can be encouraged within societies. His exploration of altruism through the lens of evolutionary biology provides a foundation for considering how a new constitutional framework might foster altruistic behavior among the citizenry.

Central Thesis: Wilson challenges the assumption that natural selection only favors selfish traits. He argues that altruism can be a product of group selection, where groups with altruistic members often outperform those without. This has implications for societal structures, suggesting that fostering group-level altruism can lead to more successful communities.

Fostering Altruism in a New Constitutional Framework:

1. *Community Focus:* Emphasize the role of smaller communities within the larger nation-state. By strengthening local governance and community initiatives, individuals can see the direct impact of their altruism, thereby reinforcing such behavior.

2. *Civic Engagement:* Encourage citizen-participation in governance and community service. This could be done by providing avenues for volunteerism to be recognized and incentivized through tax benefits or public acknowledgment.

3. *Education for Empathy:* A constitutional mandate for education that includes curricula focused on empathy, cooperation, and community service can cultivate altruistic values from a young age.

4. *Social Safety Nets:* Establishing robust social safety nets can promote a culture of care and shared responsibility. These systems exemplify institutional altruism, which can inspire individual actions that benefit the larger group.

5. *Transparency and Accountability:* Implementing transparent government practices can build trust among citizens and promote altruistic acts by showing that individual contributions to the common good are honored and reciprocated.

6. *Rewarding Altruism:* Like the concept of 'Skin in the Game' discussed by Nassim Taleb, a constitutional framework could include mechanisms that reward citizens for altruistic behavior, aligning personal interests with the welfare of the community.

We must therefore institute altruistic principles into the design of our political and social institutions; while crafting a new constitutional framework to encourage and sustain altruism, leading to a more cohesive and cooperative society; *for at the end of the day, we are: what we do, why we do, and how we do.*

Integrating the principles of altruism into the constitutional framework involves recognizing the interdependence of individual well-being and community success.

By creating structures that encourage empathetic education, reward altruistic behavior, and prioritize community engagement, the constitution can cultivate an environment where altruism not only exists but thrives.

The ultimate aim here is to create a society where individuals are motivated to act for the greater good, not just out of self-interest, but rather; the system they live-in recognizes and supports the value of altruistic endeavors.

Incorporating a Meaningful Life into the Constitutional Framework

Jonathan Haidt's 'The Happiness Hypothesis' provides a compelling examination of human well-being by drawing on wisdom from ancient philosophies and the findings of modern psychology. The book posits that happiness is a result of fulfilling human relationships, meaningful work, and a sense of connection to something larger than oneself. These insights are critical when considering the establishment of a constitutional framework that not only governs but also guides citizens towards a more fulfilling life.

Central Thesis: Haidt's thesis is that happiness comes from within and is governed by various levels of psychological well-being, which are deeply rooted in our evolutionary past. He identifies a set of universal conditions that contribute to happiness, which can be synthesized into a constitutional framework.

1. *Promotion of Virtues:* The constitution can enshrine certain virtues such as compassion, fairness, and integrity as guiding principles for citizenship, encouraging individuals to cultivate habits that lead to personal and collective happiness.

2. *Community Engagement:* Recognizing the importance of social bonds, the constitution can promote community engagement through policies that encourage social interaction, such as public spaces for communal activities and support for local organizations.

3. *Work-Life Balance:* Acknowledging the role of meaningful work in personal fulfillment, labor laws can be constitutionally guided to ensure that citizens have the opportunity for work-life balance, promoting both productivity and personal well-being.

4. *Education for Critical Thinking:* A constitutional commitment to education that fosters critical thinking and self-reflection can help individuals understand their own values and the kind of life that would bring them satisfaction.

5. *Environmental Stewardship:* Haidt emphasizes the need for a connection with nature as part of human happiness. The constitution can enshrine the protection of natural environments, ensuring access to green spaces and promoting sustainable living.

6. *Mental Health Support:* A constitutional mandate for comprehensive mental health services would support the psychological well-being of citizens, recognizing mental health as a fundamental right.

We must therefore not only create a new constitutional framework that sets out the rights and responsibilities of citizens, but also institute the conditions for leading a meaningful life, within the various constitutional incentives.

Embedding the pursuit of happiness within the constitutional framework requires a multi-faceted approach that incorporates psychological well-being, virtue ethics, and a commitment to social and environmental factors contributing to a fulfilling life.

By structuring society around these principles, the constitution can act as a blueprint for not just a well-ordered state, but a happy one, where citizens have the resources and support to pursue a life of meaning and collaborative contribution.

Uniting Persuasion and Prosocial Principles
A Pathway to Constitutional Reform

In the quest to construct a more equitable and collaborative society, the call for a constitutional convention is a formidable endeavor that requires careful orchestration of social movements and persuasive strategies.

The essence of 'Persuasion and Social Movements' lies in the understanding that social movements are fundamentally about change—whether they seek to transform laws, societal structures, or cultural norms.

The authors elucidate the mechanisms by which leaders of such movements craft messages that resonate, mobilize the masses, and exert influence on the political discourse. This persuasion is not merely about the transmission of ideas but also the coalescence of shared values and collective identities.

In the framework of a constitutional convention, this persuasive endeavor becomes critical. Leaders and advocates must not only articulate the necessity of constitutional change but also align their rhetoric with the public's deep-seated values and the ethos of the nation.

Here, the authors' analysis converges with the principles outlined in 'Prosocial,' which draws on evolutionary science to emphasize the creation of groups that are productive, equitable, and collaborative. 'Prosocial' argues that for any group to thrive, including those formed around social movements, its structure must be aligned with core design principles that facilitate cooperation and shared purpose.

At the core of 'Prosocial' is the understanding that groups function optimally when they have a strong identity and a fair distribution of influence among members, which aligns with Stewart's emphasis on democratic impulses within movement leadership. The intersection of these ideas suggests that for a constitutional convention to gain traction, it must be propelled by metacognitive leaders who not only persuade but also foster a sense of inclusivity and shared decision-making.

The narrative of 'Persuasion and Social Movements' is replete with historical examples where leaders have successfully used persuasive communication to affect change. Stewart highlights that the success of such movements often hinges on the leader's ability to adapt their strategies to changing circumstances and to maintain a connection with their grassroots base, a sentiment that resonates with the adaptive and flexible nature of group dynamics discussed in 'Prosocial.'

The journey toward a constitutional convention is one that necessitates a deep engagement with the principles of persuasion, *as outlined in 'Persuasion and Social Movements',* while also embracing the prosocial elements of group collaboration emphasized in 'Prosocial'.

It is through the synthesis of these ideas that a movement for constitutional change can gain momentum, drawing on the power of persuasive leadership to unite individuals around a common goal while ensuring that the movement itself exemplifies the principles of equity and collaboration it seeks to enshrine in the nation's most fundamental legal document.

By doing so, the movement not only argues for a change in the constitution but also *embodies the very principles of prosocial behavior that are essential for the sustained health and vitality of any democratic society.*

Fostering Constructive Dialogue

In 'The Righteous Mind: Why Good People are Divided by Politics and Religion,' Jonathan Haidt explores the psychological underpinnings of our moral judgments and how they often lead to polarized and divided societies. By understanding the moral foundations that drive our intuitions and the ensuing self-righteousness, we can learn to disagree more constructively, especially in high-stakes tasks like drafting a new constitutional framework.

Moral Foundations and Intuition: Haidt posits that our moral judgments stem from innate intuitions, not rational deliberations. These intuitions are based on various moral foundations like care, fairness, loyalty, authority, and sanctity. Our self-righteousness comes from the intuitive certainty that our moral perspective is superior, often leading to narcissistic attitudes that dismiss opposing views.

The Symptom of Narcissistic Intuitions: This intuitive certainty can manifest as a form of moral narcissism, where one's own moral framework is seen as infallible. In the context of constitutional discussions, this could stifle debate and undermine the collaborative effort required to craft a document representative of a diverse populace.

Disagreeing More Constructively: Haidt suggests that to overcome this, individuals must first recognize that their moral intuitions are not the sole arbiters of truth. This understanding is crucial for a constitutional convention, where representatives must negotiate and compromise to integrate multiple moral perspectives into a shared governance document. We must therefore underscore the importance of humility and empathy in the constitutional drafting process:

1. *Encourage Perspective-Taking:* The constitution could promote educational systems that teach perspective-taking, helping future citizens to understand and appreciate the moral intuitions of others.

2. *Institutionalize Civil Discourse:* The framework could establish forums for civil discourse, encouraging citizens to engage in open and respectful dialogue, thereby reducing the tendency to demonize those with differing views.

3. *Balance Moral Foundations:* Recognizing that different groups prioritize different moral foundations, the constitution could strive for a balance that does not overly privilege any single moral perspective but instead creates a space where different moralities can coexist and complement each other.

4. *Promote Reflective Deliberation:* The constitution could mandate reflective deliberation in legislative processes, ensuring that laws are not the product of impulsive moral reactions but are instead the outcome of careful consideration of diverse viewpoints.

By incorporating the lessons from Haidt's analysis into the constitutional framework, the founding document could help mitigate the divisiveness that stems from moral self-righteousness. It would foster a society that values empathy and open-mindedness, where citizens can disagree constructively, and where governance is based on a well-rounded understanding of the human moral spectrum.

Securing Our Future Through Responsible Stewardship

William MacAskill's 'What We Owe the Future' is a clarion call for long-termism, an ethical stance emphasizing the importance of positively influencing the long-term future. In a world facing potential global extinction events, from climate change to nuclear proliferation, MacAskill argues that current generations have a moral obligation to ensure the survival and flourishing of future humanity.

Central Thesis: MacAskill posits that our actions today have far-reaching consequences. He suggests that we should prioritize interventions that have the potential to affect the long-term trajectory of civilization. This involves cultivating a global perspective and a commitment to actions that safeguard against existential risks.

Incorporating Long-Termism into Societal Planning:

1. *Rethinking Economic Measures:* Traditional economic measures like GDP are short-term in nature. MacAskill advocates for the development of new metrics that capture long-term impacts and sustainability, guiding policy decisions towards future welfare.

2. *Investing in Research:* To change our trajectory, investment in scientific research and technologies that can mitigate existential risks is crucial. Educational policies should emphasize future-critical fields like climate science, artificial intelligence safety, and biosecurity.

3. *Global Cooperation:* MacAskill underscores the necessity of global cooperation in the face of shared risks. International treaties and organizations should be empowered to address issues that transcend national borders, such as climate change and pandemic preparedness.

4. *Policy Shift:* Governments should adopt a precautionary principle in policy-making, where the avoidance of harm to future generations is a primary consideration. This might involve stricter environmental regulations and a more cautious approach to technology deployment.

We must therefore eliminate our short-term political decision-making and shift towards a long-term perspective; while taking actionable steps for instituting long-term planning, such as fostering interdisciplinary research on long-term impacts, establishing forward-thinking policy initiatives, and promoting global stewardship.

The principles outlined by MacAskill serve as a blueprint for responsible stewardship of our planet. Instituting long-term planning is not just a philosophical ideal but a practical necessity. By taking collective action now, we can steer our trajectory towards a future that is not only sustainable but also vibrant and secure for generations to come. We must therefore nurture and cultivate a paradigm shift in how we conceive of our role in human history, urging us to be the ancestors that future generations are grateful for.

THE NEED FOR GOVERNMENT REFORM

He who experiences the unity of life,
sees his own self in all beings,
and all beings in his own self;
and looks on everything with an impartial eye.

- Buddha

Human salvation lies in the hands of the creatively maladjusted.
– Martin Luther King Jr

Synthesizing Voices Toward a New American Charter

Mike Lofgren's 'The Party is Over' sets the stage for this exploration by examining the dysfunction within the United States' political system. Lofgren, a former congressional staffer, provides an insider's view of how partisan politics and the influence of money have eroded the effectiveness of government. His insights lay the foundation for understanding the need for profound systemic change, particularly in the realm of governance and political structure.

In 'American Fascists,' Chris Hedges delves into the rise of the Christian right in American politics, arguing that their ideology borders on fascism. Hedges explores how this movement has influenced national politics and policy, often undermining democratic principles and secular governance; allowing for extremist ideologies to permeate political institutions, further supporting the need for constitutional safeguards.

Matt Taibbi's 'Griftopia' portrays the depth of corruption and greed within the American financial system. Taibbi illustrates how economic inequalities and the subversion of financial regulations have led to widespread economic injustices. Highlighting the intersection of economic policy and governance; and emphasizing the need for a constitutional framework that ensures economic fairness and accountability.

Francis Fukuyama's 'Identity' addresses the complex issues of identity politics and the struggle for recognition. Fukuyama argues that the focus on individual identities has fragmented societal cohesion and contributed to political polarization; demonstrating how the current constitutional framework is inadequate in addressing the evolving dynamics of societal identity and cohesion.

'The Fix' by Jonathan Tepperman investigates solutions to global problems that could be applied to American challenges. Tepperman presents case studies where innovative approaches have successfully addressed issues like political corruption, economic inequality, and social division. This final book offers a hopeful perspective, suggesting that solutions are possible and can be integrated into a new constitutional framework.

The synthesis of these works presents a compelling argument for a U.S. Constitutional Rewrite. The current political dysfunction, the rise of extremist ideologies, the rampant economic inequalities, the challenges of identity politics, and the examples of successful global problem-solving, all point towards the necessity for profound changes in the American political and legal system.

For without a collaborative effort to create a new U.S. Constitution, *one that addresses these contemporary challenges and incorporates mechanisms for more equitable and effective governance,* American democracy risks being subverted by an oppressive elitist cabal.

A new constitutional convention, therefore, is not just a political imperative, but a necessary step towards safeguarding the principles of democracy and ensuring a just and inclusive society for future generations.

The Threatening Psychology of Totalitarianism
https://youtu.be/ZltdPfaI5x0

'The Psychology of Totalitarianism' by Mattias Desmet presents a compelling exploration of the mechanisms and mental states that facilitate the rise of totalitarian regimes. Desmet's analysis delves into the psychological underpinnings that allow a society to become susceptible to total control, drawing upon historical examples and contemporary insights.

At the core of Desmet's thesis is the concept of mass formation, a process akin to hypnosis where a population becomes bonded in their shared feelings of discontent and fear. This psychological phenomenon is characterized by a complex interplay of factors including isolation, lack of meaning in life, free-floating anxiety, and discontent that is not connected to a specific cause. Desmet argues that when these conditions

115

are present in a significant portion of the population, a ripe ground for totalitarianism is formed.

Totalitarian systems, Desmet posits, offer a deceptive sense of unity and purpose, directing the free-floating anxiety towards a common enemy, or series of goals. This unification is achieved through narratives that simplify the complexity of the world's problems, often by designating scapegoats or insisting on ideologically driven solutions. This mass movement becomes a 'mass formation' that is self-reinforcing, often leading to a scenario where individuals willingly participate in the erosion of their autonomy.

Desmet also explores the role of the media and leaders who often utilize fear to maintain the conditions necessary for mass formation. By amplifying fears, whether of real or exaggerated threats, the psychological state of the population is kept in a place of vulnerability, where totalitarian leaders can thrive by promising security and order.

The book warns that the path towards totalitarianism is not just one of overt political and social control but is deeply rooted in psychology. Desmet's work urges an understanding of these mental processes to foster resilience against such regimes. Education, critical thinking, and the preservation of spaces for individual autonomy and skepticism are presented as vital defenses against the seductive pull of totalitarian solutions.

Desmet's conclusions are a call to vigilance, inviting readers to recognize the subtle signs of mass formation in their societies. It is a reminder that totalitarianism is not merely an external system of oppression but can be an internalized psychological state that must be actively resisted through conscious thought and collective, purposeful action that preserves the integrity of the individual within the community.

Unveiling the Deep State

David Talbot's 'The Devil's Chessboard' sets the stage for a gripping tale of power, subterfuge, and state secrets. It paints a historical panorama where key figures in the U.S. government, especially within the CIA, wield inordinate power behind the scenes. By exposing the covert operations and manipulations of the CIA, the book serves as an introduction to the concept of hidden forces within the United States government that will require a constitutional overhaul for the people to be able to check that secret power.

Douglas Valentine's 'The CIA as Organized Crime' continues the narrative by depicting the CIA not just as an intelligence agency, but as an entity engaged in clandestine activities that often skirt the edges of legality. Valentine's extensive examination of the agency's methods and impacts, *domestically and internationally,* strengthens the argument that there is a grave need for transparency and oversight. Valentine's conclusions bolsters the case for constitutional amendments to rein in such agencies, which operate outside the traditional bounds of government oversight.

In 'Surprise, Kill, Vanish,' Annie Jacobsen delves into the covert operations arm of the CIA, detailing the agency's engagement in assassination, sabotage, and other acts of espionage. Jacobsen's riveting accounts of paramilitary operations and the breadth of the CIA's global reach, add depth to our understanding of the lengths to which this 'secret government' will go. And the obvious dangers of a government within a government, demands for our urgency for constitutional action, to assert democratic control over such activities.

Annie Jacobsen's 'The Pentagon's Brain' shifts the focus to the Department of Defense and the Advanced Research Projects Agency (DARPA). Jacobsen uncovers the technological advancements and scientific research that have been conducted in the shadows, often without public knowledge or consent. This book reinforces the truth of secrecy and control among those shadowy figures that rule our world, suggesting that the military-industrial complex has evolved into a technologically advanced, semi-autonomous entity. The argument for constitutional revision is further bolstered by the need for oversight of such technological and military power.

Finally, *Mike Lofgren's 'The Deep State'* ties together the threads woven by the previous authors, describing the Deep State as a network of individuals and institutions that operate outside the view and control of the public and their elected representatives. Lofgren's analysis expands on the idea that this concealed government has a profound and unchecked influence over American life and global affairs. It solidifies our thesis that the Deep State's existence and operations represent a fundamental threat to democratic governance.

The necessity of a constitutional convention that is aimed at reining in the deep state is required of us. The Deep State has extensive power that was neither elected by the people nor acted transparently in its operations. The constitutional rewrite must therefore address:

1. The establishment of clear checks and balances on intelligence and defense entities, as highlighted by Talbot and Valentine.

2. A requirement for greater transparency and accountability in covert operations, as shown by Jacobsen.

3. Constitutional limitations on the military-industrial complex's influence and the technological autonomy of defense agencies, again brought to light by Jacobsen.

4. The dismantling of the deep state apparatus through structural reforms that restore power to elected officials and the public, as urged by Lofgren.

The greatest viable solution to the challenges posed by the deep state, is a comprehensive rewriting of the U.S. Constitution. This would involve the creation of new frameworks for accountability, oversight, and transparency that ensure all government actions are subject to democratic control.

The conclusion calls for a renewed constitution that protects the country from the overreach of hidden powers and restores the primacy of the electorate, thereby reclaiming the promise of a government of the people, by the people, and for the people.

Profit and the Push for Public Health Reform

'Evil Geniuses' by Kurt Andersen provides a foundational understanding of the transformation of the American economy and the rise of a financial elite. Andersen argues that a deliberate re-engineering of the economy occurred in the late 20th century, enabling the rich to amass greater wealth at the expense of the working class.

This introduction sets the stage for a discussion on how these economic structures have influenced the public health system, suggesting that a similar level of manipulation has occurred within healthcare, leading to the prioritization of profit, over public well-being.

Robert Kennedy's 'The Real Anthony Fauci' explores the intersection of government health agencies and the pharmaceutical industry, focusing on the influence of Dr. Anthony Fauci. Kennedy critiques the handling of the AIDS crisis and the COVID-19 pandemic, questioning the motives behind public health decisions. He suggests that financial interests have overshadowed public health goals, reinforcing Andersen's thesis of a profit-driven approach that has seeped into the public health sector.

Shanna Swan's 'Count Down' examines the declining fertility rates and the increase in reproductive health issues globally. Swan investigates the role of environmental toxins and lifestyle factors, providing a scientific perspective on how public health is being undermined. This book builds on the previous themes by highlighting a lack of regulatory action against harmful substances, pointing to a public health system that is compromised by corporate interests.

In 'Sickening,' John Abramson delves deeper into the healthcare industry, dissecting how pharmaceutical companies have influenced medical knowledge and practice. Abramson's exposé on drug company manipulations and the resulting harm to patients continues the narrative of a healthcare system in which profit motives override the goal of patient care. Thus solidifying the argument that systemic change is necessary to realign-in the healthcare system so it serves its intended purpose.

Judy Mikovits's 'The Plague of Corruption' brings a personal and controversial account of the alleged suppression of scientific research by political and corporate forces. Mikovits asserts that her work on chronic fatigue syndrome and other conditions was stymied by vested interests. Her claims prove the public health system is fraught with conflicts of interest that impede scientific progress and public welfare.

The authors collectively depict a public health system that is influenced by the 'Deep State'—a collusion of government officials and corporate entities focused on capitalizing on human health. *We must therefore:*

1. Ensure the public health system is insulated from corporate profiteering, as highlighted by Andersen and Kennedy.

2. Protect public health from environmental and other external harms, as emphasized by Swan.

3. Mandate transparency and integrity in medical research and pharmaceutical regulation, as argued by Abramson.

4. Establish robust oversight to prevent suppression and corruption in scientific research, as discussed by Mikovits.

To safeguard public health and restore trust in the healthcare system, a radical constitutional rewrite is essential. Such a rewrite must foster systems that prioritize public interest and health outcomes over private gain, ensuring a healthcare system that is transparent, evidence-based, and free from the influence of the 'deep state'.

By enshrining these values in the highest law of the land, the United States can recommit to the welfare of its citizens, embodying the principle that the health of the people is the supreme law (salus populi suprema lex).

THE NEED FOR
DEMOCRATIC REFORM

Good actions give strength to ourselves,
and inspire good actions in others.

– Plato

A Modern Democratic Reformation

by Thom Hartmann

'The Hidden History of American Democracy: Revealing the Lies That Have Distorted Our Most Cherished Values' by Thom Hartmann is a critical examination of the United States' political system, exploring the underpinnings of American democracy and the various ways it has been shaped and sometimes undermined throughout history. Hartmann, a progressive political commentator, offers a perspective that challenges mainstream narratives and seeks to uncover the less discussed aspects of the nation's democratic journey.

Part 4 of the book, titled 'A 21st-Century Democracy Agenda,' serves as Hartmann's manifesto for reforming American democracy to meet the needs and challenges of the modern era. This section of the book is particularly forward-looking, offering a variety of proposals aimed at strengthening democratic principles and ensuring that the government better serves the public interest.

In this section, Hartmann addresses several key areas where he believes democracy in the United States can be revitalized:

1. *Electoral Reforms:* Hartmann discusses the importance of making elections more accessible and representative. He advocates for the adoption of measures such as automatic voter registration, mail-in voting, and the protection of early voting to ensure that all citizens can easily participate in elections. He also supports the reform of the Electoral College system and the introduction of ranked-choice-voting to better reflect the will of the people.

2. *Campaign Finance:* To combat the influence of big money in politics, Hartmann calls for strict campaign finance reforms. He argues for the overturning of decisions like Citizens United v. FEC and suggests public funding for political campaigns to level the playing field and reduce the power of wealthy donors and special interests.

3. *Media and Information:* Recognizing the critical role of information in a democracy, Hartmann recommends policies to promote a diverse and independent media landscape. He calls for the reinstatement of the Fairness Doctrine, which required broadcasters to present contrasting viewpoints on

controversial issues, and supports efforts to counteract the consolidation of media ownership.

4. *Corporate Power:* Hartmann challenges the legal doctrine of corporate personhood and the idea that money is speech. He asserts that corporations should not have the same constitutional rights as individuals and that regulating corporate influence is essential for a functional democracy.

5. *Social and Economic Equity:* Hartmann ties the health of democracy to the well-being of its citizens. He advocates for a more equitable economic system, including the strengthening of the social safety net, fair taxation, and policies to reduce income and wealth inequality.

6. *Judicial Reforms:* Hartmann looks at the judiciary's role in shaping democratic processes and suggests reforms to ensure its independence and integrity, such as term limits for Supreme Court justices and greater transparency in the judicial appointment process.

7. *Civic Engagement and Education:* Finally, Hartmann emphasizes the need for a well-informed and engaged citizenry. He proposes investing in civic education and creating more opportunities for public participation in government decision-making.

'A 21st-Century Democracy Agenda' serves as a robust proposal for overhauling American democracy in ways that Hartmann believes will make it more inclusive, responsive, and resilient. He argues that these reforms are necessary to address the systemic issues that have historically undermined democratic ideals and to ensure that democracy remains vibrant and relevant in the modern age. Hartmann's vision is one of a revitalized democracy that is equipped to face the challenges of the 21st century and is reflective of the values and needs of all Americans.

Unveiling Monopoly

Thom Hartmann's 'The Hidden History of Monopolies' exposes the pervasive influence of monopolies in American history and how they have shaped economic and political landscapes. Hartmann meticulously charts the rise of monopolistic practices, highlighting their detrimental effects on innovation, competition, and consumer choice.

The third part of the book is particularly significant as it provides a series of solutions to counteract the monopolistic grip on the economy.

> *Monopolies Defined:* Hartmann defines monopolies as entities with exclusive control over a particular commodity or service, enabling them to manipulate markets and prices to their advantage. This control leads to an erosion of the democratic process as monopolies accrue disproportionate political power to protect and expand their dominance.

Historical Context: The book traces the history of monopolies from the Gilded Age to the present, illustrating how periods of lax regulation have allowed monopolies to flourish. Hartmann argues that monopolies have historically led to economic and social inequalities, which have sparked public and governmental backlash.
Proposed Solutions:

1. *Strengthening Antitrust Laws:* Hartmann calls for a revival and enforcement of antitrust legislation, such as the Sherman Antitrust Act and the Clayton Act, to dismantle monopolistic conglomerates and promote a more competitive market.

2. *Promoting Small Businesses:* Policies that encourage the growth and sustainability of small businesses can serve as a counterbalance to monopolies. Hartmann suggests tax incentives, grants, and access to capital for entrepreneurs.

3. *Consumer Protection:* Hartmann advocates for robust consumer protection laws that prevent monopolistic abuse and ensure fair pricing and quality of products and services.

4. *Political Reform:* Hartmann underscores the need for campaign finance reform to curtail the influence of monopoly money in politics. This would involve overturning decisions like Citizens United and instituting public funding of elections.

5. *Regulatory Vigilance:* Regular oversight by federal agencies such as the Federal Trade Commission (FTC) and the Department of Justice (DOJ) is essential to prevent the formation of monopolies and the abuse of market power.

6. *Public Ownership:* In certain sectors, Hartmann suggests public ownership as a solution to monopolistic control, ensuring that essential services like water, electricity, and internet are run in the public interest.

Thom Hartmann's solutions in 'The Hidden History of Monopolies' are a call to action to restore democratic principles and market competitiveness.

By reinvigorating antitrust laws, empowering small businesses, and ensuring regulatory diligence, Hartmann believes we can dismantle the undue power of monopolies.

The importance of vigilance and advocacy in promoting an economy that serves the many, not the few, echo's Hartmann's vision for an equitable economic future.

Reassessing Justice

Thom Hartmann's 'The Hidden History of the Supreme Court' is a critical examination of the United States Supreme Court's role in shaping the nation's destiny. The book provides an in-depth analysis of the Court's decisions and their long-term implications on American society. Hartmann's narrative reveals how the Court has often sided with corporate interests and against individual rights. In the third part of the book, Hartmann proposes several solutions to address the issues he identifies.

Supreme Court's Influence: Hartmann portrays the Supreme Court as a powerful entity that has often operated beyond the reach of public scrutiny. He asserts that the Court has played a pivotal role in consolidating power among the elite, particularly through decisions that have expanded corporate rights.

Historical Trajectory: The book details key historical moments when the Supreme Court has made controversial decisions, such as during the New Deal era or the Citizens United case. Hartmann suggests that these decisions have had profound effects on the democratic process and economic equality.

Proposed Solutions:

1. *Term Limits for Justices:* Hartmann advocates for the imposition of term limits on Supreme Court justices to prevent lifetime tenure, which he argues leads to entrenched ideologies and detachment from societal progress.

2. *Balancing Ideological Representation:* He proposes a system that ensures a balanced representation of different ideological perspectives on the Court to avoid dominance by any single judicial philosophy.

3. *Increasing Transparency:* Hartmann calls for greater transparency in the Court's proceedings, including televised hearings and mandatory disclosure of the justices' meetings with outside influencers.

4. *Reforming the Nomination Process:* The book suggests overhauling the nomination process to minimize partisan politics, possibly through a non-partisan commission that can assess the qualifications of potential justices more objectively.

5. *Expanding the Bench:* Hartmann entertains the idea of expanding the number of justices on the Supreme Court to dilute the power of individual justices and make the Court more representative of the diverse opinions in the country.

6. *Constitutional Amendments:* He recommends considering constitutional amendments to address specific decisions of the Supreme Court that have had detrimental effects on democracy and equality.

Thom Hartmann's 'The Hidden History of the Supreme Court' delves into the profound influence of the judiciary on the fabric of American society. Advocating for reformative measures, Hartmann envisions a future where the Court staunchly upholds democratic ideals and protects individual liberties, rather than reinforcing elite interests. His work calls for a reshaping of judicial authority to fortify its role in nurturing a robust and equitable democracy.

Unequal Protection: How Corporations Became 'People'...

Thom Hartmann's 'Unequal Protection' is a critical examination of corporate influence on American democracy and the concept of corporate personhood. It traces the historical development of corporations, scrutinizes their legal status as 'persons,' and assesses the impact of this designation on societal inequality and governance.

The Corporate Conquest of America: Hartmann's exploration of the rise of corporations in America, details the origins of corporations as entities chartered by the state with specific purposes and how they evolved into powerful institutions with rights akin to individuals. Hartmann argues that this transformation has led to an unprecedented level of corporate control over political processes, economic systems, and public discourse.

The Birth of Corporate Personhood: The central thesis of Hartmann's work is the legal concept of corporate personhood, which was solidified by the U.S. Supreme Court's decision in Santa Clara County v. Southern Pacific Railroad (1886; then subsequent legal interpretations granted corporations rights under the 14th Amendment—rights originally intended to protect freed slaves. Hartmann illustrates how this has allowed corporations to claim constitutional protections designed for human beings, enabling them to wield considerable influence over the democratic process.

Unequal Consequences: Hartmann's book delves into the myriad ways corporate personhood has perpetuated inequality. Hartman's arguments prove that corporate rights have overshadowed individual rights and public interest. The consequences of this imbalance include environmental degradation, economic disparity, and the undermining of labor rights. Hartmann emphasizes that the current legal framework privileges corporate profit over societal well-being.

Restoring Democracy: Hartmann presents a vision for restoring democracy by revoking the legal basis of corporate personhood, implementing campaign finance reform, and reasserting the power of the people to regulate corporations. Hartmann believes these steps are crucial for creating a more equitable society where the government is responsive to the will of its citizens, rather than corporate interests.

Conclusion for a New U.S. Constitution: We must therefore clarify the distinction between corporate entities and human beings in the eyes of the law; while making white-collar crime a police enforcement priority. Furthermore, we must revitalize our democracy by ensuring that elected officials serve the electorate instead of corporate donors.

The Erosion of the American Dream

Thom Hartmann's 'The Hidden History of American Neoliberalism' presents a chilling account of how the United States is being systematically undermined by a neoliberal oligarchy. Hartmann's thesis centers on the insidious ways in which neoliberalism, under the guise of economic progress, has facilitated the concentration of power and wealth in the hands of a few.

This oligarchic elite, through deregulation, privatization, and tax policies favoring the wealthy, has not only amassed immense economic power but also gained significant influence over political and social structures. Hartmann argues that this has led to the erosion of the middle class, increased income inequality, and the dismantling of the social safety net, all of which have been detrimental to the fabric of American society.

The Subversion of the American Ideals: Neoliberalism, as outlined by Hartmann, is more than an economic theory; it is a mechanism that has subverted the core American ideals of democracy and equal opportunity. The relentless pursuit of profit and efficiency has overridden considerations of social justice, community welfare, and environmental sustainability. Hartmann paints a foreboding picture of a society where the collective good is sacrificed at the altar of individual gain, leading to a fragmented and polarized nation.

Reverting to Keynesian Economics and Hamilton's Vision: Hartmann advocates a return to Keynesian economics as a countermeasure to the neoliberal agenda. This approach emphasizes government intervention in the economy to stabilize markets, create jobs, and promote equitable growth. Hartmann argues that a Keynesian framework, characterized by robust public investment in infrastructure, education, and healthcare, is vital to rebuilding the American economy in a way that benefits all citizens, not just the elite.

> Furthermore, Hartmann draws on Alexander Hamilton's 'American Plan,' advocating for policies that support domestic industry, protect workers, and foster innovation. This includes reversing free trade policies that have often favored multinational corporations at the expense of local businesses and workers.

Raising Taxes on the Rich: A pivotal element of Hartmann's proposal is the call for a more progressive tax system, where the wealthy pay their fair share. He argues that reversing the trend of tax cuts for the rich is essential to fund public services and social programs that are crucial for a balanced and just society.

The ultimate goal, as articulated by Hartmann, is to build a society that works for everyone, not just the privileged few. This involves not only economic reforms but also a cultural shift towards values of solidarity, community, and mutual responsibility. Hartmann's work is a call to action for economic justice and a reaffirmation of democratic principles in the face of a growing neoliberal oligarchy.

The Shadowy Eyes of Surveillance

In 'The Hidden History of Big Brother in America,' Thom Hartmann paints a chilling portrait of the invasive surveillance tactics employed by what he terms the American Deep State, and how these practices are encroaching on the fundamental rights of citizens.

Hartmann's book delves into the alarming expansion of surveillance technologies by the American Deep State, a term he uses to describe a covert alliance between government agencies and private corporations. This nexus, Hartmann argues, has led to widespread violations of citizens' right to privacy. From indiscriminate data collection to intrusive monitoring practices, Hartmann paints a picture of a society where every action, communication, and movement can be tracked, analyzed, and potentially used for manipulative purposes.

> Hartmann goes further, asserting that these surveillance mechanisms are not just about gathering information but are tools for social control and behavior modification. He suggests that the knowledge and fear of being watched can lead to self-censorship and conformity, subtly influencing the behavior and decisions of individuals, thereby undermining the principles of a free and open society.
>
> Thus drawing an ominous parallel with China's Social Credit System, which Hartmann uses as a cautionary example of surveillance taken to an extreme. In China, citizens are scored based on their behavior, with repercussions affecting their access to services and societal privileges. Hartmann warns that while America's system is not as overt, the incremental encroachment of surveillance could lead to a similarly dystopian reality.

Hartmann's analysis brings into sharp focus the need to reaffirm and protect the Constitutional right to privacy. He advocates for robust legal frameworks that limit the reach of government and corporate surveillance, ensuring that technology serves the people rather than controls them. Hartmann calls for citizen engagement in policymaking processes and supports grassroots movements that push for transparency and accountability in surveillance practices.

Hartmann's 'The Hidden History of Big Brother in America' serves as a stark reminder of the threats posed by unchecked surveillance; underscoring the urgent need for vigilance and action to protect the right to privacy and prevent the descent into a surveillance state. Hartmann's work is not just a critique but a call to arms for citizens to defend their civil rights and restore the foundational values of privacy and freedom in the face of the ever-looming shadow of Big Brother.

The Diseased Roots of Sickness for Profit

In his probing work, 'The Hidden History of American Healthcare,' Thom Hartmann lays bare the unsettling journey of the U.S. healthcare system, tracing its origins to a greed-fueled and racially discriminatory past.

Hartmann's analysis begins with a dissection of how a racist and greedy oligarchy shaped the early American healthcare system. He argues that the system's inception was marred by profit-driven motives and racial exclusion, creating disparities that persist to this day. Hartmann highlights how these oligarchic influences prioritized financial gain over public health, leading to a system more concerned with balance sheets than patient care.

> This 'sickness for profit' model, illustrates how this system incentivizes illness over health; where healthcare providers and pharmaceutical companies benefit financially from ongoing patient ailments. Hartmann contends that this model not only undermines the quality of care but also drives up costs, making healthcare inaccessible to many, especially marginalized communities.

> Hartmann does not shy away from the racially charged history of American healthcare. He chronicles how systemic racism has been ingrained in healthcare policies and practices, leading to significant health disparities among racial and ethnic minorities. This aspect of the history is critical, as it underscores the deep-seated inequities that any reform must address.

Hartmann presents 'Medicare for All' as not just a healthcare reform, but a moral imperative to rectify the historical wrongs of the system. He outlines the potential benefits of Medicare for All, including universal coverage, cost savings, and the elimination of the profit motive in healthcare, which would lead to more equitable and effective care.

Hartmann emphasizes that Medicare for All would not only improve health outcomes but also bolster the economy. By alleviating the burden of healthcare costs, individuals would have more disposable income, leading to increased spending and economic growth. Moreover, a healthier workforce would be more productive, further benefiting the economy.

Thom Hartmann's 'The Hidden History of American Healthcare' serves as a clarion call to recognize and address the deep flaws in the U.S. healthcare system; underscoring the urgent need for a comprehensive overhaul through Medicare for All, not only as a matter of public health, but as a moral obligation to create a more equitable and just society. Hartmann's work compels us to confront the past, understand the present, and work diligently towards a future where healthcare is a right, not a privilege.

Ending 'Money Is Speech' Is the Only Way to Restore Democracy

'Ending 'Money Is Speech' Is the Only Way to Restore Democracy' by Thom Hartmann argues that the current interpretation of money as free speech under the First Amendment is detrimental to American democracy.

Hartmann highlights the Supreme Court's ruling that categorizes money as speech, thereby allowing large corporations and billionaires to have disproportionate influence in politics through financial means. This ruling has led to the neglect of public will in favor of corporate and wealthy interests.

Hartmann uses the analogy of his own money to illustrate the absurdity of considering money as speech, noting that while money can influence politicians, it does not equate to the expressive power of speech. He contends that this doctrine has led to a range of societal issues, including exorbitant pharmaceutical prices, expensive internet services, and homelessness, among others.

> Hartmann also points to the Tillman Act of 1907, which once made corporate political donations a felony, to demonstrate how far current practices have strayed. Hartmann emphasizes that such laws were effective in creating a government responsive to voters, leading to the establishment of social security, unions, Medicare, and other beneficial programs.

Hartmann compares the U.S. with other countries like Finland, Germany, France, Canada, Denmark, Norway, and Taiwan, where money is not equated with speech, and as a result, more democratic and equitable policies prevail. These countries have successfully implemented policies like free or affordable education, healthcare, and internet services without the corrupting influence of money in politics.

He concludes by citing Justice John Paul Stevens' dissent in the Citizens United case, warning of the dangers of corporate and foreign influence in American politics. Hartmann argues that the doctrine of money as speech not only corrupts domestic politics but also exposes the U.S. to foreign manipulation and interference.

Hartmann's analysis is a call to action for a constitutional convention to redefine the role of money in politics, asserting that only by ending the equivalence of money to speech can American democracy be truly restored.

The Struggle for the Middle Class and the Path to Democratic Restoration

In 'Screwed: The Undeclared War Against the Middle Class,' Thom Hartmann presents a critical analysis of the socio-economic challenges facing the middle class in the United States. Hartmann argues that the middle class, once the backbone of American democracy, is under siege due to the actions of the corporatocracy, and the weakening of regulatory frameworks.

Hartmann explores the concept of an undeclared war against the middle class, illustrating how policies and practices favoring large corporations have systematically eroded the economic stability and political influence of middle-class Americans. This includes wage stagnation, job outsourcing, and the diminishing power of labor unions, all of which have contributed to increasing income inequality and a declining standard of living for many.

A significant part of Hartmann's argument focuses on the role of multinational corporations in this dynamic. He explains how these entities, driven by profit motives and often lacking allegiance to any particular nation, have exploited global labor markets, manipulated trade agreements, and lobbied for policies that serve their interests at the expense of the broader population.

> Hartmann emphasizes the environmental and social repercussions of such corporate activities, highlighting their contribution to global crises like climate change and economic disparity.

Central to Hartmann's thesis is the assertion that a strong, prosperous middle class requires robust government regulations. He advocates for policies that protect workers' rights, ensures fair wages, and maintain environmental standards. Hartmann argues that such regulations are not antithetical to economic growth but are, in fact, essential to creating a more equitable and sustainable economic system that benefits a wider section of society.

In the concluding part of his book, Hartmann outlines a roadmap for restoring American democracy and revitalizing the middle class. He calls for a renewed commitment to democratic principles and civic engagement, urging individuals to become more politically active and informed. Hartmann emphasizes the importance of reversing the trend of corporate influence in politics and restoring the power of the vote to the average citizen.

Hartmann ultimately posits that the restoration of democracy and the revitalization of the middle class may require a radical step: the writing of a new U.S. Constitution through a constitutional convention. He believes that such a move could provide an opportunity to embed protections for the middle class, enforce stricter regulations on corporations, and realign the nation's policies with the needs and aspirations of its citizens.

This, according to Hartmann, is not just a path to restoring democracy, but a necessary journey towards creating a more equitable and sustainable future for all Americans. *Hartmann's message serves as a call to action, urging readers to recognize the power they hold in shaping the direction of their country and the welfare of generations to come.*

The Shadow of Oligarchy in America

In Thom Hartmann's critical examination, 'The Hidden History of American Oligarchy,' a foreboding narrative unfolds, revealing how the United States stands at a precipice, threatened by the insidious rise of an oligarchic structure. Hartmann meticulously dissects the alarming ways in which elitist control has permeated the media, the unrestrained flow of money in political campaigns, and the gradual oligarchic co-opting of the judicial system.

The Creeping Elitist Control: Hartmann's research uncovers a disturbing trend: the elite's increasing dominance over the media. This control is not just about shaping news and information but also about molding public opinion to serve the interests of a few. The situation is exacerbated by the phenomenon of unlimited campaign contributions, a practice that has transformed the democratic process into a playground for the wealthy, where policies and politicians can be 'bought'. Equally troubling is the oligarchic takeover of the judicial system, where justice seems increasingly skewed in favor of the elite.

America at a Crisis Point: The cumulative effect of these elements places America at a crisis point. Hartmann argues that this oligarchic tide is not just a political or economic issue; it is a threat to the very fabric of American democracy. The ideal of 'government of the people, by the people, for the people' is being eroded, replaced by a system where the elite dictate policies and decisions that serve their interests, often at the expense of the majority.

Hartmann's Call to Action: However, Hartmann's narrative is not one of despair, but a call to action. He outlines practical measures to counter this oligarchic surge. Key among these is breaking up media monopolies to ensure a diverse and independent press that can serve as a bulwark against elite propaganda. Limiting the influence of money in politics is another critical step; this includes reforming campaign finance laws to prevent the wealthy from having disproportionate influence over the political process.

> Hartmann also advocates for the reclamation of wealth that has been systematically siphoned by the oligarchy over decades. This involves more equitable tax policies and closing loopholes that have allowed the elite to accumulate vast wealth while contributing little to the societal fabric.

Building a Movement: The cornerstone of Hartmann's thesis is the necessity of building a grassroots movement - a coalition of the informed and engaged citizenry. This movement's goal is to return control of America to 'We the People'. It involves not just political engagement, but also societal and cultural shifts; where the values of democracy, equity, and justice are reinstated at the core of American life.

A Call for Vigilance and Action: Thom Hartmann's 'The Hidden History of American Oligarchy' is a stark reminder of the challenges facing American democracy; serving as a clarion call for vigilance and action. By adopting Hartmann's practical measures, there is a path forward to dismantle the oligarchic structures and restore the democratic ideals that are the bedrock of American society. The future of America hinges on the ability of its people to recognize, resist, and reverse the tide of oligarchy.

THE CRITICAL ROLE OF IMMIGRATION IN RESTORING AMERICAN DEMOCRACY

It will be worthy of a free, enlightened, and, at no distant period, a great nation, to give to mankind the magnanimous and too novel example of a People always guided by an exalted justice and benevolence.

- George Washington

Suketu Mehta's 'This Land is Our Land' provides a profound narrative on immigration, challenging the preconceived notions and misconceptions surrounding this contentious issue. Mehta underscores the historical and ongoing contributions of immigrants to various nations, particularly the United States, and addresses the unfounded fears and hostility they often face. His work is a clarion call to recognize the indispensable role of immigration in societal development and national prosperity.

Mehta vividly portrays the ongoing, albeit undeclared, war against immigration. He describes the systemic barriers, stringent policies, and often xenophobic rhetoric that create an unwelcoming environment for immigrants. This war is not only against the immigrants themselves but against the very ethos of diversity and opportunity that many nations, especially the U.S., were built upon. By highlighting individual stories and historical patterns, Mehta illustrates how these actions are counterproductive to the nation's progress and ideals.

> Immigration is a key driver of population growth in many developed countries, including the United States, which faces an aging population and declining birth rates. Immigrants not only contribute to population growth but also play a vital role in sustaining the social safety net. They often occupy essential roles in the economy, paying taxes that fund social security, healthcare, and other public services. These contributions are crucial in maintaining the economic balance and supporting the aging native population.

Successfully integrating immigrants into the social, economic, and cultural fabric of the nation is vital for maximizing their contributions. Mehta argues for policies and practices that facilitate this integration, such as language education, recognition of foreign qualifications, and anti-discrimination measures. He emphasizes that when immigrants thrive, they bring innovation, entrepreneurial spirit, and a diversity of perspectives that significantly benefit the nation.

Drawing on external sources, statistics show the undeniable impact of immigration on national development.

For instance, according to the American Immigration Council, immigrants in the U.S. paid over $458 billion in taxes and had over $1.2 trillion in spending power in one single recent year.

Furthermore, the National Academy of Sciences reports that immigrants and their children are essential in counteracting the demographic challenges posed by an aging population.

Linking this to the concept of a new U.S. Constitution, it's clear that the principles and policies surrounding immigration will be crucial in shaping a more inclusive, democratic, and prosperous society.

The very act of rewriting the Constitution through a constitutional convention can be seen as a symbolic and practical step towards embracing the diversity and dynamism that immigration brings. It's an opportunity to enshrine values of inclusivity and equal opportunity, ensuring that the nation's laws and policies reflect the reality of its demographic makeup and the invaluable contributions of immigrants.

'This Land is Our Land' by Suketu Mehta provides compelling evidence and narratives underscoring the importance of immigration to the United States. The discussion extends beyond just acknowledging the contributions of immigrants to actively advocating for their inclusion and integration into the societal fabric.

The path to restoring and enhancing American democracy, as Mehta suggests, lies in recognizing and valuing the diversity brought by immigrants. This realization is not only a moral imperative but a practical necessity for the nation's continued prosperity and democratic renewal.

A Constitutional Rewrite Through Chomsky's Vision

The more you can increase fear of drugs and crime,
welfare mothers, immigrants and aliens,
the more you control all the people.

- *Noam Chomsky*

Noam Chomsky's 'What Uncle Sam Really Wants' serves as the introduction to this exploration. In this book, Chomsky unveils the often-hidden motives behind U.S. foreign policy, highlighting a consistent pattern of self-interest and power consolidation at the expense of democratic ideals and global welfare. This sets the stage for an argument that underscores the necessity for a constitutional rewrite, as current policies do not adequately reflect the principles of democracy and equality.

Building on the initial critique, *'The Prosperous Few and the Restless Many'* delves into the growing economic disparities and the concentration of wealth and power in the hands of a few. Chomsky argues that this imbalance undermines the democratic process and leads to a restless majority, disillusioned by the growing chasm between the affluent and the common people. This analysis points to the need for constitutional reforms that address economic inequality and ensure fair representation.

In *'Secret, Lies, and Democracy,'* Chomsky explores the deception and misinformation that permeate political discourse. He emphasizes how these tactics are used to manipulate public opinion and serve the interests of the elite. This book suggests that for a true democracy to flourish, a constitutional rewrite must include mechanisms to enhance transparency, accountability, and truthful communication in governance.

'The Common Good' shifts the focus to the concept of communal welfare. Chomsky argues that current policies and practices often prioritize individual or corporate gains over the collective well-being. He advocates for a reorientation towards the common good, a principle that should be embedded in a new constitutional framework, ensuring that laws and policies serve the broader interests of society rather than a privileged few.

In *'Profit Over People,' Chomsky* critiques the prevailing neoliberal ideology that places profit and market efficiency above human needs and social values. He argues that this approach has led to significant social and economic injustices. This perspective underscores the need for constitutional changes that prioritize people over profits, ensuring that economic systems serve the wider community, not just the corporate sector.

Synthesizing the arguments from Chomsky's works, it becomes evident that a comprehensive rewriting of the U.S. Constitution is necessary. The current constitution, according to Chomsky's analysis, fails to address the deep-seated issues of inequality, misinformation, lack of transparency, and the prioritization of profit over people.

The proposed solution lies in a constitutional convention, facilitated by an incorruptible self-governing social network, LUVRules.com. This platform would enable the citizenry to collaborate directly, ensuring a democratic and inclusive process. Such a rewrite would not only address the shortcomings highlighted by Chomsky but also pave the way for a truly democratic society that prioritizes the common good, transparency, and economic justice.

In essence, this exploration articulates the need for a constitutional revolution, guided by the principles laid out by Noam Chomsky, and executed through a modern, participatory platform that embodies the democratic ideals the new constitution seeks to uphold. This revolutionary approach could indeed be the key to resolving the systemic issues Chomsky identifies, ushering in an era of true democracy and social justice.

Shaping a Resilient and Adaptive Constitutional Convention

We have it in our power to begin the world over again.

– Thomas Paine

John Hamilton's 'Manipulating the Masses' lays a critical foundation for this analysis by examining the history and methods of mass media manipulation in shaping public opinion and political landscapes. Hamilton delves into the strategies used by governments and corporations to influence the masses, revealing the vulnerabilities in public perception and the susceptibility of democratic institutions to manipulation; thus setting the stage for understanding the need to reinforce democratic safeguards in a revised U.S. Constitution.

Robert Cialdini's 'Influence' expands upon the theme of persuasion, but with a focus on the psychology behind why people say 'yes' and how this can be ethically applied. Cialdini's principles of persuasion (reciprocity, commitment and consistency, social proof, authority, liking, and scarcity) elucidate the subtle ways in which individuals and groups can be influenced. This understanding is crucial in rethinking constitutional provisions to protect citizens from undue influence.

In 'The Person and the Situation,' Lee Ross explores how social contexts and environments influence individual behavior. Ross argues that behavior is less about personal traits and more about situational factors. This insight is vital in framing a constitution that not only addresses individual rights, but also considers the impact of social structures and institutions on human behavior.

Jonah Berger's 'The Catalyst' introduces the concept of change without resistance. Berger examines how to reduce barriers to change and encourages innovative approaches to problem-solving. In the context of a constitutional rewrite, Berger's insights offer strategies on how to effectively implement changes in a system resistant to alteration, emphasizing the need for flexibility and adaptability in constitutional design.

'Nudge' by Richard Thaler focuses on 'choice architecture' and how small design changes in the way choices are presented can significantly impact decision-making.

Thaler's concept of 'nudging' people towards beneficial behaviors without restricting freedom of choice can inform how a new constitution might better structure societal choices towards more desirable outcomes.

Synthesizing these works presents a compelling case for a U.S. Constitutional Rewrite. The combined insights into mass manipulation, principles of influence, the power of situational factors, strategies for fostering change, and the impact of choice architecture underline the vulnerabilities in the American democratic system.

A collaborative effort to create a new U.S. Constitution that is informed by these insights, is imperative. The new constitution should not only safeguard against the subversion of the American paradigm by an elitist cabal, but also utilize the wisdom from these books to build a system that is resilient, adaptive, and better aligned with the evolving needs and challenges of a modern democracy.

The goal is to forge a constitution that is robust in protecting democratic values, while being flexible enough to nudge societal progress in a direction that benefits all of our citizens.

Envisioning an Evolutionary Metacognitive Society

I wish the Constitution, which is offered, had been made more perfect...
And, as a constitutional door is opened for amendment hereafter, the adoption of it,
under the present circumstances of the Union, is in my opinion desirable.

– George Washington

In 'The Invisible Gorilla,' Christopher Chabris presents the concept of attentional blindness, revealing how people can miss obvious things in their visual field when focused on something else. This book sets the tone for understanding the gaps in societal awareness, especially concerning the U.S. Constitution. It highlights the need for heightened collective awareness to recognize and address the shortcomings in our current constitutional framework.

Chip and Dan Heath's 'Made to Stick' delves into why some ideas survive and others die. The book's exploration of simplicity, unexpectedness, concreteness, credibility, emotions, and stories (SUCCESs principles) serves as a blueprint for effectively communicating the need for a constitutional rewrite; so as to express the need for a constitutional renewal that is understandable and compelling to the American public.

In 'Switch,' Chip and Dan Heath examine how to change things when change is hard. They discuss the rational mind (the Rider), the emotional mind (the Elephant), and the path both must traverse. We must therefore align rational understanding and emotional engagement among the populace, ensuring that both aspects are addressed in our drive toward constitutional change.

Chip Conley's 'Peak' introduces the idea of maximizing human satisfaction through transformative experiences. Translating this to a national level, Conley's framework discusses how a rewritten constitution could focus on maximizing satisfaction and engagement, thus moving America towards an evolved societal structure that fosters both individual and collective fulfillment.

Noam Chomsky's 'Optimism over Despair' provides a critical lens on current global issues, including economic disparity, climate change, and political dysfunction. Chomsky's insights underline the urgent need for systemic change, reinforcing the argument for a constitutional convention. His emphasis on optimism suggests that despite the challenges, a path forward is possible through collective action and enlightened leadership.

The awareness of our cognitive blind spots, as illustrated in 'The Invisible Gorilla,' combined with the communication strategies from 'Made to Stick,' the change management insights from 'Switch,' the focus on peak experiences from 'Peak,' and Chomsky's call for optimism and action, together provide a powerful framework for motivating Americans to collaboratively engage in rewriting the Constitution.

This effort is not just about legal and political renewal, but about fostering a society that is more aware, communicative, emotionally intelligent, satisfying, and hopeful. The ultimate goal is an evolutionary leap towards a society that supports a metacognitive state – one where individuals and the collective are not only aware of their thought processes, but can also adapt and evolve these processes for the greater good.

This proposed rewriting of the Constitution would serve as a foundation for an evolved society, one where people are equipped to face current and future challenges with insight, empathy, and resilience.

THE PROPOSED BEGINNING
OF THE CONSTITUTIONAL MODEL

The wave of the future is not the conquest of the world by a single dogmatic creed,
but by the liberation of the diverse energies of free nations and free men.

– *John F. Kennedy*

CONSTITUTIONAL MODEL ABSTRACT
Towards a Resilient and Enlightened Self-Governing System

When the business interests pushed through the first installment of civil service reform in 1883, they expected that they would be able to control both political parties equally.

- Carroll Quigley

For us to develop a comprehensive self-governing structure, while transitioning towards a resource-based economic model, it is imperative to examine the fundamental issues that predispose humanity towards self-destructive behaviors; **notably narcissism** (an excessive preoccupation with personal status) **and avarice** (the apprehension surrounding insufficient financial power to secure elevated status).

Methodology: **To address these tendencies, a systems-engineering approach is essential. This methodology should integrate mechanisms that encourage altruistic, status-driven incentives, aiding citizens in their evolution towards achieving a metacognitive state. The aim is to transform our narcissistic self-interest, into compassionate actions of impartial self-sacrifice, so as to effectively reduce our long-term suffering.**

Strategic Approach: **The strategy involves guiding citizens towards the Aristotelian 'golden mean'—a divine metamorphosis of self-centeredness, into altruistic behaviors. This can be achieved within a resilient framework that incentivizes acts driven by both personal gain and compassion.**

Transitional Systems Engineering: **The proposal calls for an integrative systems engineering strategy, that employs transitional methodologies, which focus on the transformation of our: current 'illusory economy' (predicated on money and power), our 'systems of injustice' (founded on power and control), along with the full utilization of incorruptible blockchain and smart contract technologies.**

Structural Design: **To achieve this lofty goal, a clear, anti-fragile structural design with status-driven incentives, and a meritocratic hierarchy, must be established. This structure should encourage risk-taking behavior; while also embracing a certain degree of chaos, as a natural part of creation and innovation.**

144

Holistic-Humanism: This mission calls for decisive action; and emphasizes 'holistic-humanism'—an approach that combines individual and societal well-being within a dynamic system of incentives. This ethos emphasizes the importance of reciprocal care, encapsulated in the principle, 'We must take care of those who take care of us.'

Process Streamlining: Consequently, we must devise more streamlined processes for assessment, verification, certification, integration, and social justice, allowing individuals' past transgressions to be transmuted through open-reconciliation and self-forgiveness. This cultivates humility, an essential aspect of the proposed system.

The integration of an advanced resilient Self-Governing System, *that encompasses both a Social Capitalistic Economic System and a Mercifully Oriented Justice System*, is essential and must be elucidated without recourse to legal jargon, to foster a society *balanced in 'self-interest and compassion', along with 'autonomy and interdependence'.*

145

Constitutional Reformation

The NSA routinely lies in response to congressional inquiries
about the scope of surveillance within America.

- Edward Snowden

The path towards a resilient self-governing system is complex and multifaceted. It demands a collective effort to transcend our current limitations and evolve into a society that is not only self-regulating, but also deeply grounded in principles of interdependence and humanism.

> We must therefore transition from our current institutionalized mindset, into an interdependent framework that cultivates both antifragility and metacognition into the development of our citizenry.

This societal shift is crucial in the face of 'mass formation', where widespread consumer-driven narcissism supplants our lack of meaning in life, where patriarchal leadership structures cause free-floating anxiety, and where a scarcity of resources causes us to suffer from a discontent we just can't place.

As a result of these complex psychological factors, this societal shift requires us to emerge as self-regulating citizens, who not only embrace, but also nurture the diversity in our communities and tribes.

This societal evolution demands a dynamic system that upholds autonomy, nurtures critical thinking, and instills a backbone of collaborative combativeness, as we contemplate our conflicts, their roots, and the dignity with which we confront them; thereby leading us towards a more noble and harmonious existence.

Several pressing issues must be addressed to pave the way for this transformation:

1. *Unchecked International Capitalism:* creates an economic caste system.

2. *Accumulation of Inherited Wealth:* creates a concentration of power.

3. *Racial Segregation and Sexism:* perpetuates division and strife.

4. *Sexual Oppression and Repression:* often results in perversion and abuse.

5. *Problematic Agricultural Practices:* contribute to widespread health issues.

The resolution to these challenges lies in the strategy of 'Quantum Perception Manipulation', encompassing:

1. *Transitional Economy and Governance Foundations:* Building resilient self-governing systems grounded in the interdependent principles of humanism.

2. *Community Success Frameworks:* Laying the foundations for success in various organizational structures and guidance systems.

3. *Co-creation and Role Embracement:* Establishing a framework that supports the acceptance and execution of both chosen and assigned roles.

4. *Structuring Role Implementation:* Developing systems within anti-fragile frameworks that support successful role implementation.

5. *Flexibility for Continuous Development:* Recognizing that change is the only constant; while leaving room for ongoing evolution and adaptation.

Synergizing the Integration

To synergize this transitional systems-engineering approach, it is crucial to:

1. Harness the potential of mass media.
2. Implement a values-based social-capitalistic model.
3. Promote social entrepreneurship through societal engineering.

The primary challenge in executing this self-governing system lies in the unification of disparate institutional indoctrinations into an integrated, synthesized, and synergized societal system. This system must adopt an inclusive methodology that cultivates shared values and guides us towards virtuous autonomy through an anti-fragile, values-oriented approach.

In essence, establishing an interdependent global society entails:

1. Integrating our diversity with a passionate purpose serving the greater good.
2. Synthesizing micro-cultural norms through shared missions.
3. Synergizing the societal values system with societal roles and objectives.
4. Utilizing antifragility to self-actualize fulfillment, and to co-create peak experiences.
5. Attaining metacognition via the progressive evolution of a transformative society.

The achievement of such an objective necessitates adherence to a humanistic framework, one that adopts the 'diversely-interdependent spectrum of balance'—a modern interpretation of the Aristotelian mean—while concurrently pursuing a paradoxical, yet harmonious, quest for joy; through the self-actualization of a metacognitive mindset.

> The application of principles such as antifragility, honorable authenticity, compassionate confrontation, self-forgiveness, and open reconciliation is imperative.

These principles constitute the bedrock of a comprehensive care system, which in turn is the cornerstone of an efficacious societal framework. Without these foundational methodologies, society risks perpetual revolution, as opposed to progressive evolution.

The 'LUVRules Self-Governing Systems Framework' is poised to facilitate the emergence of a new world order characterized by actualizing individual peak experiences within a robust societal system that acknowledges and leverages our interdependently synergized collective action.

However, the prerequisite for this enlightening transition is the eradication of corruption within public service. This demands a decisive pivot towards the establishment of a more resilient form of representative democracy, one less susceptible to degradation.

It is envisaged that this will be achieved through the construction of a Constitutional System committed to employing Ethereum blockchain and smart contract technologies to foster a more delegative and incorruptible democracy.

CONSTITUTIONAL MODEL DESCRIPTION

In the pursuit of an advanced society, it is essential to integrate an antifragile Self-Governing System that encompasses both a 'Social Capitalistic Economic System' and a 'Mercifully Oriented Justice System'.

To effectively facilitate this transformation, a strategic approach is required. This involves: 1) maximizing the influential capacity of mass media, 2) implementing a social-capitalistic framework that is fundamentally values-based, and 3) fostering social entrepreneurship through deliberate societal engineering.

To elaborate, it is imperative to cultivate a business ecosystem that ranges from small (fewer than 153 individuals) to medium-sized (fewer than 1,813 individuals) enterprises. Within this social-entrepreneurship ecosystem, the ethos of values-based capitalism must be instilled to achieve metacognition among the populace.

Moreover, the spirit and intent behind legislative frameworks should be anchored in both impartial nobility and merciful justice. And such an undertaking necessitates the pre-existence of a values-based framework to serve as the operational foundation for this envisioned society.

Constitution Preamble

We the People of the United States, in order to form a more resilient and equitable Union, establish an Anti-Fragile Self-Governing System that embodies the principles of Social Capitalism and Merciful Justice.

We commit to fostering an economy that rewards innovation and hard work, while ensuring that prosperity is shared among all citizens. Our Economic System shall encourage the growth of wealth alongside social responsibility, balancing individual initiative with the common good.

Our Justice System shall be mercifully oriented, ensuring fairness and rehabilitation over punishment, emphasizing restorative practices that heal communities and individuals alike. This system shall strive to prevent harm and rectify injustice, ensuring that every person is treated with dignity and respect.

Integral to our Union is the pursuit of Total Quality Management in all sectors, ensuring that our construction is green, our air and water are pure, our soil fertile, and our food organic.

We shall therefore practice Regenerative Agriculture to renew our earth, meet our Sustainable Energy Needs to power our future, and implement Green Sewage and Garbage Systems to protect our environment.

We shall maintain a ready and professional Military, well-regulated Militia, and dedicated Police, Fire, EMT, and Coroner Services, all committed to the safety and welfare of our citizens.

Our Healthcare and Insurance Systems shall be Social Capitalistic Institutions backed by the Nation's Public Banking System, designed to provide quality care and financial protection to all, recognizing health as a public good, not merely a commodity.

A web of Social Capitalistic Public Banks shall offer low-interest loans to serve the public interest, fueling innovation and development without burdening future generations with unsustainable debt.

Corporate Reformation, Regulation and Oversight shall ensure that businesses operate ethically, contribute positively to society, and respect the dignity of labor.

In these endeavors, we pledge to uphold the principles of liberty, equal dignity, and justice for all, creating a society that not only endures but thrives amidst the challenges of a changing world. Thus, we lay down the foundation for a constitution that governs not just for today, but for the sustainable prosperity of all future generations.

Proposed Articles, Sections, and Subsections

Article I.

The Citizens shall embrace the role of stewards of the Earth, fostering the growth and vitality of the diverse peoples within our communities and tribes. They shall endeavor to implement an evolutionary structural system, which shall include, but not be limited to, the following strategies:

Section 1.

A Top-Down approach shall be adopted for the management of resources and fiscal affairs, which shall encompass the formulation of budgets and guidelines, the provision for oversight and transparency, along with the encouragement of experimentation and innovation.

Section 2.

A Middle-Way course shall be pursued for enlightened governance, where leadership shall consist of a Principal Leader and two Adjunct Leaders, with collaborative guidance provided by the collective wisdom of tribes and villages, all operating under a constitution rooted in our ethos of holistic humanism.

Section 3.

A Bottom-Up strategy shall be employed for the cultivation of human resources, embracing an antifragile framework, ensuring diversity, fostering community by synergizing physical proximity, and through the establishment of anonymous, and yet transparent, committee systems.

Article II.

All legislative Powers herein granted shall be vested in a Congress of our Nation-State, which shall be composed of a Senate and a House of Representatives, and within it, a tripartite system distinguished by the designations of 'the Independent', 'the Fiscal', and 'the Social' parties, each to serve the common good with due diligence and integrity.

Article III.

The Nation-State shall establish and maintain a system of governance comprising a Legislative Branch, an Executive Branch, and a Judicial Branch. These branches shall be coequal in their powers and responsibilities, and together they shall regulate and oversee a collaborative total quality management system.

Section 1.

The quality management system shall prioritize the following sectors to ensure the sustainability and welfare of the Nation-State:

Subsection i.

The construction industry shall adhere to environmentally responsible and sustainable practices, known as Green Construction.

Subsection ii.

The maintenance of Air, Water, and Soil Quality shall be of paramount concern to protect and enhance the natural environment.

Subsection iii.

The cultivation and distribution of Organic Food Systems shall be supported to provide healthy sustenance for all citizens.

Subsection iv.

Transportation systems shall be held to high standards of Quality, ensuring safety, efficiency, and minimal environmental impact.

Subsection v.

The energy needs of the Nation-State shall be met through Sustainable methods, reducing dependency on non-renewable resources.

Subsection vi.

Waste management systems, including Green Sewage and Garbage disposal, shall be implemented to minimize ecological footprint.

Subsection vii.

Defense and emergency services, including Military, Militia, Police, Fire, Emergency Medical Technicians (EMT), and Coroner Services, shall be provided to ensure public safety and order.

Subsection viii.

A Social Capitalistic framework shall govern Healthcare and General Insurance Systems to ensure accessibility and quality care for all citizens.

Subsection ix.

A Social Capitalistic Web of State Banks shall be established to provide Low-Interest Government Loans, stimulating economic growth and stability.

Subsection x.

Corporate entities shall be regulated to establish Humane Business Practices, ensuring that commerce operates with integrity and respect for all stakeholders.

Article IV

The United States shall be organized into distinct subdivisions based on population and geographic boundaries. These shall include, in ascending order of size, Villages, Townships, Communities, Provinces, Regions, and Territories. The aggregation of these subdivisions shall maintain the Nation's cohesiveness, notwithstanding non-contiguous geographies.

Section 1: Organizational Hierarchy and Limitations

Villages, as the foundational unit, shall consist of housing clusters, with Townships uniting up to twelve Villages. Townships in turn unite under Communities, with a maximum of twelve per Community, and similarly, up to twelve Communities may form a Province. Furthermore, Territories and Regions are delineated by the 12-Supreme Councils of the Executive Branch; and are subject to alterations only with a supermajority in Congress, following the arbitration process delineated in Article I, Section 1, Part 4, Subsection 2.

Section 2: Population and Membership Caps

The United States shall not exceed a population of 818,159,616 citizens, distributed across a maximum of twelve Territories, each containing no more than twelve Regions, and so forth down to the Villages, which are the smallest unit and may contain up to 274 members each.

Section 3: Governmental Tribes and Committee Membership

Each Citizen may affiliate with a maximum of 144 Governmental Tribes, serve on 48 Government Committees, be a primary member of 12 Supreme Councils, and be the Prime Minister of 12 Supreme Councils - *each with a maximum of 13 primary members, a maximum of 26 secondary assistant members, and a maximum of 234 tertiary research members.*

Article V

Section 1: The Legislative Power

Legislative authority shall be vested in the Congress of the United States, comprising a Senate and House of Representatives, to legislate and oversee key sectors including but not limited to environmental quality, infrastructure, military and emergency services, healthcare, banking, and corporate regulation.

Section 2: The Executive Branch

The Executive power shall reside in a Prime Minister of the United States, serving a maximum of three eight-year terms without limitation on age. The appointment of Vice Prime Ministers shall follow the consent of an Electoral College and they must have prior experience as Community Mayors.

Section 3: The Tripartite Party System

The political system shall be structured around three primary parties - the Fiscal, the Social, and the Independent. These parties shall adhere to specified representation limits in both houses of Congress and are subject to campaign regulations as prescribed by the 12 Supreme Councils of the Executive Branch, and validated by the Supreme Court.

Section 4: The Elections System

Elections shall be mandatory, occurring every four years, with specific guidelines for voting procedures, campaign conduct, and debate requirements. The right to vote shall be inviolable, save for individuals convicted of treason.

Section 5: The Separation of Church and State

The United States shall maintain a strict separation between Religion and State. Tax exemption for religious organizations shall be contingent upon adherence to specific leadership composition (50% Women) and the fulfillment of community service requirements. Religious entities must comply with the laws of the land without exception.

These articles shall be ratified and integrated into the Constitution of the United States, thereby ensuring a structured, equitable, and functional governance system in perpetuity.

AUTHENTIC LEADERSHIP ASSESSMENT

Section 1: Establishment of Narcissistic Personality Disorder Assessment

In recognition of the perils posed by malignant narcissism in positions of power, as elucidated in detailed research and analysis, including the insights of Frank Yeomans, this Article of the United State Constitution mandates the implementation of a rigorous Narcissistic Personality Disorder (NPD) Assessment for all individuals elected to government leadership positions in the United States of America.

Section 2: The Assessment Protocol

    i.   The NPD Assessment shall be a comprehensive psychological evaluation, designed to accurately diagnose the presence of Narcissistic Personality Disorder traits that could be detrimental to public service.

    ii.   The assessment shall be conducted over a period of 90 days, commencing from the day of election or appointment to a government position.

    iii.   The evaluation process shall be conducted by a panel of qualified mental health professionals, appointed and regulated by an independent federal body.

Section 3: Probationary Period for Elected Officials

    i.   The first 90 days of an elected official's term shall be considered a probationary period, during which the NPD Assessment is conducted.

    ii.   During this period, the elected official shall assume all roles and responsibilities of the office, subject to the results of the NPD Assessment.

Section 4: Assessment Failure and Succession

    i.   Should an elected official fail the NPD Assessment, they shall be deemed unfit for the office and immediately removed from their position.

ii.   In such an event, the candidate who received the second-highest number of votes in the election shall assume the position and undergo the same NPD Assessment during their initial 90 days in office.

iii.   This succession process shall continue until a candidate who passes the NPD Assessment occupies the office.

Section 5: Confidentiality and Transparency

i.   The results of the NPD Assessment shall be confidential but the final decision regarding the fitness of the official for the office shall be public.

ii.   The process shall be transparent, with regular updates provided to the public about the ongoing assessment, without revealing specific psychological details.

Section 6: Appeals and Reassessments

i.   An official who fails the NPD Assessment may request one reassessment after a period of six months.

ii.   The reassessment shall follow the same protocols and standards as the initial assessment.

Section 7: Implementation and Oversight

i.   The implementation of this Article shall be overseen by a newly established Federal Psychological Assessment Office (FPAO), which shall be responsible for the development, administration, and oversight of the NPD Assessments.

ii.   The FPAO shall also be tasked with ensuring the continuous improvement and accuracy of the assessment methods.

Section 8: Amendment and Modification

This Article may be amended or modified by a two-thirds majority vote in both the House of Representatives and the Senate, followed by ratification by three-fourths of the states.

This amendment aims to safeguard the integrity of the United States government by ensuring that its leaders possess the psychological and emotional stability necessary to empathetically and effectively serve the public. It represents a proactive step towards fostering ethical, empathetic, and effective governance for the benefit of all citizens.

The Perilous Path of Malignant Narcissism

https://youtu.be/x3zaA6BA_Is   /   https://youtu.be/xoRuzpsLzTU

Understanding Malignant Narcissism: *Frank Yeomans Perspective*

According to Frank Yeomans, malignant narcissism is an extreme form of narcissistic personality disorder, characterized by grandiosity, a lack of empathy, and a ruthless pursuit of power. Yeomans underscores the danger this presents when such individuals assume leadership roles. Malignant narcissists in power can inflict unprecedented damage due to their inability to consider the welfare of others and their tendency to foster divisive ideologies.

Historical Context: *The Jonestown Massacre*

- Yeomans uses the Jonestown Massacre as a profound example to explain the catastrophic potential of malignant narcissistic leadership. Jim Jones, a quintessential malignant narcissist, led his followers into a mass murder-suicide, demonstrating the terrifying extent to which such leaders can manipulate and destroy. This event serves as a chilling reminder of the destructive power of pathological narcissism when combined with charismatic authority.

The Narcissistic 'Will to Receive' and Its Threats

- Malignant narcissists are driven by a 'will to receive' – an unquenchable thirst for admiration, status, and entitled comfort. This relentless pursuit often comes at the expense of ethical considerations and societal well-being. In positions of power, such individuals prioritize personal gain over collective interests, exacerbating issues like inequality, environmental degradation, and social unrest.

Primitive Appeal of Splitting and Societal Impact

- Yeomans discusses the concept of splitting – a primitive psychological mechanism that divides the world into 'good' and 'evil'. Malignant narcissists exploit this by creating a strong in-group (us) versus out-group (them) dynamic, often leading to social polarization and conflict. Figures like Trump and Hitler exemplify this through their rhetoric and policies, which have deepened societal divisions and fueled hatred and bigotry.

Global Implications and the Road Ahead

- Extrapolating Yeomans' observations to a global scale, illustrates how malignant narcissism in leadership can potentially lead to catastrophic consequences – from authoritarian governance and human rights abuses to the exacerbation of global crises such as climate change and pandemics. *It stresses the importance of recognizing and mitigating the influence of such individuals in power.*

Frank Yeomans' analysis of malignant narcissism presents a stark warning about the risks posed by such individuals in leadership roles. The survival of our species hinges on our ability to identify, understand, and counteract the influence of malignant narcissism.

This involves promoting psychological awareness, fostering empathetic and ethical leadership, and creating robust systems that prevent the ascent of such destructive personalities to positions of power.

The analysis calls for a collective effort to safeguard our societies and planet from the dire consequences of malignant narcissistic leadership, advocating for a future where empathy, cooperation, and ethical governance prevail.

CHILDREN'S BILL OF RIGHTS

Recognizing that every child deserves a healthy start to life, a nurturing environment, and the opportunity to reach their full potential, this Children's Bill of Rights is established. It is founded on the principle that the well-being of children is paramount and that society has an obligation to safeguard, educate, and empower its youngest members.

Section 1: Right to a Healthy and Desired Birth

    i.   Every child has the right to be born to a healthy mother who has willingly chosen to bring a child into the world.

    ii.   Prospective parents have the right to access comprehensive reproductive healthcare, including the right for the mother to safely terminate a pregnancy.

    iii.   Expectant mothers shall have access to quality prenatal care and nutrition to ensure the healthiest possible start for their child.

Section 2: Parental Education and Training

    i.   Prospective and current parents have the right to receive education and training in child-rearing, including aspects of physical, emotional, and cognitive development.

Section 3: Right to Comprehensive Education

    i.   Every child has the right to free, high-quality education from Pre-Kindergarten through to an Associate's Degree or its equivalent.

    ii.   Educational systems shall aim to develop each child's personality, talents, and mental and physical abilities to their fullest potential.

Section 4: Right to Nutritional Knowledge and Healthy Food

    i.   Children have the right to access healthy, balanced, and nutritious food.

    ii.   Education systems shall provide knowledge about epigenetics, the gut-brain axis, and the impact of nutrition across generations, emphasizing the importance of healthy eating habits, the gut microbiome, and homeostasis.

Section 5: Right to Emancipation

    i.   Recognizing the diverse maturity levels of children, those aged 9 and above shall have the right to seek emancipation under specific, legally defined conditions that ensure the child's safety, well-being, and continued development.

Section 6: Protection and Welfare

    i.   Children have the right to be protected from physical, mental, and emotional abuse or neglect.

    ii.   Societies shall establish systems to safeguard children from harm and provide necessary support for their welfare and development.

Section 7: Right to Healthcare

    i.   Every child has the right to access comprehensive healthcare services, including preventative care, organic functional foods, basic dental care, psychological mental health services, and medical treatments with an emphasis on Osteopathic manual manipulation.

Section 8: Right to a Voice

    i.   Children have the right to express their views freely in all matters affecting them, with their opinions given due weight in accordance with their age and maturity.

Section 9: Right to Identity and Nationality

i.   Every child has the right to a name, a nationality, and, as far as possible, to know and be cared for by their parents.

Section 10: Right to Leisure, Play, and Culture

i.   Every child has the right to rest, leisure, play, and participation in cultural and artistic activities.

This Bill of Rights commits to the holistic development and well-being of all children, recognizing their unique needs and potentials. It calls upon parents, educators, healthcare providers, and policymakers to uphold these rights and ensure that every child can thrive in a supportive and nurturing environment.

The Impact of Legalized Abortion on Crime Rates

The assertion that the legalization of abortion leads to a significant decrease in crime rates years later is a topic of considerable debate and analysis within social science and criminology. Central to this discussion is the study of various factors including demographic changes, societal shifts, and policy alterations that might contribute to this phenomenon.

The hypothesis that legalized abortion can lead to a decrease in crime rates was popularized by the work of economists Steven Levitt and John Donohue, who in 2001, proposed that the United States' drop in crime during the 1990s could be attributed to the legalization of abortion following the Roe v. Wade decision in 1973.

Their argument centered around the idea that unwanted children, who may have been more likely to grow up in adverse conditions, were less likely to be born, potentially leading to a reduction in the number of individuals prone to criminal behavior.

Analysis of Statistical Data:

-    *Trends in Crime Rates:* A detailed examination of crime statistics in the 15 years following the legalization of abortion reveals a significant decrease in crime rates, particularly in violent crimes and property crimes. This trend appears to align temporally with the period when children born post-legalization would reach the age of potential criminal activity.

- *Control Variables:* To attribute these changes exclusively to the legalization of abortion, one must control for other variables that could influence crime rates, such as economic factors, changes in policing methods, drug use trends, and other social policies.

- *Demographic Shifts:* The hypothesis suggests that the decrease in crime is partly due to the reduction in the number of children born into potentially high-risk environments. This aspect involves analyzing demographic shifts, including the number of births, socioeconomic conditions, and child-rearing environments.

A recent study, as reported in an article titled 'Economic Research Resurfaces Debate about the Link Between Legalized Abortion and Crime Reduction,' revisits Donohue and Levitt's hypothesis – https://journalistsresource.org/economics/abortion-crime-research-donohue-levitt/

This study reaffirms the original findings, suggesting a strong correlation between the availability of legal abortion and a reduction in crime rates 15 to 20 years later.

The research reinforces the notion that access to abortion, *thus reducing the number of unwanted children in the world,* leads to a decrease in the number of children growing up in environments that could predispose them to criminal activity.

STATE-SANCTIONED MARRIAGES

Section 1: Purpose and Scope

This amendment is crafted to redirect the trajectory of state-sanctioned marriages towards a secular, child-centered framework, transcending the boundaries of the couple's gender or sexual orientation. It underscores the paramount significance of adopting a secular approach within the realms of both marriage and child-rearing.

Backed by compelling scientific evidence, this approach recognizes the adverse effects of religious indoctrination on child brain development, while being firmly committed to cultivating critical thinking and metacognition in young minds.

Scientific studies consistently demonstrate that religious indoctrination during childhood can have profound and lasting effects on 'calcifying' neural pathways and preventing positive childhood experimentation and exploration. For it is the imposition of rigid religious beliefs that often restricts a child's ability to engage in critical thinking and metacognitive processes. And the latest research in neuroscience suggests that early exposure to dogmatic religious teachings can lead to cognitive inflexibility, inhibiting the development of open-mindedness and independent thought.

Moreover, psychological studies highlight the importance of fostering an environment that encourages children to question and explore different perspectives. Religious indoctrination, with its emphasis on unquestioning faith, can hinder the development of these essential cognitive skills. By redirecting the focus of state-sanctioned marriages towards a secular and child-centric approach, this amendment aligns with the scientific consensus on promoting intellectual autonomy and metacognition in young individuals.

Section 2: Defining State-Sanctioned Secular Marriage

i. State-sanctioned marriages are hereby legally defined as unions established for child-rearing, whether through biological means or adoption.

ii. These marriages will be purely secular, legally binding agreements, devoid of religious affiliations, rituals, or doctrines, thereby promoting a metacognitive approach to family life.

Section 3: Incentives and Protections for Secular Child-Rearing Marriages

i.   Legal and financial incentives are designated solely for couples committed to raising children within the secular, metacognitive framework of this amendment.

ii. Such incentives are extended to couples actively engaging with the state-hosted social network that provides resources on prenatal care, child development, nutrition, and metacognitive parental education, up to the child's 26th year.

iii. Incentives are reserved for secular marriages with children, excluding childless civil unions and 'marriages' solemnized through religious ceremonies. This provision underscores the amendment's commitment to secularism and the metacognitive upbringing of children, free from religious coercion or indoctrination.

Section 4: Adoption and Social Support Networks

i.   A state-hosted social network and adoption system will be established, facilitating a speedy adoption process, exclusively for state-sanctioned married couples.

ii. This state-hosted social network also serves as the mandated platform for sharing best practices in child-rearing, while also providing speedy adoption processes that minimize harm.

Section 5: Support for Unwed Pregnant Teens and New Mothers

i.   The government will establish and fund secular and holistic group-home dormitories specifically for unwed pregnant teenagers and new mothers, focusing on the crucial first 7-years of a child's life—a period scientifically recognized as vital for cognitive, emotional, and social development. The provided care, education, and nutritional support will foster the optimal development of both the child and mother, emphasizing the importance of the mother-child bond during these formative years.

ii. These centers prioritize physical and holistic development, offering a natural, sunlit environment conducive to healthy growth and bonding. This setting is designed to promote the well-being of children and mothers, acknowledging the importance of nature in early childhood development and maternal health.

iii.   Recognizing that humans are inherently social beings, these facilities will also provide communal spaces and programs for mothers to engage with each other. This aspect of the program acknowledges the importance of adult social interaction and support for maintaining mental health and personal growth. Mothers will have access to adult education and life skills training, offering them opportunities to adapt to and navigate the challenges of a fulfilling adult life. This ensures that the focus is not solely on child-rearing, but also on the personal and social development of the mothers, facilitating a balanced approach to family and personal life.

Section 6: Educational and Supportive Resources for Parents

i.   A state-hosted social network will offer resources on prenatal care, childhood development, nutrition, and parental education.

ii.   The platform will include empathy training programs to combat societal issues like narcissism, focusing on fostering responsible and compassionate parenting.

Section 7: Implementation and Oversight

i.   Government agencies will transparently oversee the implementation of this constitutional article, ensuring adherence to its principles.

ii.   Regular assessment and updates of the policies and programs will be conducted to ensure their effectiveness and relevance.

Section 8: National Interest and Justification

i.   This amendment aligns with the national interest in promoting the welfare of children and responsible parenthood.

ii.   By focusing on child-rearing as the primary purpose of secular state-sanctioned marriages, it aims to enhance the societal fabric by nurturing and cultivating metacognition in the citizenry who are also well-rounded and empathetic.

This proposed constitutional amendment seeks to transform the concept of state-sanctioned marriage, focusing it squarely on the responsibilities and benefits associated with child-rearing. It aims to create a secular, inclusive, and supportive framework that prioritizes the well-being of children, whether through biological means or adoption. The amendment also incorporates significant support systems for parents and prospective parents, emphasizing the importance of education and empathy in child-rearing.

MARITAL DISSOLUTION AND CHILD WELFARE

Section 1: Purpose and Scope

This amendment is designed to establish a constitutional process for divorce of pair-bonded adults; prioritizing the well-being of children, and the equitable treatment of spouses.

Recognizing the diversity of modern marriages, *including those without intentions of having children,* this amendment seeks to provide a fair and harm-minimizing framework for marital dissolution.

Section 2: Principles Guiding Marital Dissolution

   i.   The primary focus in divorce proceedings involving children is to minimize emotional and psychological harm to the children.

   ii.   In cases without children, the process emphasizes fair and equitable division of assets and responsibilities through the mandated arbitration process.

Section 3: Child-Centric Approach in Custody

   i.   Children over 9 years of age have the right to choose their primary caregiver.

   ii.   Children may choose to modify their living arrangements as needed or desired, emphasizing their need for security, comfort and emotional well-being, but both parents must agree on the change via the use of the mandated government social network.

   iii. Measures are to be further developed and implemented to protect children from being used as leverage, or from being subjected to emotional manipulation, by either parent.

Section 4: Addressing Parental Fitness and Child Safety

    i.   In cases of alleged emotional abuse or manipulation, a thorough investigation is required to assess the child's best interests.

    ii.   A parent proven to engage in such behavior may face restrictions on custody, determined by the severity of the issue.

    iii.   Special attention is given to identifying and protecting children from risks of domestic abuse and sexual exploitation, recognizing the alarming statistics of familial child molestation.

Section 5: Divorce Proceedings Without Children

    i.   Divorces without children are directed to utilize the mandated arbitration process which focuses on equitable asset division, ensuring fair treatment of both parties.

    ii.   Spousal support and asset division are swiftly adjudicated with the aim of minimizing financial conflicts and encouraging a fair resolution.

Section 6: Implementation and Enforcement

    i.   Family courts are tasked with the implementation of these guidelines, ensuring they align with the principles of fairness, child welfare, and justice.

    ii.   Regular training and updates for judges and legal practitioners in family law will be mandated to stay informed on best practices in child welfare and family dynamics.

Section 7: National Interest and Justification

    i.   This amendment acknowledges the evolving nature of family structures and the need for a modern legal framework that reflects these changes.

ii.   It balances the interests of children and adults in marital transitions, fostering a more harmonious and just process.

iii.   The emphasis on child welfare and equitable treatment aligns with the nation's commitment to human rights and family stability.

This proposed constitutional amendment seeks to modernize the legal framework surrounding marriage and divorce, placing a strong emphasis on the well-being of children and the equitable treatment of adults. It aims to address the complexities of contemporary family dynamics, ensuring that the process of marital dissolution upholds the principles of justice, fairness, and compassion.

FAMILIAL EQUITY AND LEGACY PRESERVATION

Section 1: Establishment of Familial LLC-Trust

Upon the birth of their first child or the legal adoption of any child, each parent shall automatically become a special Familial Limited Liability Company Trust (Familial LLC-Trust). This innovative financial instrument ensures that the parent's assets and estate are managed within each individual parent's Familial LLC-Trust.

Section 2: Trustee and Inheritance Rights

i. Each biological or legally adopted child of the parent shall be designated as a trustee-owner of each individual parent's designated Familial LLC-Trust.

ii. No child may be excluded or excommunicated from each individual parent's trust, ensuring equitable treatment of all progeny, adopted or otherwise, upon the death of a parent.

iii. Upon an unmarried parent's death, the estate will be divided equally among all trustees (up to $3.5M each), either through liquidation of assets or division of assets based upon fair market discounted cash flow valuations; nullifying the legality of any other wills or trusts previously established.

    a. If the unmarried deceased parent owns controlling interest or has super voting rights in a company, those shares may be sold at fair market value.

- However, the employees of the company can form a legal cooperative to purchase those shares, and in doing so, they will have first right of refusal.

- Or those shares can be inherited by the trustees, but all inherited shares lose voting rights, unless a trustee is familiar with the financials of the company, and has substantial 'hands-on' know-how to assume the power accorded with the trustee's portion of such inherited ownership.

Section 3: Spousal Rights in Inheritance

    i.   Division of Joint Assets Upon Spousal Death: Upon the death of one spouse, all officially designated 'joint property', including real estate, bank accounts, investment accounts, and other financial instruments, will be inherited by the surviving spouse.

        a. This inheritance is contingent upon the surviving spouse integrating all child-trustees listed in the deceased spouse's Familial LLC-Trust into their own Familial LLC-Trust. These child-trustees must be accorded equal status alongside the surviving spouse's existing child-trustees.

    ii.   Surviving Spouse with Children Under 21: When a surviving spouse is responsible for children under the age of 21, and there are no officially designated 'joint properties', they shall inherit the deceased spouse's estate.

        a. This inheritance is contingent upon the surviving spouse integrating all child-trustees listed in the deceased spouse's Familial LLC-Trust into their own Familial LLC-Trust. These child-trustees must be accorded equal ownership status alongside the surviving spouse's existing child-trustees.

        b. If the deceased spouse has controlling interest or super voting rights in a company, those shares may be sold at fair market value.

            ▪ However, the employees of the company can form a legal cooperative to purchase those shares, and in doing so, they will have first right of refusal.

            ▪ Or those shares can be inherited by the surviving spouse, but all inherited shares lose voting rights, unless the spouse is an officially designated joint-owner of the shares, and is familiar with the financials of the company, and has substantial 'hands-on' know-how to assume the power accorded with such inherited ownership.

    iii. Surviving Spousal Parent with No Children under 21: In situations where no children under 21 are being raised by the surviving spousal parent, and there are no officially designated 'joint properties', the surviving spousal parent is entitled to the primary residence, plus their fair share of the remaining estate.

a. This entitlement also requires the surviving spousal parent to incorporate all trustees from the deceased spouse's Familial LLC-Trust into their own Familial LLC-Trust, treating them equally with their existing child-trustees.

b. The remainder of the estate is to be divided among the child-trustees who are 26 years of age or older, with each eligible trustee receiving up to $3.5 million.

c. Child-trustees below 26 years of age are not directly eligible for inheritance, which is to be held in trust, but can access their portion for sanctioned medical and educational expenses.

iv.   Tax Exemption: All inheritances and distributions outlined in this article are exempt from any form of taxation.

Section 4: Allocation of the Remaining Estate to Governmental Agencies

This section outlines the distribution of the residual estate, following the maximum distributions for the spouse and children of $3.5M each. The remaining assets will be allocated to specific governmental agencies, with the explicit purpose of building infrastructure and enhancing the humanistic development of the residents, aiming to foster virtue and autonomy:

i.   Residential Village and Township: 12% of the remaining estate will be allocated to the local Village (6%) and the local Township (6%).

ii.   Residential Community, Province, and Territory: 36% of the remaining estate will be distributed among the wider Community (12%), Provincial (12%), and Territorial (12%) governmental bodies.

iii.   Residential Region and Nation State: The Regional (26%) authority and the National (26%) government will together receive 52% of the remaining estate.

These distributions are intended to directly contribute to programs and initiatives that build infrastructure and promote the human development of the citizens in these respective areas.

Section 5: Fair Wealth Gifting and Blockchain Control

In this section, we outline a system that allows a single citizen of sound mind, without children; or a married couple, both of sound mind, without children, to gift up to $1 million annually, or a home valued at no more than $1 million, to individual human recipients before their passing. To prevent potential abuse and ensure fairness, specific conditions must be met:

i.   Unconditional Gifting: The gifting must be unconditional, with no strings attached, ensuring that the wealthy cannot exploit the less fortunate for personal gain.

ii. No Coercion: The citizen making the gift should not be under any form of coercion, ensuring that the process remains voluntary and ethical.

iii. Recipient Criteria for Gifting: The gifting recipients cannot be religious leaders, corporate entities, trusts, pets, or any other non-human entities.

To implement these measures, we have structured the taxation of these gifts as follows:

-   Initial Exemption: A gifted home valued at less than $1M, as well as the first $35,000 of an annual gift, of up to $1M, is exempt from a gifting taxation, reflecting research that small gifts have minimal impact on wealth disparity.

-   Progressive Taxation: The subsequent $965,000 of the maximum annual gift is subject to a 35% gifting tax rate. This rate is aligned with recent statistical data highlighting significant income disparities in the United States. The gifting tax revenue generated will be allocated to specific governmental agencies, as detailed in Section 4 of this reformation.

Section 6: Regulated Gambling and Blockchain Oversight

In this section, we establish a comprehensive system governing gambling activities, with a focus on fairness and responsible participation. The guidelines are as follows:

i.   Prohibition for Parents with Children Under 26: Parents with dependent children under the age of 26 are prohibited from engaging in gambling activities. This measure aims to protect families and ensure the well-being of young dependents.

ii.   Eligibility for Gambling: Eligibility for gambling activities is restricted to two categories of individuals or couples:

    a. *Single Citizens:* Any single citizen of sound mind, without dependent children, is allowed to engage in gambling.

    b. *Married Couples:* Married couples, where both spouses are of sound mind and without dependent children, are also eligible to participate in gambling. However, both must agree is using funds from a joint-designated account.

iii.   Annual Gambling Limit: All eligible individuals and couples may gamble up to a maximum of $120,000 annually ($10,000 monthly) without incurring an up-front luxury tax of 20%. This is designed to prevent excessive gambling and to reduce financial harm.

iv.   Location of Gambling:

    a. *Sanctioned Gambling Facilities:* All forms of gambling, excluding sports betting, must be conducted physically within regulated gambling facilities. These American facilities are exclusively situated in designated areas, namely Atlantic City and Las Vegas.

    b. *Regulated Online Sports Gambling:* For sports betting, individuals are required to transact their bets online through state-regulated sports betting websites. This ensures a secure and regulated environment for sports gambling.

These measures are established to promote responsible gambling, protect families with young dependents, and maintain fairness and transparency within the gambling industry. Additionally, the oversight and enforcement of these regulations will be facilitated through the utilization of blockchain technology, providing transparency and accountability in the gambling ecosystem.

Section 7: Regulated Drug Use and Blockchain Controls

In this section, we introduce a comprehensive framework to govern recreational drug and alcohol activities while emphasizing responsible consumption and medicinal use. These guidelines are established to address the ongoing drug abuse epidemic, fund innovative drug rehabilitation facilities, and promote overall public safety. The key provisions are as follows:

i. Prohibition for Parents with Children Under 26: To safeguard families and ensure the well-being of young dependents, parents with children under the age of 26 are prohibited from recreational drug use involving decriminalized substances (e.g., cocaine, meth, heroin) within their residence or in the presence of their children, whether at home or away. However, the responsible use of prescribed drugs for medicinal purposes is permitted. Additionally, both medicinal and recreational use of cannabis, psilocybin, and MDMA is entirely legal, can be sold as a microdosing food supplement, and carries no legal repercussions. Moderate alcohol consumption in the presence of children remains socially acceptable.

ii. Eligibility for Decriminalized Drug Consumption: Participation in decriminalized drug consumption is limited to two specific categories of citizens:

a. *Single Citizens:* Any single citizen of sound mind, without dependent children, is allowed to engage in decriminalized drug use.

b. *Married Couples:* Married couples, where both spouses are of sound mind and without dependent children, are also eligible to partake in decriminalized drug use.

iii. Annual Drug Consumption Limit: To prevent excessive drug use and protect participants from potential financial harm, all eligible citizens are subject to an annual limit (via blockchain controls) of $13,000 for decriminalized drug consumption.

iv. Locations for Decriminalized Drug Use of Eligible Citizens:

a. *In the Privacy of Home:* Decriminalized drug use is permitted within the confines of one's private residence.

b. *Sanctioned Lodging and Event Spaces:* Specifically designated and regulated lodging and event spaces are authorized for decriminalized drug consumption. These spaces adhere to stringent quality and safety standards and are closely monitored to ensure safe consumption.

These measures serve a dual purpose: firstly, to encourage responsible drug consumption and secondly, to protect the welfare of families with young dependents. Furthermore, this framework promotes the development and maintenance of quality and safety standards within the regulated drug manufacturing industry.

And to enhance oversight and enforcement, blockchain technology will be utilized, providing transparency and accountability in the state-sanctioned drug manufacturing ecosystem. This comprehensive approach addresses the urgent need to combat drug abuse, fund innovative drug rehabilitation facilities, and disempower the drug cartels so as to retask the DEA towards human trafficking.

Section 8: Death of a Single Unmarried Citizen with Living Relatives and no Children

In situations where a single unmarried citizen with no children, but with living parents, siblings, nieces, and/or nephews; half of the estate will be distributed equally among the living parents, siblings, nieces and nephews; with a maximum distribution of $3.5M each (to be held in trust for anyone under the age of 26). The other half of the estate, plus any residuals, will be allocated to specific governmental agencies (as directed in Section 4).

Section 9: Death of a Single Unmarried Citizen with No Children or Living Relatives

In situations where there is a death of a single unmarried citizen with no living parents, siblings, nieces, or nephews; the distribution of the entire estate will be allocated to specific governmental agencies (as directed in Section 4).

Section 10: Enforcement and Regulation

The scientific research on wealth inequality in America consistently demonstrates alarming levels of disparity, with a small portion of the population holding a substantial share of the nation's wealth. Recent statistical data on wealth disparity emphasizes the urgency of these measures in creating a fairer and more prosperous society for future generations.

Furthermore, the enforcement of these limitations will be facilitated through the utilization of Ethereum Blockchain and Smart Contract technologies. These technologies provide transparency and accountability, preventing manipulation and exploitation of the system.

These limitations on wealth are a part of a larger stratagem in directing investments into small to medium-sized businesses that practice Social Capitalism. This multi-pronged approach will contribute to a more equitable society, and foster a thriving Social Capitalistic Ecosystem which acknowledges the existence of the two-tier economy, while setting-in motion societal remedies that ensure a more balanced and prosperous nation.

This proposed amendment seeks to ensure equitable distribution of assets among family members, safeguarding the interests of children and spouses while also contributing to local communities and government entities through the structured distribution of larger estates.

Generational Wealth Concentration
And the Impending Economic Repercussions

The unprecedented accumulation of wealth among Baby Boomers and older Americans has far-reaching implications for the American economy. Over the past three decades, this demographic has amassed a staggering $35 trillion, accounting for 27% of all U.S. wealth, which is a significant increase from 20% thirty-years prior. This wealth accumulation is equivalent to 157% of U.S. gross domestic product, more than doubling the proportion from thirty-years ago, according to federal data.

This concentration of wealth is not merely a statistic; it is a harbinger of a potential economic imbalance that threatens to destabilize the foundational principles of equitable economic growth and social mobility. The current trajectory affirms the establishment of a two-tier economy; characterized by a significant divide between the asset-rich older generation, and the comparatively asset-poor younger generations.

The economic disparity can be traced to several factors, including the post-World War II economic boom, favorable tax policies, the rise in property values, and the stock market growth that older generations have experienced and benefited from throughout their lives. These factors, coupled with changes in pensions and the shift towards individual retirement accounts, have allowed wealth to concentrate heavily at the top of the age spectrum.

However, this wealth concentration, which continues to enlarge, presents several challenges:

- *Reduced Wealth Mobility:* With a significant portion of wealth locked with older generations, younger individuals face barriers to accumulating wealth. This can lead to reduced consumer spending, investment, and overall economic dynamism, as the younger generations struggle with student debt, rising housing costs, and stagnant wages.

- *Economic Inequality:* As wealth begets wealth, those without access to inherited or accumulated capital are increasingly marginalized, exacerbating socioeconomic disparities and fostering economic environments that can lead to social unrest.

- *Unsustainable Economic Model:* An economy that relies on continuous wealth accumulation by a shrinking demographic is unsustainable. As the Baby Boomers age, the withdrawal of their capital from the economy to fund retirement could lead to a decrease in investment and a potential liquidity crisis.

- *Dependency and Autonomy Loss:* The younger generations' reliance on the wealth of their predecessors for economic advancement undermines their autonomy. This dependency can stifle innovation and entrepreneurship, vital drivers of economic growth.

While the accumulation of wealth by older generations is a testament to being born within a privileged race and/or generation, it poses a threat to the economic stability and social fabric of the nation.

Policies and practices that promote intergenerational equity and wealth distribution are crucial to maintaining a balanced and fair economy. Without such measures, we risk creating an economy where the majority are not stakeholders, but rather cogs in a wheel, serving a system that is not designed for their benefit.

EQUITABLE COMPENSATION IN EDUCATION

Section 1: Purpose and Intent

The purpose of this amendment is to address the growing disparity in compensation between school administrators and teachers in both public and private educational institutions.

> This amendment seeks to remedy the detrimental effects of bloated bureaucracies on educational outcomes, and the overall well-being of the educational system.

This is in response to increasing concerns about administrative overheads that significantly outpace investments in direct educational activities and teacher compensation.

Section 2: Compensation Cap for Administrators

i.   The maximum compensation for any administrator in public and private educational institutions, including but not limited to superintendents, principals, and department heads, shall not exceed the median income of the top quartile of teachers within their respective institutions.

ii. This compensation includes all forms of salary, bonuses, and other financial benefits.

Section 3: Rationale and Supporting Data

i.   Studies have shown that excessive administrative costs can divert crucial resources away from classrooms, negatively impacting student learning and teacher effectiveness.

ii. Data indicates that high administrative pay does not correlate with improved educational outcomes. Instead, investment in teacher training, educational materials, and classroom facilities has a more direct and positive impact on student achievement.

iii.   The discrepancy in pay between administrators and teachers has been linked to decreased morale among educators, leading to higher turnover rates and affecting the quality of education.

iv.   Ensuring more equitable compensation structures aligns financial incentives with educational priorities, fostering a more collaborative and effective educational environment.

Section 4: Implementation and Oversight

i.   The Department of Education, in collaboration with state and local educational authorities, shall establish guidelines for the implementation of this compensation cap.

ii.   Regular audits and reports will be conducted to ensure compliance and assess the impact of this policy on educational outcomes.

Section 5: Justification and National Interest

i.   Education is a critical factor in the nation's socio-economic development, and ensuring effective allocation of resources in education is of national interest.

ii.   This amendment aligns with the principles of fairness, equity, and efficient use of public funds, ensuring that the educational system operates in the best interest of students and teachers alike.

iii.   By addressing the imbalance in compensation, this amendment aims to attract and retain talented educators, foster educational excellence, and ultimately contribute to the health and prosperity of the nation.

This proposed constitutional amendment reflects a commitment to restoring balance in educational administration, prioritizing resource allocation towards direct educational services, and reinforcing the nation's dedication to quality education for all.

Transformation of Higher Education Research Institutions

Section 1: Purpose and Intent

This amendment is aimed at transforming colleges and universities in the United States into primarily teaching-focused institutions, rather than for-profit research entities.

It seeks to address the concerns related to the commercialization of academic research and its impact on the quality of education and public welfare.

The intent is to cultivate a higher education system that upholds academic integrity, prioritizes teaching excellence, and contributes responsibly to scientific advancement and community stewardship.

Section 2: Restructuring Research and Teaching Priorities

i.   All colleges and universities shall primarily function as teaching institutions, with the primary objective of providing high-quality holistic education.

ii.   Research activities conducted by these institutions must adhere to the highest standards of scientific integrity, with a focus on peer-reviewed, incorruptible research.

iii. Direct hiring of faculty or researchers by government agencies or corporations, *other than by independent commercial research institutions that adhere to stringent scientific standards,* is prohibited.

Section 3: Compensation Regulation

i.   The compensation of college and university faculty involved in research shall not exceed the median income of the top quartile of teachers within their respective institutions.

ii.   This ensures equitable distribution of resources and aligns the incentives of faculty members with teaching and responsible research.

Section 4: Rationale and Supporting Data

    i.   There is growing concern over the influence of profit motives in academic research, leading to conflicts of interest and compromised research integrity.

    ii.   Instances such as the OxyContin scandal, where corrupted scientific research contributed to the opioid epidemic, underscore the dangers of profit-driven research. This epidemic has cost countless lives and demonstrated the catastrophic consequences of compromised scientific integrity.

    iii.   Studies have shown that the commercialization of research in higher education can detract from teaching quality and academic freedom, impacting student education and broader societal interests.

Section 5: Oversight and Implementation

    i.   The Department of Education, in collaboration with independent academic bodies, shall oversee the transparent implementation of these guidelines.

    ii.   Regular audits and assessments will be conducted to ensure adherence to teaching priorities and integrity in research.

Section 6: Justification and National Interest

    i.   The amendment aligns with the nation's commitment to educational excellence and responsible scientific inquiry.

    ii.   By prioritizing teaching and integrity in research, this amendment aims to foster a more ethical and transparent academic environment.

    iii.   The transformation of higher education institutions serves the long-term interests of society by promoting informed, critical thinking, and innovation free from undue commercial influences.

This proposed constitutional amendment represents a commitment to redefining higher education in the United States, emphasizing the role of colleges and universities as bastions of learning and responsible, ethical research. It aims to safeguard the interests of students, educators, and the public by ensuring that higher education serves as a pillar of societal progress and integrity.

TRANSFORMATION OF THE PUBLIC EDUCATIONAL SYSTEM

Section 1: Purpose and Scope

This constitutional amendment stands as a response to mounting scientific evidence highlighting the inadequacies of our current school system and underscores the critical importance of implementing the proposed educational reform for the future success of the American citizenry.

Research consistently demonstrates that our existing educational model falls short in adequately preparing students for the challenges of the modern world. High dropout rates, declining academic performance, and disparities in educational outcomes are clear indicators of the system's limitations. Furthermore, studies reveal that traditional teaching methods often fail to foster metacognition and critical thinking, essential skills for navigating today's complex society.

This amendment's purpose is to revolutionize our nation's educational system by integrating a holistic approach that blends both traditional and boarding school experiences, while simultaneously discontinuing the funding of school vouchers for private and charter schools.

The scientific consensus supports the need for comprehensive reform to address these educational shortcomings and equip students with the skills and knowledge necessary for success in the 21st century.

Section 2: Year-Round Schooling for Enhanced Student Development

This section explores the profound impact of a year-round schooling system, organized in quarters, within a hybrid self-paced educational model. It delves into how this system promotes student development, fosters metacognition, and aligns with the natural biorhythms of the seasons.

    i.   *Early Education (PreK to 2nd grade):* The focus on foundational skills, *including music literacy, instrument playing, and chess,* aligns with cognitive development research. Studies indicate that early exposure to music and strategic games enhances brain development and critical thinking skills.

ii.   *Boarding School Format (3rd to 12th grade):* The transition to a boarding school setting for part of the week, *from Monday to Wednesday nights, with classes from Monday to Thursday,* is supported by research suggesting that immersive educational environments can deepen learning and foster independence.

iii.   *Extended School Year (44 weeks with specified breaks):* The extended school year, with shorter, more frequent breaks, reduces learning loss compared to traditional long summer vacations, as indicated by educational research. Furthermore, strategic placement of breaks synchronizes students' biorhythms with natural cycles.

      a. *1 week off for Spring Break; week of March 1st.*

      b. *1 week off for May Day; week of May 1st.*

      c. *2 weeks off for Summer Break; weeks of July 4th and after.*

      d. *1 week off for Halloween; week of October 31st.*

      e. *1 week off for Thanksgiving; week of November 24th.*

      f. *2 weeks off for Christmas/New Year; weeks of December 24th and after.*

iv.   *Comprehensive Quarterly Schooling System:* The quarterly schooling system aligns with cognitive and developmental psychology, sociology, and educational research; emphasizing the importance of balanced, continuous learning environments in developing metacognition, emotional intelligence, and holistic student development.

      a. Spring Quarter (New Beginnings): This quarter underscores the concept of revitalization and reenergizing, aligning with the psychological phenomenon of seasonal affective patterns. Studies reveal that the arrival of spring is associated with increased motivation, as exposure to natural light stimulates the release of serotonin, a neurotransmitter linked to mood elevation and cognitive function. The cyclical nature of this quarter mirrors the inherent human need for renewal and fresh starts, optimizing the learning environment.

      b. Summer Quarter (Self-Discipline and Self-Leadership): During the summer quarter, the emphasis is on self-discipline and authentic leadership. Summer traditionally embodies relaxation and leisure, making it an ideal time to challenge students to balance their recreational activities with academic responsibilities. Research in self-regulation and goal-setting supports the significance of cultivating these skills, as they are critical for long-term success.

   c. Autumn Quarter (Completion and Achievement): **The autumn quarter coincides with the harvest season, symbolizing the fruition of efforts and the completion of long-anticipated goals.** Psychological studies on delayed gratification underscore its vital role in character development and academic achievement. By assigning integrated projects that span three quarters and culminate in the autumn, students learn the value of sustained effort and patience, developing essential skills for goal attainment.

   d. Winter Quarter (Reflection and Transition): **Dedicated to science fiction reading assignments, an annual review, and standardized test preparation; the winter quarter aligns with the introspective nature of the season.** Research on metacognition emphasizes the importance of reflection in the learning process. The portfolio presentations and graduation ceremonies serve as opportunities for students to reflect on their achievements, fostering self-awareness and self-assessment skills.

- Scientific consensus in cognitive and developmental psychology, sociology, and education supports the notion that a comprehensive quarterly schooling system optimally aligns with the natural rhythms of human learning and development.

- This approach is scientifically sound, as it enhances cognitive development, emotional intelligence, and overall student well-being, preparing them to navigate the complexities of the modern world with metacognitive proficiency.

Section 3: Curriculum Core and Life-Skills Development

   i. Experiential Learning and Joyful Fulfillment: This component integrates physical, intellectual, and emotional experiences into the learning process. Studies indicate that experiential learning enhances memory retention and understanding. It also contributes to holistic well-being, as supported by research showing the benefits of joyful and engaging education in fostering long-term academic success.

ii.   Critical Thinking and Metacognitive Self-Analysis: This element emphasizes the ability to independently evaluate various situations. According to educational research, critical thinking skills are crucial for problem-solving and decision-making in complex environments. Metacognitive Self-analysis, in turn, enhances self-awareness and personal growth, as indicated by psychological studies.

iii.   Perception Manipulation and Relationships: This section emphasizes the importance of understanding cultural determinism, where long-standing institutional influences shape our perceptions and realities. Achieving a metacognitive state, where individuals are conscious of both their own and others' thought processes, is key. Neuroscientific studies show that grasping various viewpoints is essential for social cognition and healthy relationships.

iv.   Empathy Training and Public Service: Involving game theory approaches, this part of the curriculum seeks to cultivate and nurture empathy. Empathy training is linked to better emotional intelligence and social harmony, as evidenced by psychological studies. Involvement in public service further reinforces community engagement with diverse perspectives bolsters critical thinking and problem-solving abilities by prompting individuals to question their biases.

v.   Creative Thinking and Teamwork: This segment encourages collaborative and innovative problem-solving. Research in educational psychology demonstrates that teamwork and creativity not only foster cognitive skills but also improve social interaction and conflict resolution abilities, prompting individuals to question their implicit biases.

vi.   Public Speaking, Teaching, and Diplomatic Debate: These components focus on refining communication skills. The ability to articulate ideas clearly and engage in constructive debate, or 'good arguments', is essential in diverse professional contexts, as shown by communication studies. Teaching skills further enhance understanding and clarity of thought.

vii.   Nutrition, Regenerative Farming, and Cooking: Emphasizing the adage 'you are what you eat,' this part of the curriculum is grounded in the scientific understanding of nutrition's impact on epigenetics, health, and cognitive function. Agricultural education connects students to food sources, promoting sustainable practices, as highlighted by environmental studies.

viii. Sports, ROTC, Police/Fire/EMT Cadets, Performing and Visual Arts: **This diverse range of recreational skills supports physical fitness, discipline, teamwork, and artistic expression. Studies in sports psychology and arts education show that such activities enhance physical health, mental resilience, and creative skills.**

Section 4: Operational Logistics

i. Boarding schools operate three nights a week with detailed scheduling.
    a. *Classes Start at 9:30 am for Monday Brunch.*
    b. *Classes End at 8:30 pm Thursday, after student cleanup.*
    c. *Sports and Clubs are to meet and play Tuesday through Thursday from 3pm to 5pm; and all day on Fridays and Saturdays (Sun-Mon Off).*

ii. All Schools are required to serve fresh organic meals and maintain small class sizes (25 students maximum) with a robust staff structure:
    a. *Each School can teach a Maximum of 150 students per grade level.*
    b. *Each grade level requires 6 classrooms of 24 students each.*
    c. *Each grade level requires 6 teachers.*
    d. *Each grade level requires 12 teaching-assistants / tutor-counselors.*
    e. *Each School requires 8 department chairs / hybrid class developers.*
    f. *Each School requires 1 Managing Director with 2 Associate Directors.*

Section 5: Progressive Doctrinal Education for Developing Students

This section delves into the critical importance of evolving doctrinal teaching strategies across different educational stages (Elementary, Junior High, and High School) to foster metacognition and authentic self-leadership in students. This approach aligns with scientific understanding of developmental psychology and educational theory, emphasizing the need for diverse educational experiences to cultivate virtuous, autonomous individuals who embody 'the way of impartial nobility'.

i.   *Grades 3 to 6 (Elementary Boarding School):* Focuses on self-awareness education, incorporating practical tasks like cleaning and autonomy training, aligned with values orientation. This stage introduces cadet training to instill discipline and resilience, including activities like pellet gun and expedition experiences. A significant feature is the personal crafting of knives and machetes, symbolizing autonomy and skill mastery, culminating in a ceremonial knife gifting at the end of the 3rd grade.

ii. *Grades 7 to 9 (Junior High Boarding School):* This phase intensifies with a comprehensive physical training regime, hike-in camping, international travel, and exposure to foreign arts, music, and literature. Physical defense skills, including jiu-jitsu and .22 caliber gun training, are integral, emphasizing self-defense and responsibility.

iii. *Grades 10-12 (Technical Boarding High School):* This stage is designed for real-world experiences and advanced training, such as intensive 'warrior of the rainbow' training, sniper training with long rifles, A.I. guided computer programming, diesel engine mechanics, and home-building skills. This phase is critical for developing technical proficiency, strategic thinking, and a sense of responsibility towards community and environment.

-   Scientifically, these progressive educational stages are crucial for cognitive and personal development. Research in developmental psychology suggests that such diverse and hands-on experiences enhance critical thinking, problem-solving, and emotional intelligence. The gradual increase in complexity and responsibility across the stages prepares students for adult life, embedding a sense of duty, ethical conduct, and leadership.

-   This model aligns with the principles of experiential learning and cognitive development theories, advocating for practical, real-world experiences to supplement traditional 'high-tech' classroom learning, thereby fostering well-rounded, capable, and conscientious individuals.

Section 6: Grading and Evaluation

Assignments will be graded anonymously to minimize biases, ensuring fair assessment of students' work. And grading is about being able to move onto the next level of self-paced education, and has nothing to do with advancing to the next grade level, which every student does regardless of where they are in their self-educational tract; *regarding each subject matter.*

Section 7: Culturally Integrated and Balanced Education System

This section addresses the integration of cultural protocols in a self-paced educational system, aimed at achieving a metacognitive state of mind and a balanced approach to life planning. The emphasis on humanistic values, a higher purpose, challenging missions, honorable intentions, self-sacrificing goals, noble roles, and impartial norms; is critical in evolving the effects of cultural determinism, and in guiding students towards a holistic interdependency.

    i.   *Emphasis on balancing masculine and feminine energies, empathy training, and authentic leadership skills:* This approach is grounded in psychological research suggesting that emotional intelligence, empathy, and gender balance are key to effective leadership and interpersonal relationships.

    ii.   *Hands-on, project-oriented approach across disciplines:* Studies in educational psychology highlight the benefits of experiential learning in enhancing cognitive skills and promoting deeper understanding of complex concepts.

    iii.   Integration of a culture code focusing on metacognition, effective kindness, virtuous autonomy, interdependent diversity, and holistic humanism:

        a. Effective-kindness: Research in social psychology underscores the importance of kindness in fostering social cohesion and individual well-being.

        b. Virtuous-autonomy: Psychological studies link autonomy with higher motivation, better performance, and personal growth.

        c. Interdependent-diversity: Sociological research supports the value of diversity in promoting creativity, problem-solving, and resilience.

        d. Honorably-authentic and metacognitive intention: Cognitive science reveals that authenticity and metacognition are crucial for personal development and effective decision-making.

e. Self-sacrificing goal: Altruism has been shown to enhance social bonds and personal satisfaction.

f. Responsible roles: Educational research emphasizes the importance of responsibility in developing maturity and social awareness.

g. Holistic-humanism norms: Humanistic psychology promotes a holistic view of individuals, emphasizing personal growth and self-actualization.

h. Community success and belonging: Social psychology research illustrates the power of belonging and its impact on individual and communal success.

Incorporating these elements into an educational framework aligns with scientific findings from psychology, sociology, and cognitive science. This integrative approach not only fosters academic excellence but also equips students with the skills needed to navigate and contribute positively to an increasingly complex and interconnected world.

Section 8: Integrated Core Educational Competencies

This section advocates for an educational approach that blends eight core competencies—history, philosophy, psychology, sociology, science, economics, mathematics, and language—into a self-paced, technologically aided system. This integration aims to foster metacognition in students, enabling them to understand and regulate their thought processes effectively.

i. History: Taught from the perspective of those who lived it, this approach helps students understand the subjective nature of historical narratives, encouraging critical thinking and empathy.

ii. Philosophy: Explored through the four dyadic levels of consciousness, philosophy education enhances students' ability to contemplate and question their existential and ethical surroundings.

iii. Psychology: Focusing on the influences of environment, epigenetics, and genetics, this aspect helps students understand human behavior and mental processes, aiding in self-awareness and understanding of others.

iv.   Sociology: Examining different institutional indoctrinations, sociology education promotes awareness of societal structures and their impact on individuals and groups.

v.   Science: Approached from a paradigm of holistic-humanism, science education fosters an understanding of the interconnectedness of life and the importance of ethical considerations in scientific endeavors.

vi.   Economics: Centered around entrepreneurial and legal aspects, this component equips students with practical understanding of economic systems and their role in society.

vii.   Mathematics: Emphasizing practical application linked to the eight core competencies, this approach makes mathematics relevant and engaging, enhancing problem-solving skills.

viii.   Language: Focused on effective communication, language education is crucial for expressing ideas clearly and understanding others, a key component of social interaction and collaboration.

- Incorporating these competencies within a 'sticky' teaching methodology—techniques that make learning memorable and engaging—is vital for a comprehensive education reform.

- This method is supported by research indicating that such integrative and interactive learning environments enhance cognitive skills, critical thinking, and empathy, key components of a well-rounded educational experience.

Section 9: Empowering Students through Peer-Led Educational Roles

This section underscores the critical importance of peer-led tutoring, coaching, and mentoring within the educational framework, fostering metacognitive development and teaching efficacy among students. Scientifically, this approach aligns with research in cognitive development, social psychology, and educational theory, suggesting that teaching others is a powerful method for consolidating one's own learning while contributing to the holistic development of the entire 'learning organization'.

By engaging students in roles of tutors, coaches, and mentors; the educational system transcends traditional learning paradigms, fostering a culture of mutual growth, empathy, and collaborative success. This aligns with the scientific consensus on the benefits of personalized support, expressive skills development, and identity formation in students.

i.   Teacher-Assisted Counseling/Tutoring: Mandating teacher-assisted counseling and tutoring sessions for all students, aligns with educational psychology findings that highlight the benefits of personalized support in enhancing learning outcomes and emotional intelligence.

ii. Public Speaking: The requirement for mandatory public speaking is supported by communication studies, which emphasize the development of expressive skills and confidence as foundational for effective leadership and community engagement.

iii. Life Portfolio Creation: The development of a 'Life Portfolio' by each student not only encourages self-reflection and personal growth, but also fosters a sense of accomplishment and identity formation, as supported by developmental psychology research.

iv. Peer Tutoring: Having each boarding school student tutor a student one grade below in core competencies, is grounded in the educational theory of peer-assisted learning. This approach is shown to reinforce the tutor's own knowledge and skills, while fostering a sense of responsibility and empathy.

   a. Tutoring is about helping the younger students successfully advance with the eight core-competencies.

v.   Peer Coaching: The coaching of students two grades below in critical life skills and team playing, reflects the principles of experiential learning and social development theory. It emphasizes the importance of practical, real-world skills development in a supportive peer environment.

   a. Coaching is about cultivating team playing, critical thinking, life skills, teaching, and public speaking skills in the younger student.

vi. Peer Mentoring: Mentoring students three grades below in areas such as life planning and collaboration, is rooted in the concepts of social learning theory and mentorship studies. This method promotes leadership, civic responsibility, and the development of strong interpersonal relationships.

    a. Mentoring is about roles identification and co-creation, life planning, collaboration, good debate, and travel in the younger student.

- This peer-led educational structure, not only aids in achieving a metacognitive state of mind, but also equips students with the skills to effectively impart knowledge and support others, a crucial aspect of community building and cultural evolution.

- Scientifically, this approach aligns with research in cognitive development, social psychology, and educational theory; suggesting that teaching others is a powerful method for consolidating one's own learning, while contributing to the holistic development of the community.

- By engaging students in roles of tutors, coaches, and mentors; the educational system transcends traditional learning paradigms, fostering a culture of mutual growth, empathy, and collaborative success.

Section 10: Implementation, Oversight, and Child Safety Enhancement

In this section, we outline the crucial steps for implementing and overseeing the transformative educational system. Additionally, a cutting-edge child safety program will utilize advanced GPS trackers and video monitoring systems. The key provisions are as follows:

i. Department of Education Oversight: The Department of Education will play a pivotal role in the nationwide rollout of this innovative educational system. Their responsibilities include monitoring its effectiveness, ensuring compliance with educational standards, and coordinating with relevant authorities to address any emerging issues.

ii. Regular Evaluations and Updates: To maintain the system's relevance and effectiveness, regular evaluations and updates will be conducted. These assessments will follow best practices in educational policy implementation and assessment, ensuring continuous improvement in the quality of education provided to students.

iii. Child Safety Enhancement - GPS Trackers and Video Monitoring: **As part of our commitment to the safety and well-being of students, we propose the integration of GPS trackers and video monitoring systems within school premises. This enhancement allows parents and guardians to log onto the video monitoring system at any time, providing them with real-time information about their child's whereabouts within the school.**

iv. Geofence Tracking: **The GPS trackers will employ geofence tracking technology, which defines specific boundaries within the school. This technology ensures that students remain within designated areas, enhancing their safety and security.**

v. Partially Automated Merit-Demerit System: **To maintain a safe and orderly school environment, a partially automated Merit-Demerit System will be implemented. This system is designed to focus on consequentialism rather than punishment, encouraging positive behavior and responsible actions among students. Students will earn merits for exemplary conduct and participation in school activities, while demerits may be extracted for behaviors that deviate from established guidelines.**

- Research in educational psychology and child development has shown that a secure and supportive school environment is essential for student well-being and academic success. Implementing GPS trackers and video monitoring systems will provide parents with peace of mind while promoting accountability among students.

- Additionally, the Merit-Demerit System aligns with studies in behavioral psychology, emphasizing the effectiveness of consequences in shaping behavior and fostering a positive school atmosphere.

- This combined approach not only ensures the continuous improvement of the educational system, but also reinforces the safety and well-being of students, promoting a conducive learning environment for all.

Section 11: National Interest and Justification

This amendment aims to foster well-rounded, holistic development in students, preparing them academically, emotionally, physically, and socially for the challenges of

196

the future. It seeks to redefine the structure and core of public education to create a generation of well-informed, empathetic, and responsible citizens; a goal supported by extensive research in education, psychology, and sociology.

This proposed amendment is a bold step towards reimagining public education in the United States. It integrates various facets of learning and personal development, ensuring that students are not only academically proficient, but also equipped with critical life skills. The amendment seeks to build a robust, inclusive, and empathetic educational framework that aligns with the evolving needs of society and the individual.

BRIDGING WEALTH DISPARITIES THROUGH SOCIAL CAPITALISM

"No society can surely be flourishing and happy,
of which the far greater part of the members are poor and miserable."

- Adam Smith

Our contemporary world is grappling with the harsh realities of coercive behavioral economics and staggering wealth inequality; a situation exacerbated by corporate greed synergizing with our society's prevailing narcissism. *Rigorous scientific studies in the field of behavioral economics underscore the critical role that status and vanity play as core motivators for our detrimental behaviors.*

This innate 'will to receive,' driven by narcissistic desires, fuels an insatiable appetite for power and control. Paradoxically, the more distress we endure, the stronger the yearning for power becomes, as it represents an illusory means to regain control over our lives. However, it is vital to acknowledge that control is a mirage, as the complexities of our environment, and the diversity of people, defy complete mastery.

Yet, an elitist class often seeks to homogenize society, to make us more amenable to control. These elites employ coercive behavioral economics, often exploiting religious and societal indoctrination, to incite chaos, thereby eliciting public clamor for order; *and, inevitably, a new world order dominated by the same elites who ramped-up the chaos in the first place.*

Section 1: The Role of Social Capitalism

   i. Minimizing Wealth Disparity: Social Capitalism offers a path to mitigate wealth disparities by recognizing the existence of a two-tier economy and implementing systemic reforms to level the playing field. At its core, Social Capitalism represents 'values-based capitalism,' where the focus shifts toward uplifting individuals living within Tier-Two (the disadvantaged). Government oversight of the economic system, facilitated by blockchain and smart contract technologies, ensures a more fair and equitable playing field.

       a. *Humanistic Aspiration:* Fundamentally, our innate human desire revolves around the opportunity to harness our unique talents for the collaborative creation of something greater than ourselves. It is an aspiration best realized when we are free from arbitrary constraints imposed by coercive institutions.

b. *Cultivate and Nurture:* The fundamental flaw in our current economic system lies in its failure to incorporate the feminine aspects of nurturing and cultivation. Without this balance, our society inadvertently perpetuates a 'sink or swim philosophy' rooted in the malevolent notion that 'might makes right'.

c. *Transcending Suffering:* To create an effective and transparent hierarchical system, we must establish a self-sustaining framework for Tier-Two citizens, aiding them in transcending their hardships while leading lives characterized by an ever-evolving liberty. The entirety of strategies outlined in this proposed constitutional rewrite, serve as the blueprint for realizing this transformative vision.

d. *Health Insurance Funding:* Tax rates are increased to take care of last-years shortfalls, and rates are decreased when budgeted needs have already been met.

- Recent research in behavioral economics highlights the negative impact of wealth inequality on societal health. Studies indicate that societies with narrower wealth gaps generally experience stronger social cohesion, reduced crime rates, and greater happiness among citizens. Additionally, psychological research points to the role of significant wealth disparities in aggravating narcissistic tendencies, hindering the achievement of societal harmony.

- Incorporating blockchain and smart contract technologies into economic governance has been endorsed by leading economists and technologists as a means to enhance transparency, reduce corruption, and ensure equitable resource distribution. These technological innovations provide data-driven insights and safeguards against unfair economic practices, aligning with the principles of Social Capitalism.

The adoption of Social Capitalism, supported by empirical data and visionary strategies, represents a pivotal step toward addressing wealth inequality, nurturing human potential, and fostering a more harmonious and prosperous society for all.

Section 2: Ensuring Health & Financial Security

Currently, a staggering 25% of annual healthcare expenditures are directed toward end-of-life care, with one-third of this cost incurred in the last month of life. The prevailing health insurance system has come under scrutiny as an apparent racket, further exacerbated by the profit-driven practices of both the pharmaceutical and insurance industries. It's crucial to highlight that hospital errors rank as the third leading cause of death, following heart disease and cancer, which are often linked to chronic inflammation caused by the overconsumption of processed foods, meat, bread, dairy, and sugar.

i. Nationwide Health & Home Insurance: Scientific data and expert analysis underscore the urgent need for a comprehensive Social Capitalistic 'Medicare for All' health insurance plan, as well as innovative home and car insurance plans tailored to the needs of Tier-Two citizens.

ii. Social Capitalistic Healthcare: Social Capitalistic Hospitals and Care Centers are envisioned as a transformative solution to these challenges, incorporating the following principles:

   a. *Administrator Compensation:* Administrators within these institutions will not earn more than the median income of practicing physicians in their facility. This measure ensures that financial incentives align with the well-being of patients and the equitable distribution of resources.

   b. *Holistic Health:* A focus of care centers will prioritize holistic well-being, including the promotion of daily exercise and organic food consumption rich in fruits, nuts, vegetables, legumes, and cannabinoids. While advising the elimination of processed foods, while limiting meat, bread, dairy, and sugar intake, for the purpose of bringing our bodies into homeostasis so we can self-heal.

   c. *Osteopathic Manual Manipulation:* Osteopathic Manual Manipulation will become the standard of care for total health, addressing the 'log jams' in our musculoskeletal framework, including joints, muscles, and the spine; for the purpose of bringing our bodies into homeostasis so we can self-heal. This approach emphasizes prevention and the preservation of well-being.

d. *Professional Obligation:* Medical professionals engaged in private medical facilities catering to the wealthy with private insurance plans, will be required to allocate at least 35% of their total weekly hours to serve at local Social Capitalistic Hospitals and Care Centers for standard pay. This commitment ensures that expertise is shared equitably across the healthcare system.

iii. Pharmaceutical and Vaccine Regulation: Medical errors in healthcare facilities, particularly in hospitals, have risen alarmingly, now ranking as the third leading cause of death in the United States. Annually, these errors lead to approximately 251,000 deaths, a figure higher than fatalities from respiratory diseases, strokes, and Alzheimer's. Notably, these errors are often linked to incorrect prescriptions and dosages of pharmaceuticals, accounting for over one million serious injuries or deaths in the U.S. each year. The proposed reforms seek to address these issues by integrating social capitalistic solutions to mitigate profit-driven motives in medical experimentation, especially on older populations:

a. *Rigorous Safety Trials:* Mandatory double-blind safety trials for all pharmaceuticals and vaccines to ensure their safety and efficacy. Plus mandatory transparency in ingredient disclosure, enabling citizens to understand the composition and purpose of medical treatments.

b. *Child Immunization Policies:* Mandating only the safest and most effective pharmaceuticals and vaccines for children with healthy immune systems, based on solid scientific evidence to prioritize child health.

c. *Upholding Individual Choice:* The reforms emphasize the right of citizens to opt-out of experimental vaccines without facing discrimination. Moreover, it prohibits members of the governmental health ministry from financial gains linked to medical products, ensuring decisions are motivated by health and safety rather than monetary gains.

d. *Universal Healthcare and Dietary Focus:* Social Capitalistic healthcare, that emphasizes the role of nutrition in disease prevention, improves health outcomes, reduces mortality, and lowers healthcare costs.

e. *Strengthening Pharmaceutical Industry Oversight:* This amendment focuses on addressing the issue of corporate influence on regulatory agencies and the safety of drugs. It underscores the necessity for rigorous regulatory oversight within the pharmaceutical industry. By advocating for transparent clinical trials and clear ingredient disclosure, these measures align with the foundations of evidence-based medical practices.

These reforms are designed to overhaul critical aspects of healthcare and insurance, informed by scientific evidence and expert analysis. By implementing these changes, the aim is to improve the well-being and financial security of Tier-Two citizens. The focus is on creating a more equitable and health-oriented society, reducing the influence of profit motives in social-capitalistic medical practices, and ensuring the safety and efficacy of medical treatments for all.

Section 3: Fostering Health Through Agriculture Reform

i. Regenerative Agriculture and Hemp Biochar: Expert analysis and scientific data emphasize the pivotal role of regenerative agriculture and hemp biochar in promoting both the health of Tier-Two citizens and the nation as a whole:

    a. *No-Till Regenerative Agriculture:* The Department of Agriculture will oversee the implementation of a no-till regenerative agricultural system, incorporating hemp biochar to create microorganism habitats. This approach has profound implications for soil health and ecosystem sustainability. Scientific research consistently shows that no-till farming improves soil structure, enhances carbon sequestration, and reduces the need for synthetic fertilizers and pesticides. Moreover, it contributes to increased crop yields and the restoration of biodiversity.

    b. *Hemp Cover-Crop Program:* A vital component of this system is the hemp cover-crop program, *offering subsidies for the cultivation of hemp botanical flower, hemp seed, and hemp fiber.* Hemp serves both industrial and medical purposes, providing versatile and sustainable resources.

    c. *Hemp Animal Feed Program:* The inclusion of hemp in animal feed, *supplemented with bioavailable hemp botanical flower,* ensures animal health without the use of antibiotics. Research supports the efficacy of hemp-based animal feed in reducing the release of stress hormones while improving overall livestock well-being.

d. *Prohibition of GMOs and Non-Organic Pesticides/Herbicides:* Recognizing the impact of GMOs and non-organic pesticides/herbicides on human health through the disruption of the gut microbiome, this reform strictly forbids their use. Scientific studies highlight the potential risks associated with GMO consumption and pesticide/herbicide exposure, emphasizing the need for precautionary measures to safeguard public health.

e. *Subsidy Reformation and Organic Farming:* Subsidy reformation abolishes support for toxic ingredients and unsafe products while removing seed patents and streamlining the patent process. Organic, regenerative, biodynamic permaculture farming becomes a legal requirement, fostering sustainable and environmentally friendly agriculture. The subsidization of greenhouse farming aligns with research findings on its potential for year-round crop production and reduced resource consumption.

f. *Human Safety Trials for Chemicals:* To ensure public safety, all unique and novel chemicals undergo thorough human safety trials conducted by accredited research institutions for extended periods before use. This rigorous testing process prioritizes health and well-being, preventing potential harm from unsafe chemicals.

ii. Open Fuel Standard and Hemp-Based Fuels: Implementing an open fuel standard is vital for promoting fuel diversity and reducing dependence on fossil fuels. Expert analysis highlights the significance of this standard, especially when coupled with hemp subsidies:

a. *Hemp Subsidies for Sustainable Fuels:* Hemp serves as a versatile and sustainable resource that can be converted into plastic, biodiesel, methanol, and ethanol. Scientifically, these fuels align with modern vehicle capabilities, requiring only simple software updates for compatibility. Hemp subsidies support the growth of a sustainable fuel industry, reducing carbon emissions and environmental impact.

iii. Industrial Hemp and Sustainable Plastic Alternatives: Industrial hemp has emerged as a promising raw material for producing biodegradable and sustainable plastic alternatives. Unlike conventional plastics derived from fossil fuels, hemp-based plastics are biodegradable, thereby significantly reducing pollution and the accumulation of non-degradable waste in landfills and oceans.

By integrating these reforms for a holistic approach to agriculture and energy, the aim is to pave the way for a more sustainable future. Embracing hemp as a resource for both fuel and plastic alternatives represents a significant step toward environmental conservation and the reduction of harmful emissions. This approach aligns with the goals of reducing the environmental impact of human activities and moving towards a more sustainable and ecologically responsible society that is economically robust for all citizens, with a particular focus on the well-being of Tier-Two individuals.

Section 4: Dismantling Concentrations of Wealth for Economic Health

This strategy promotes the creation of a small to medium-sized business ecosystem with a focus on social entrepreneurship, a DIY-Maker culture, apprenticeship programs that also act as trade unions, along with infrastructure management for utilities, telecommunications, mass production, and security is entrusted to regional governance, ensuring efficient and secure operations.

i. Small Business Ecosystem for Economic Health: **Expert analysis highlights the critical importance of fostering social entrepreneurship within a small-business ecosystem to enhance the health and vibrancy of the nation's economy.**

    a. *Anti-Trust Enforcement*: Understanding the historical tendency of powerful entities to form monopolies and cartels, this reform focuses on decentralizing and dismantling corporate conglomerates. A regionalized 'Total Quality Management (TQM)' systems-engineering-approach, coupled with a computerized 'Just-in-Time (JIT)' inventory system for manufacturing supplies, is proposed.

    b. *Big Sports Reform*: This reform emphasizes equitable sharing of advertising revenues across high school, college, and professional sports, with public-private oversight. Regionalized bracketing systems for all playoff competitions. And player contract regulations are enforced by 'regional sports trade unions' to enhance fairness and transparency. Tax-breaks and incentives for professional sports venues are prohibited, and all online sports gambling is conducted on the state-hosted social network, utilizing the blockchain currency and smart contract technologies of Ethereum.

ii. Corporate Structure Reform: This restructuring initiative aims to enhance corporate governance, improve operational effectiveness, and ensure more agile and responsive management structures within large organizations. By breaking down large corporations into smaller units, the reform seeks to foster a more sustainable and efficient business ecosystem. The restructuring process is delineated as follows:

   a. *Size Classification:* Corporations will be classified into two categories based on employee count: small businesses with fewer than 153 employees, and medium-sized businesses with fewer than 1,813 employees.

   - Large-scale manufacturing companies will fall under the rigorous supervision of a dedicated Resource Facilitation Agency. The focus will be on equitable distribution and sustainable use of resources, prioritizing societal welfare and environmental sustainability.

   b. *Transformation into Series LLC Management Companies:* Large corporations will be divided into multiple Series LLC Management Companies. Each of these companies will be capped at a maximum of 153 employees to ensure more effective management and operational efficiency.

   c. *Establishment of a 'Mother Management Company LLC':* A 'Mother Management Company LLC' will be created to oversee up to 12 separate Management Company LLCs. This structure ensures centralized oversight while maintaining operational independence for each LLC.

   d. *Leadership and Management Structure:* Each Management Company LLC will be directed by a team of three operations managers, including one Chief and two Vice-Chiefs. These managers will also serve as managing members of the 'Mother Management Company LLC'.

   - This arrangement results in a maximum of 36 senior operations managers who are collectively responsible for the oversight of all 12 management companies within the framework.

iii. Disempowering Multi-Nationals and Resource Management: **This section addresses the need to disempower multi-national corporations and prioritize resource management for a healthier economic landscape:**

   a. *Removing Corporations from Legislative Process*: Corporate influence in the legislative process is curtailed through the elimination of corporate lobbying, the abolition of money as free speech, and the denial of corporate personhood. This measure restores the integrity of the legislative process.

   b. *Government Oversight of Mass Production*: Government oversight of mechanized mass production as part of the 'National Resource Management System' promotes transparency, accountability, and fair resource allocation.

   c. *Subsidies for DIY & Maker Movements:* Subsidizing the DIY & Maker Movements fosters innovation, creativity, and economic diversification, reducing dependence on large corporations.

   d. *Promoting a Resource-Based Economy:* By eliminating the oligarchy's ability to manipulate societal values, this reform shifts the prevailing worldview away from Darwinian Capitalism and patriarchal paradigms, promoting a more equitable and resource-based economy.

Incorporating these reforms is critical for creating an economic landscape characterized by competition, fairness, and empowerment of small and medium-sized businesses. It also seeks to disempower conglomerates and align societal values with the principles of fairness, sustainability, and economic diversity, ultimately benefiting all citizens and ensuring a brighter future for the nation.

Section 5: Banking Reformation for a Social Capitalistic Economy

i. Disempowering Investment and Commercial Banks: Expert analysis underscores the critical need to disempower investment banks, commercial banks, and the central banking cartel for the success of a social capitalistic economic reformation:

a. *Abolishing Investment Banking:* Investment banks will be dismantled and regulated out of existence using new anti-trust laws. This measure eradicates banking speculation, promoting financial stability, and protecting the economy from excessive risk-taking.

b. *SEC-Certified Brokers:* Investment firms will be required to employ SEC-certified brokers with fiduciary responsibilities to their clients and their nation. These brokers will prioritize serving humanity while making reasonable profits, ensuring ethical and responsible financial practices.

c. *Eliminating Speculative Practices:* A range of speculative practices including compound interest, usury, debt trading, market-driven money valuation, reserve currency dominance, inflation, unfair resource exploitation, concentration of power, debt slavery, trading regulations, trading centers, and processing fees will be strictly regulated and managed through the Ethereum-based government social network. This approach ensures transparency, fairness, and accountability in financial transactions.

ii. Embracing Public Banking and Central Banking Reformation: **To further support the success of the social capitalistic economic reformation, this section advocates the institution of public banking, and the reformation of central banking:**

a. *Return to Honest Mortgages:* Public banking will provide honest commercial and home mortgages that serve community development principles. Commercial Banks will be required to convert to credit unions, forming a network of Social Capitalistic banks supported by the state, modeled after institutions like the Bank of North Dakota.

b. *Disempowering the Central Banking Cartel:* The central banking cartel, characterized by its concentration of financial power, will be disempowered. A network of state-backed public banks, utilizing a blockchain digital dollar, will replace the negative influence of central banks, fostering economic autonomy and decentralization.

c. *Promoting Financial Equity:* This reform ensures that banks prioritize the needs of communities and individuals, facilitating responsible lending, investment in local development, and equitable access to financial resources.

Recent scientific research and economic analysis support these measures, highlighting their potential to mitigate financial instability, prevent exploitative banking practices, and promote the values of social capitalism. By implementing these reforms, the nation can embark on a path toward a fairer, more transparent, and socially responsible economic system that benefits all its citizens.

Section 6: Social Justice Reform

i. Addressing Structural Violence and Core Issues: The success of a social capitalistic economic reformation hinges on comprehensive social justice reform, acknowledging the inherent structural violence of poverty, and addressing core issues; such as limited resources, fossil fuel scarcity, fresh water scarcity, and environmental pollution. Expert analysis underscores the importance of the following measures:

   a. *National Resource Management System:* Implementing a National Resource Management System for Sustainability is crucial to efficiently allocate resources, promote sustainability, and reduce environmental stressors. This system ensures responsible resource management, safeguarding the well-being of citizens and the environment.

   b. *Supreme Court Judiciary Code of Ethics:* Establishing a Supreme Court Judiciary Code of Ethics with term limits enhances the integrity and accountability of the judicial branch, ensuring fair and impartial justice.

   c. *Abolishing Minimum Mandatory Laws:* The abolishment of 'Minimum Mandatory Laws' promotes a justice system that focuses on individual circumstances and the principle of proportionality and merciful justice, rather than rigid sentencing requirements.

   d. *Eliminating Statute of Limitations for Certain Crimes:* Removing the 'Statute of Limitations' for criminals over the age of 25, ensures that serious offenses are not shielded by arbitrary time constraints, contributing to a fair and just legal system.

e. *Ending Influence of Super PACs and ALEC:* Publicly funding elections while ending money as speech and abolishing 'Super PACs and ALEC', prevents the undue influence of corporate entities in legislative processes, preserving the integrity of democratic decision-making.

ii. Empowering Workers and Fostering Economic Equity: Social justice reform involves empowering workers and promoting economic equity, aligning with the principles of social capitalism:

   a. *Increasing Union Rights and Collective Bargaining:* Mandating trade union rights, and collective bargaining abilities, allows workers to negotiate fair wages and working conditions, contributing to a more equitable distribution of wealth.

   b. *Implementing Resource-Based Economy:* A resource-based economy with a blockchain-based smart contract currency, akin to Bitcoin, supports transparency, efficiency, and sustainable economic practices.

   c. *Reducing Work Week and Mandatory Public Service:* A reduced work week (four six-hour days) with mandatory public service and continuing education hours, ensures employment opportunities for all citizens, while promoting continuous learning and community engagement.

iii. Transforming the Justice System: The implementation of a private-public preliminary justice system, referred to as 'Trade Union Bars,' is integral to transforming the justice system:

   a. *Consequentialism Over Punishment:* 'Bars' empower trade unions and apprenticeship programs to facilitate and manage a 'jury of peers,' emphasizing consequentialism over ineffective monolithic punishment for minor crimes. This approach promotes rehabilitation and societal reintegration.

iv. Lifelong Public Education: Public education becomes a lifelong endeavor, facilitated through the government social network and localized continuing education programs, ensuring continuous learning and personal development as all citizens embrace the role of student-teacher.

v.   Ensuring Strategic Resource Access: The timesharing of basic goods for Tier-Two citizens creates strategic access to essential resources, promoting decentralized use and returning goods to regionalized community centers, fostering responsible care of shared resources, resource efficiency, and equitable distribution.

vi.   Legalizing and Regulating Prostitution: Legalizing and regulating prostitution through government oversight; empowers sex workers, reduces the influence of middle-men (pimps and organized crime), and combats human trafficking, while promoting societal well-being.

vii.   Decriminalization, Sales, Taxation, and Rehabilitation: Recognizing addiction as a neurological disorder, the proposed constitutional reforms are grounded in scientific evidence that supports the therapeutic potential of organic plant-based diets, functional foods, MDMA, kratom, cannabis, psilocybin-mushrooms, and moderate daily exercise. These methods, along with personalized cannabis cultivation, have been shown to offer significant health benefits, including relief from depression, reduction of chronic inflammation, promotion of homeostasis, and enhancement of neuroplasticity and brain cell growth.

   a. *Drug Decriminalization:* The full legalization of cannabis and psilocybin-mushrooms, coupled with the decriminalization of hard drugs like opiates and cocaine, is aimed at dismantling the profit motive for organized crime and minimizing societal harm. Scientific studies indicate that such decriminalization can lead to decreased crime rates, reduced burden on the criminal justice system, and provide improvements in public health outcomes.

   b. *State-Managed Drug Processing & Sales*: Implementing federal oversight for the production and sale of opiates and cocaine. The revenue generated from these sales, in the form of taxes, will be allocated to fund rehabilitation centers. These centers will specialize in a comprehensive approach to treating addiction disorders, combining various therapeutic methods. Research supports the efficacy of government-regulated drug markets in controlling substance quality, reducing public health risks, and generating funds for public welfare initiatives.

   c. *Hemp Flower Rehabilitation for Tobacco Users:* In response to the severe impact of tobacco smoking, which includes high mortality rates, widespread diseases, and significant economic costs, the introduction of smokeable hemp flower (enriched with delta 8 THC) is proposed as a tobacco replacement therapy. This initiative addresses the tobacco epidemic responsible for over 480,000 deaths annually in the U.S. and aims to alleviate its extensive economic burden. Studies have shown that alternative therapies like hemp flower can be effective in smoking cessation efforts, contributing to reduced tobacco-related health issues.

- *These reforms, backed by scientific data and expert analysis, are designed to comprehensively address the complex issues surrounding drug use and addiction. The goal is to shift drug policy towards a more humane, health-focused approach, thereby enhancing public health and promoting social justice. By implementing these changes, the reforms aim to create a more equitable and health-conscious society.*

viii.   Strategic Redirection of Law Enforcement Agencies: The proposed constitutional amendments advocate for a significant reorientation of federal law enforcement agencies like the Drug Enforcement Administration (DEA) and the Bureau of Alcohol, Tobacco, Firearms and Explosives (ATF). This shift is aimed at refocusing their resources and expertise from drug, tobacco, and firearm offenses to addressing more critical societal challenges:

   a. *Human Trafficking:* Elevating the fight against human trafficking to a top priority. This crime, a severe violation of human rights involving labor and sex exploitation, represents a global humanitarian crisis. Redirecting law enforcement efforts to tackle human trafficking aligns with international human rights standards and addresses an urgent need to significantly disrupt trafficking networks and aid in victim recovery.

   b. *Immigration Control:* Modifying the approach to immigration control to emphasize human rights and public safety. This approach advocates for a balanced strategy that respects individual dignity and upholds the integrity of national borders, moving away from purely punitive measures. Studies suggest that humane and effective immigration policies can enhance national security while respecting human rights, fostering better international relations and community integration.

   c. *Firearm and Explosives Regulation:* Focusing on the effective regulation of firearms and explosives to ensure public safety. This will involve enforcing existing laws more rigorously, closing legal loopholes, and developing well-regulated militias that align with modern societal demands and technological advancements. Research supports the need for comprehensive firearm regulation to reduce gun violence and enhance public safety.

d. *Tackling White Collar Crime:* With advancements in blockchain and smart contract technologies, coupled with digital oversight by government licensing committees and continuous education requirements, white-collar crime enforcement will evolve. Rather than relying on selective prosecution by district attorneys, these crimes will now fall under direct police enforcement. Technological advancements in monitoring and enforcement can significantly improve the detection and prevention of white-collar crimes, as indicated by expert analysis in the field of digital law enforcement.

- *This reform aims to establish a more balanced, humane, and effective law enforcement system. It emphasizes the importance of focusing on serious crimes with broad social implications, such as human trafficking, and advocates for respecting individual liberties while minimizing governmental overreach in personal affairs. The realignment of law enforcement priorities seeks to foster a safer, more just society that aligns with libertarian principles, ensuring a more equitable approach to law and order.*

ix. Reforming the Prison Industrial Complex: The amendment proposes a targeted and impactful transformation of the prison industrial complex, underpinned by a blend of holistic and humanistic principles. This comprehensive approach is supported by scientific research and expert analysis, ensuring that the reforms address deep-rooted systemic issues:

a. *Eradicating For-Profit Prison Models:* This critical reform aims to abolish for-profit prisons, removing the profit incentive from incarceration. Research has shown that for-profit prisons can lead to longer sentences and higher incarceration rates, which is counterproductive to public safety and rehabilitation goals.

b. *Decriminalization of Non-Violent Drug Crimes:* In the context of drug legalization and decriminalization, non-violent drug offenses, except those contributing to the delinquency of a minor, will no longer result in imprisonment. This shift is in response to studies that reveal the socio-economic factors often driving drug-related offenses, advocating for more rehabilitative rather than punitive responses.

c. *State-Managed Drug Production and Sales:* The state will assume responsibility for the production and sale of legalized drugs, focusing on quality control, safety, and ethical distribution. Evidence suggests that state-regulated drug markets can effectively reduce the harms associated with drug use and limit illegal drug trade.

d. *Funding Drug Rehabilitation with Drug Sales Profits:* Proceeds from government-regulated drug sales will be channeled into drug rehabilitation programs. This strategy emphasizes a rehabilitative approach over punitive measures, aligning with studies that underscore the effectiveness of treatment over incarceration in reducing drug-related harm.

e. *Re-evaluating the Concept of Punishment:* The amendment calls for a societal reevaluation of the concepts of crime and punishment. It challenges traditional punitive approaches, advocating for approaches rooted in self-forgiveness and communal accountability, as supported by criminological research emphasizing restorative justice.

f. *Addressing Systemic Issues in Crime and Punishment:* Recognizing the role of economics and gangs in perpetuating crime, the amendment promotes social-capitalism and community-centric leadership. This approach aligns with research advocating for holistic solutions to crime, emphasizing social and economic reforms.

g. *Statistical Evidence of Systemic Failure:* America's disproportionately high incarceration rates and the prevalent lack of fair trials are critical issues highlighted by the amendment. International comparisons and criminal justice studies point to the need for substantial reforms to address these systemic failures.

By implementing these reforms, the aim is to transition from a predominantly punitive system to one that prioritizes compassion, rehabilitation, and effectiveness. This reformed system will value human dignity, prioritize rehabilitation, and encourage community responsibility, aspiring to foster a more equitable, enlightened, and just society.

x.   Reforming the American Police State: The amendment proposes a comprehensive reform of law enforcement practices, focusing on bias elimination, enhanced training, and a reorientation towards serious crimes:

a.   *Addressing Bias and Corruption in Law Enforcement:* Acknowledging the impact of biases, group think, racism, and a gang mentality on policing, particularly in the treatment of disenfranchised communities. The amendment calls for measures to counteract these issues, recognizing the corrupting influence of power.

b.   *Requiring an Associate's Degree in Criminal Justice:* Providing foundational knowledge in law enforcement, legal processes, constitutional law, and conflict resolution to produce well-rounded police officers.

c.   *Restraining Use of Lethal Force:* Emphasizing the need for restraint in the use of lethal force. Most law enforcement situations do not require lethal responses, necessitating a shift in tactics and equipment.

d.   *Enhanced Training and Transparency:* Providing extensive training to police officers requiring transparency, particularly with regards to body camera footage; aims to increase accountability and improve policing methods.

e.   *Equipping Law Enforcement with Effective Tools:* Ensuring police officers have access to the most effective equipment to perform their duties safely and responsibly.

f.   *Upholding Founding Principles:* Reaffirming the principles of 'innocent until proven guilty' and 'protection from unreasonable search and seizures.' While also addressing the disparities in the bail system and the overreliance on plea bargains, which disproportionately impact the poor and minorities.

g.   *Abolishing For-Profit Prisons and Decriminalizing Drug Consumption:* Eliminating the for-profit prison model and decriminalizing non-violent drug consumption to focus on rehabilitation rather than punishment.

h. *Refocusing on Major Crimes:* Redirecting law enforcement resources towards major crimes such as physical harm, death, grand larceny, rape, and white-collar crimes involving harm or fraud for financial gain. This shift emphasizes the need for law enforcement to tackle serious offenses that pose significant threats to public safety and economic stability.

By implementing these reforms, the amendment aims to transform the American police force into a more just, effective, and community-oriented institution; representing a commitment to the principles of equity, accountability, and the rule of law, while aligning law enforcement practices with the foundational values of the nation.

Section 7: Taxation and Social Capitalistic Economic Reform

i. The Need for Tax Reform: Social capitalistic tax reform is pivotal for the success of our national economy. The current system faces challenges, including a large government workforce and impending issues with Social Security's financial sustainability; clearly indicating the necessity for comprehensive tax and entitlement program overhauls:

   a. *Government Workforce Reduction:* With over 22 million Americans working for the Federal, State, and Local Governments, the bloated bureaucracy imposes a fiscal burden while corrupting the democratic process. However, the implementation of a state-hosted social network using Ethereum blockchain and smart contract technologies can streamline government operations, while simultaneously reducing the need for a large workforce.

   b. *Social Security Sustainability:* Social Security faces financial strain due to an increasing number of beneficiaries compared to contributors. By 2033, the program's trust fund reserves are projected to be depleted, necessitating a solution to completely transform Social Security.

   c. *Entitlement Spending:* In fiscal year 2022, the federal government spent $1.19 trillion on more than 80 different welfare programs; representing almost 20% of total federal spending and a quarter of tax revenues in 2022, or $9,000 spent per American household. That number is expected to go up to $2.6 trillion in new entitlement spending for 2023; highlighting the urgency of reforming these programs.

d. *Federal Government Spending:* In fiscal year 2023, the federal government is estimated to spend $6.3 trillion, amounting to 24.2% of the nation's gross domestic product (GDP). Of that $6.3 trillion, over $4.8 trillion is estimated to be financed by federal revenues. The remaining $1.5 trillion will be added to the growing national debt of $33.8 trillion (costing the taxpayer even more money in fraudulent interest and fees). The continued deficit spending raises concerns about the sustainability of such expenditures.

ii. A Path to Economic Transformation: This constitutional rewrite aims to address these issues and establish a more sustainable economic framework. Key elements include:

    i. *Public Banking System:* The institution of a public banking system eliminates the interest and fees paid on borrowed funds, benefitting the American people.

    ii. *Flexible Graduated Tax Rate:* A flexible graduated tax rate is introduced to fund economic transformation, cover shortfalls, and reduce tax burdens during prosperous times. Tax credits are exclusively provided to tier-two parents raising children under the age of 26.

    iii. *Tax Parameters:* The tax parameters are outlined as follows:

- Capital Gains Tax: *Set at 20%; adjustable from 15-30%.*

- Luxury Goods Sales Tax: *Set at 20%; adjustable from 15-30%.*

- Normal Purchases Sales Tax: *Set at 5%; adjustable from 3-8%.*

- Property Tax: *Set at 0.5%; adjustable from 0.25% to 1%.*

- Graduated Income Tax: *A tiered income tax structure ranging from 5% to 40%, with adjustable rates within a +/- 5% range.*

  - 0% tax on income from $1 to $55K;
  - 10% tax on total income of $55K to $85K; *adjustable to +/- 5%*
  - 15% tax on total income of $85K to $115K; *adjustable to +/- 5%*
  - 20% tax on total income of $115K to $145K; *adjustable to +/- 5%*
  - 25% tax on total income of $145K to $185K; *adjustable to +/- 5%*
  - 30% tax on total income of $185K to $315K; *adjustable to +/- 5%*

      o   35% tax on total income of $315K to $515K; *adjustable to +/- 5%*

      o   40% tax on total income of $515K+; *adjustable to +/- 5%*

iii.   Allocation of Tax Revenues: **All tax revenues are dedicated to funding governments at various levels, from Villages to Regions.** The funds support humane business practices, green construction, high-quality healthcare, robust public transportation, top-tier education, affordable housing, and an organic food system. Additionally, tax revenues are allocated for public utility infrastructure, air, water, and soil quality protection, and defense and emergency services.

iv.   Interest-Free Loans for Deficit Spending: **Our network of state-backed public banks will provide interest-free government loans for short-term deficit spending, ensuring financial stability and flexibility.**

This comprehensive tax reform aims to create a sustainable and equitable economic system that benefits all citizens and fosters a social capitalistic economy grounded in fairness and prosperity.

Section 8: Reforming Work, Retirement, and Social Security

Incorporating blockchain and smart-contract technologies, this section proposes a transformative approach to work, retirement, and social security within a delegative democratic framework. The aim is to create a more adaptive, equitable, and socially responsible economic system, substantiated by scientific data and expert analysis.

i.   Reformed Societal Work Structure: **Full-time work hours are tailored to the individual's age and health, with mandatory 1.5X overtime pay.**

    a. *Adaptive Full-Time Work Hours:* **Studies in occupational health suggest that adjusting work hours based on age and health can improve workforce productivity and well-being:**

        - Maximum 48-hour workweek for ages 16-44.

        - Maximum 36-hour workweek for ages 45-64.

        - Maximum 18-hour workweek for ages 13-15 and 65+.

        - Maximum 9-hour workweek for ages 11-12 and 75+.

b. *Partial Retirement and Community Service*: Research on aging indicates that continued engagement in community activities can enhance the quality of life for seniors.

  - Setting the partial retirement age at 70, inclusive of required community service and continuing education.

c. *Health-Based Full Retirement Benefits:* Economic studies support personalized retirement benefits based on health, reflecting the varying needs of retirees.

  - Full retirement benefits are determined by individual health status.

d. *Disability and Work Integration:* Integration of disabled individuals into the workforce, as per their capacity, is supported by research showing positive impacts on self-esteem and societal contribution.

  - People receiving disability benefits will be employed in roles and for hours suitable to their abilities.

e. *Mandatory Public Service Work:* This model of civic duty aligns with sociological research emphasizing the benefits of community involvement for societal cohesion and individual fulfillment:

  - An additional 20% of paid work hours (8-hours for a 40-hour week) are mandated as unpaid public service, assigned by the Township Grand Council of 12 Village Chieftains.

  - Decisions by chieftains can be appealed to the village council every four months for a council vote; a 50% yea vote upholds the chieftain's decision.

f. *Mandatory Continuing Education:* All citizens will engage in ongoing education in the humanities, liberal arts, history, and community scientific research. This initiative aligns with sociological and educational research, highlighting the benefits of continuous learning for personal development, societal cohesion, and community engagement; while enhancing cognitive skills, empathy, and a deeper understanding of cooperative societal dynamics.

  - *Citizens as Part-Time Student-Teachers;* The model encourages citizens to adopt dual roles as both learners and educators throughout their lives. This approach is aimed at creating a more informed, engaged, and versatile populace; while significantly improving knowledge retention and application.

- *Life-Long Participation, Learning, and Teaching:* The commitment to lifelong education is not just about formal learning but involves active participation in community and societal development; leading to better health outcomes, increased social capital, and greater adaptability in an ever-changing world.

By integrating these reforms, the goal is to establish a socially responsible work, education, and retirement system that aligns with humanistic values and scientific evidence. This new framework aims to enhance social equity, improve quality of life across different age groups, and foster a sense of community responsibility. The reforms reflect a commitment to building a more balanced and participatory society.

Section 9: Innovative Approach to Affordable Housing on Federal Lands

In response to the housing affordability crisis, the proposed constitutional amendment introduces a groundbreaking initiative to develop affordable housing communities on federally leased lands. This approach is supported by urban planning research and economic analysis, ensuring a sustainable and equitable solution for low-income residents.

i. Development of Affordable Housing Communities: The U.S. government will establish affordable housing on federal lands, leasing the land to individual home buyers. These communities will be designed to high construction standards with defined minimum and maximum square footage, promoting efficient and sustainable living spaces.

    a. All buildings must adhere to green building standards and be designed for longevity, with an aim of lasting 1,000 years. Research in sustainable architecture underscores the environmental and economic benefits of green building practices.

ii. Housing Specifications and Community Integration: Homes will be financed with an 88-year land lease, transferable under certain conditions, aligning with long-term housing security objectives.

a. The transfer or sale of homes will require Homeowners' Association (HOA) approval. In cases of non-approval, the community will purchase the home at fair market value, ensuring stability and fairness in housing transactions.

iii. Resident Responsibilities and Community Engagement: Residents will contribute to their monthly HOA fees through work in greenhouse farming, integrating sustainable agriculture with community living.

a. An additional 20% of residents' hours will be dedicated to community service, fostering civic engagement and community development.

b. Participation in the LUVRules.com social network and self-governing system will be mandatory, promoting digital democracy and community cohesion.

c. Utilization of a blockchain-based Social Capitalist economic system alongside a digital U.S. Dollar wallet will be implemented, aligning with modern financial technologies and promoting economic transparency and efficiency.

d. Prospective Village Chieftains undergoing a 90-day probationary period will be assessed for clinical narcissism, with provisions for refund and excommunication from the HOA if necessary. This measure is in place to ensure ethical and psychologically sound leadership within the communities.

This comprehensive approach to affordable housing on federal lands aims to create sustainable, integrated, and self-governing communities. By combining innovative construction standards, green initiatives, and a focus on community engagement and governance, the amendment seeks to address housing affordability while promoting social responsibility and environmental stewardship.

Section 10: Comprehensive Media Reform for Enhanced Public Discourse

The proposed constitutional amendment introduces a far-reaching media reformation strategy, driven by the need to counteract corporate influence in media and to evolve public discourse. Supported by findings from behavioral economics and social psychology, these reforms aim to diversify media sources, protect journalistic integrity, and redefine threat narratives.

i. Diversification of Media Sources: Encouragement of journalism that seeks a variety of sources, especially those representing marginalized or dissenting voices. This approach aims to enhance cultural diversity and provide a more comprehensive view of societal issues, to foster a more inclusive society.

ii. Building Resilience Against 'Flak': Strengthening the defense against negative responses to media stories ('flak'), by protecting journalists and media organizations from undue legal and financial pressures; safeguarding journalistic freedom for maintaining media integrity and promoting public trust.

iii. Redefining Threat Narratives: Mandating a constitutional clause that compels media to portray a more accurate and less sensationalized depiction of global and domestic threats, moving away from fear-based narratives; reducing societal anxiety and division, and contributing to a more informed and cohesive society.

iv. Mandatory Fairness and Balance in Media: Requiring all media companies to adhere to standards of fairness and balance, and to enforce truth in advertising and news reporting; so as to prevent misinformation, and ensure responsible journalism.

v. Implementation of 'Journalism Bars': Establishing 'Journalism Bars' to regulate journalist trade-unions, ensuring adherence to ethical standards and journalistic integrity; enhancing accountability and professionalism in journalism.

vi. Restrictions on Advertisements: Prohibiting pharmaceutical, tobacco, or recreational drug/alcohol advertisements in media; reducing harmful consumption behaviors while protecting vulnerable populations.

vii. Advertisement-Free Programming: Mandating one hour of fair and balanced nightly news without advertisements, and kid-friendly programming without commercial interruptions; benefiting children's development and the public's understanding of news.

viii. Support for Local PBS Stations: Funding and mandating local PBS stations to provide three hours of nightly localized programming from 7pm to 10pm, serving each geographic community; fostering community engagement and cultural representation.

ix.   Size Limitation for Media Companies: Restricting privately held media companies to a medium-sized business framework, not exceeding 1,813 employees; contributing to a healthier democratic discourse.

x.   Compliance with Public Sphere Operations: Ensuring that all media companies operating in the public sphere comply with First Amendment rights, enforce truth in advertising, and contribute to the development of an impartial and noble citizenry; promoting civic virtues through media content.

Through these reforms, the amendment aims to cultivate a media landscape that is more diverse, truthful, and focused on fostering an informed and noble citizenry. The intent is to create a media environment that supports democratic values, encourages critical thinking, and enhances the quality of public discourse.

THE NEED FOR
GLOBAL GOVERNANCE

Of all the means I know to lead men, the most effectual is a concealed mystery.

- Adam Weishaupt, Founder of the Illuminati

THE ILLUMINATI'S PATRIARCHAL DELUSION OF ENLIGHTENMENT

The head of every family will be what Abraham was, the patriarch, the priest and the unlettered lord of his family, and Reason will be the code of laws to all mankind.

- Adam Weishaupt, Founder of the Illuminati

Adam Weishaupt's founding of the Illuminati in 1776, under the guise of Enlightenment principles, presents a paradoxical narrative in the history of philosophical thought. While claiming to advocate for reason and rationalism, Weishaupt's vision, reveals a deeply ingrained patriarchal mindset that negates the very essence of enlightened equality and freedom.

Weishaupt's assertion, "The head of every family will be what Abraham was, the patriarch, the priest and the unlettered lord of his family, and Reason will be the code of laws to all mankind," unveils a deeply rooted patriarchal worldview. This vision glorifies the male head as an unquestionable authority, reminiscent of Abraham's biblical role, but strips away the element of divine guidance, replacing it with human reason. This shift, while seemingly progressive, subtly perpetuates male dominance and authority, effectively sidelining the role and importance of the feminine perspective in family and society.

This ideology not only reinforces traditional patriarchal structures, but also cloaks them in the deceptive garb of rational enlightenment. It negates the balance and harmony that the integration of both masculine and feminine principles could bring to societal progress. By positioning reason as the ultimate law, Weishaupt inadvertently promotes a form of intellectual narcissism, where rationality becomes a tool for asserting superiority and control, rather than a means for collective enlightenment and progress.

The second quote, "Of all the means I know to lead men, the most effectual is a concealed mystery," further unveils Weishaupt's manipulative and narcissistic traits. His strategy of employing mystery as a leadership tool reflects a desire to control and dominate through secrecy and elitism. This approach not only contradicts the Enlightenment ideals of transparency and humility, but also reveals a lack of empathy and vulnerability – qualities essential for authentic leadership.

Weishaupt's desire to lead through mystery and intrigue aligns with a Satan-like aspiration to ascend to a position of unparalleled authority. This aspiration betrays a profound fear and rejection of the divine feminine – the nurturing, empathetic, and collaborative aspect within humanity. His philosophy actually becomes an embodiment of an unbalanced pursuit of power, devoid of the harmonizing and compassionate qualities that are vital for a truly enlightened and just society.

Adam Weishaupt's vision for the Illuminati, *far from being a beacon of enlightenment*, reveals a deeply flawed and unbalanced perspective, steeped in patriarchal arrogance and narcissistic control. His rejection of the divine feminine and overemphasis on patriarchal rationalism demonstrate a fundamental misunderstanding of what true enlightenment entails – the harmonious integration of all aspects of human nature, including both the masculine and feminine.

Weishaupt's legacy, therefore, serves as a cautionary tale of how noble ideals can be distorted by unaddressed personal biases, along with a misguided desire for dominance and control.

Unraveling the Roots of Patriarchy

Patriarchy is a bully notion, which if you will notice never attacks a nation that can defend itself... Zionism is patriarchal and sets Judaism on its head.

- Roseanne Barr

Angela Saini's 'The Patriarchs' offers a profound exploration into the origins and evolution of patriarchy. Saini's analysis begins in prehistory, challenging the traditional narrative that patriarchal structures are a natural order.

The Genesis of Gendered Oppression

Archaeological evidence suggests that early human societies may have been more egalitarian, with gender roles not strictly defined. The shift towards agriculture and the subsequent establishment of permanent settlements marked a turning point. These developments brought about resource accumulation and inheritance, laying the groundwork for male-dominated hierarchies. This transition highlights a key theme in Saini's work: patriarchy is not an inherent human condition, but a societal construct that evolved under specific economic and social conditions; influenced by migration, conquest, and cultural exchange.

Global Spread of Patriarchal Ideologies

These patriarchal systems spread globally, influenced by migration, conquest, and cultural exchange. Then as empires expanded and religions spread, so did the concept of male dominance. Societies that once may have practiced more egalitarian gender relations were gradually assimilated into patriarchal norms. This spread was not just a transfer of power, but also an ideological shift, where patriarchal values were increasingly seen as universal truths.

The Naturalization of Male Dominance

Central to Saini's argument is the idea that male domination was naturalized in human societies. Through religious texts, legal systems, and cultural narratives, the male authority was presented as a divine or natural order. This naturalization process, Saini argues, is a key factor in the resilience and ubiquity of patriarchal structures. It rendered the questioning of male dominance not just a social challenge, but a confrontation against perceived natural laws.

Adam Weishaupt and the Illuminati

Integrating the earlier analysis of Adam Weishaupt's vision for the Illuminati, even movements founded on principles of enlightenment and rationalism were not immune to patriarchal biases. Weishaupt's envisioning of a society led by 'unlettered lords' and his reliance on secrecy and elitism were manifestations of a deeper patriarchal conditioning. His ideals mirrored the broader societal beliefs in male superiority and control, illustrating how patriarchy can permeate even those ideologies that claim to challenge the status quo.

Reckoning with the Legacy of Patriarchy

Angela Saini's 'The Patriarchs' offers a critical lens through which to view the historical and cultural roots of patriarchy. It challenges the notion of male dominance as a natural human condition, revealing it as a construct that evolved under specific socio-economic conditions and was perpetuated through cultural and ideological systems. And the example of Adam Weishaupt and the Illuminati, underscores the pervasive and often insidious nature of patriarchal ideology.

Envisioning a Future Beyond Patriarchal Constructs

Angela Saini's 'The Patriarchs' provides not only a critical examination of the entrenched history of patriarchy but also serves as a beacon of hope. By meticulously uncovering the diverse tapestry of human social arrangements throughout history, the book disrupts the longstanding grand narratives that have often painted male supremacy as a fixed and immutable aspect of human society. Saini's work exposes male dominance as one element in a larger, ever-evolving system of control and power dynamics.

This revelation is empowering; it suggests that just as patriarchal systems were constructed and solidified over time, they can also be deconstructed and reimagined. 'The Patriarchs' thus stands as a profoundly hopeful testament to the potential for societal transformation, a call to recognize and challenge the patriarchal structures that have shaped our past, and an invitation to envision a more equitable future.

The Sovereignty-Destruction Project

The history of the last century shows, that the advice given to governments by bankers, like the advice they gave to industrialists, was consistently good for bankers, but was often disastrous for governments, businessmen, and the people generally.

- Carroll Quigley

'Tragedy & Hope 101' by Joseph Plummer is a distilled version of Carroll Quigley's monumental work, 'Tragedy and Hope,' focusing on the influence and operations of global power elites.

Plummer's book, organized into nine chapters, examines the workings of what he terms 'The Network Leaders'—a group of influential and interconnected individuals who, according to the author, manipulate global events for their benefit.

1. *Introduction to 'The Network':* The book opens by setting the stage for the discussion of a cabal of elite leaders. Plummer suggests these individuals possess an enormous, often unseen influence over global political and economic systems. He introduces the concept that these elites view the general population as mere pawns in their grand strategy of global dominance.

1) *The Ideological Foundation:* Here, Plummer delves into the philosophical underpinnings of the network. He posits that their worldview is rooted in a Machiavellian approach to power, where the end justifies the means; crucial in understanding the alleged motives behind The Network's actions.

2) *The Rise of Financial Power:* Plummer examines the historical ascent of financial institutions and their proprietors, arguing that control over money supply and economic systems is central to The Network's influence.

3) *Consolidation of Control:* This chapter discusses how The Network has allegedly co-opted various institutions, including governments and international bodies, to centralize power and advance their agenda.

4) *Instruments of Influence:* Plummer points to specific tools used by The Network, including propaganda, educational control, and manipulation of the media, to shape public opinion and maintain their power structure.

5) *War and Conflict:* Plummer argues that wars and conflicts are often orchestrated and exploited by The Network to reshape global power dynamics and profit from the ensuing chaos.

6) *The Path to Totalitarianism:* Here, Plummer suggests that The Network's ultimate goal is the establishment of a global totalitarian system, where dissent is crushed, and individual freedoms are curtailed.

7) *The Networks and Modern Crises:* This chapter connects historical events to contemporary issues, asserting that many modern crises can be traced back to the manipulations of The Network.

8) *Solutions and Hope:* Contrasting the book's largely grim analysis, this final chapter proposes ways in which individuals and societies might counteract the influence of The Network and reclaim sovereignty.

Plummer's narrative in 'Tragedy & Hope 101' reaches its apex with the discussion of the Sovereignty-Destruction Project, positing that the network achieved a significant milestone in their agenda with the establishment of the Federal Reserve in 1913. This event, according to Plummer, symbolizes the culmination of a long-standing plan to exert covert control over political and economic systems, influencing media, education, and public perception.

This analysis takes a more ominous turn when synthesizing Plummer's views with the concept of 'mass formation' as detailed by Mattias Desmet in 'The Psychology of Totalitarianism.' According to Desmet, mass formation occurs when a significant portion of a population is hypnotized into a totalitarian mindset, often facilitated by fear and isolation, leading to a society where rational thought and individual critical analysis are suspended.

When considering the COVID-19 pandemic, or the 'plandemic' as termed by some theorists, this synthesis suggests a strategic utilization of the crisis by the alleged 'Network'. The pandemic, in this view, served as an ideal environment for fostering mass formation. The global fear, uncertainty, and social isolation created a fertile ground for manipulating public perception and behavior. This, according to the synthesis of Plummer and Desmet's theories, was not a mere consequence of the pandemic, but a calculated move by The Network to further their total control.

The idea is that the pandemic accelerated the network's agenda, pushing societies towards greater acceptance of restrictive measures, surveillance, and a curtailment of freedoms under the guise of public health and safety. This situation could be seen as a real-time execution of the Sovereignty-Destruction Project, where individual rights and national sovereignties are increasingly eroded.

This foreboding perspective raises questions about the balance between public health measures and civil liberties, the integrity of global leadership, and the power dynamics at play in times of crisis. It also underscores the importance of critical thinking and the need for vigilance against potential abuses of power.

AN ELITIST ONE-WORLD GOVERNMENT

Nothing in all the world is more dangerous than
sincere ignorance and conscientious stupidity.

- Martin Luther King Jr

'The Empire of the City' by Edwin Knuth offers a deep dive into the intricate workings
of what he perceives as a shadowy cabal of global elites operating a super-
government, that operates behind the scenes of global politics and finance.

- In the opening chapters, Knuth lays the groundwork for his thesis. He describes
  a secret society, composed of the world's most influential figures, who have
  formed an unacknowledged super-government.

- This cabal, according to Knuth, possesses immense political and financial
  power and orchestrates major global events to serve its interests. Knuth traces
  the historical roots of this group, back to various secret societies and influential
  families.

- Knuth delves into the mechanisms through which this elite group exerts its
  influence. He suggests that they control key financial institutions, manipulate
  major economies, and dictate international policies.

- According to Knuth, wars and political upheavals are tools used by this group to
  maintain and extend their control, often under the guise of promoting
  democracy or protecting national interests.

- Knuth believes that this cabal has directly influenced global events, leading to
  conflict, economic crises, and political upheaval. He argues that the ultimate
  goal of these actions is to weaken national sovereignties and consolidate power
  in the hands of the few.

- Knuth explores how the cabal allegedly maintains its influence in the modern
  world. He points to their control over media, education, and cultural institutions,

which he believes are used to indoctrinate the public and suppress dissenting voices.

- The final chapter speculates on the overarching plans of this group, which Knuth claims, includes the establishment of a one-world government, and the erosion of individual freedoms. This vision, according to Knuth, is marked by a world where democratic values are supplanted by the dictates of an unelected elite.

In synthesizing the narrative of 'Tragedy & Hope 101' by Joseph Plummer with Knuth's 'The Empire of the City,' one can see parallels in their portrayal of a global elite manipulating events for their gain. Both suggest that the COVID-19 pandemic, or 'plandemic', was used as an opportunity by this cabal to further their control, aligning with the Sovereignty-Destruction Project detailed by Plummer.

Positing that the pandemic was leveraged to advance the agenda of consolidating power and eroding national sovereignties, as outlined by Knuth, it is more than probable that the 'plandemic' served as an effective tool for creating mass formation among the populace, while accelerating the move towards a one-world government; thus diminishing the relevance of national borders, and centralizing authority.

The Luciferian Illuminati and Global Conflict

I know not with what weapons World War III will be fought,
but World War IV will be fought with sticks and stones.

- Albert Einstein

'Pawns in the Game' by William Carr presents an international conspiracy led by a group described as Satanistic global leaders. Carr's narrative is built around the idea that this cabal aims to destroy existing governments and religions, creating chaos by dividing people on various fronts.

The Foundations of the Conspiracy: Carr begins by outlining the historical background of the conspiracy. He traces its roots to ancient secret societies, suggesting that these groups have long sought to manipulate world events; and discusses the formation and evolution of these societies, emphasizing their alleged desire to create a world divided and in constant turmoil.

Strategies of Division: Carr delves into the tactics used by the cabal. He argues that they deliberately foster divisions among people based on politics, race, social status, and economic disparities. According to Carr, these divisions are tools to weaken societies, making them more susceptible to manipulation and control.

The Wider Impact: Carr extends his theory to a global scale, asserting that major historical events, including wars and revolutions, have been orchestrated by this group. He suggests that these events are not spontaneous but are part of a calculated plan to destabilize nations and advance the cabal's agenda.

The Endgame and Vision: The concluding chapters of the book discuss what Carr perceives as the ultimate goal of the conspiracy: the establishment of a one-world government led by this elite group. He paints a picture of a future where traditional forms of government and religion are eradicated, replaced by a totalitarian regime.

Synthesizing Carr's 'Pawns in the Game' with 'The Empire of the City,' and 'Tragedy & Hope 101,' we observe a recurring theme: the notion of a secretive, powerful patriarchal elite orchestrating global events.

This synthesis posits that the Luciferian Illuminati, as described by Carr, have indoctrinated 'Network Leaders' into believing that only a one-world government, run by white men, can end the global conflicts and tribulations.

A pinnacle of this grand plan is the COVID-19 'plandemic'; which demonstrated their success in achieving totalitarian mass formation, by manipulating the global population into a state of compliance and control.

A GLOBALIST SUBVERSION OF OUR AMERICAN DEMOCRACY

A Literature Review

Here in America we are descended in blood and in spirit from revolutionists and rebels
- men and women who dare to dissent from accepted doctrine.
As their heirs, may we never confuse honest dissent, with disloyal subversion.

- Dwight D. Eisenhower

Rethinking Global Governance through a Libertarian Federation

The purpose of this literature review is to delve into the insights of the following books to explore the evolution and challenges involved in the governance of modern societies; while also developing a cohesive argument for institutional reformation that leads us towards a federation of libertarian nation-states, within the context of a reformed United Nations. The aim is to counterbalance the alleged dominance of an elitist cabal and promote a world governed by libertarian principles.

Part 1: 'The Open Society and Its Enemies 1' by Karl Popper

Popper's first volume critically examines the philosophies of Plato, Marx, and Hegel, arguing against their deterministic and collectivist views. He advocates for an 'open society' that embraces liberal democracy, individual freedom, and critical rationalism. This foundation is crucial for understanding the need for societies that are open to change and resistant to authoritarian control.

Part 2: 'The Open Society and Its Enemies 2' by Karl Popper

Continuing his argument, Popper in this volume warns against the totalitarian dangers inherent in historicism and utopianism. He emphasizes the importance of piecemeal social engineering over revolutionary changes. This perspective underscores the need for gradual, reasoned reforms in building resilient, open societies.

Part 3: 'The Great Transformation' by Karl Polanyi

Polanyi's work offers a contrasting view, critiquing the unregulated free market and advocating for a more socially responsible economic system. He discusses the dislocation and upheavals caused by the industrial revolution and market capitalism, suggesting the need for protective countermeasures by the state. This work provides a nuanced understanding of the balance required between market forces and social needs.

Part 4: 'Why Nations Fail' by Daron Acemoglu and James Robinson

Acemoglu and Robinson explore the reasons behind the success or failure of nations. They argue that inclusive political and economic institutions, as opposed to extractive ones, are crucial for prosperity. This insight is key in understanding how institutional designs can foster or hinder the development of resilient, free societies.

Part 5: 'The Narrow Corridor' by Daron Acemoglu and James Robinson

This book builds on the previous one, discussing the 'narrow corridor' to liberty – a balance between state and society where rights and freedoms are protected. It emphasizes the delicate balance required to maintain liberty, suggesting that vigilant societies are necessary to keep states accountable.

Synthesizing these texts, the need for a reformation of global governance structures become apparent. The dominance of an elitist cabal represents a significant threat to the ideals of open, free societies. By embracing the libertarian ideals of individual freedom, limited government, and inclusive institutions, there is a pathway to counter this dominance.

> *The proposed reformation of the United Nations into a federation of libertarian nation-states, aims to create a global governance structure that is anti-fragile, resistant to authoritarian control, and dedicated to safeguarding individual liberties.*

This new United Federation of Nations would seek to balance the needs of global cooperation with the principles of libertarianism, ensuring that no single power or elite group can dominate or dictate the global agenda; thus proposing a transformative vision for a new libertarian world order, one that prioritizes participatory collaboration, interdependent inclusivity, and resilience in the face of global challenges and authoritarian threats.

The Cold-Blooded Architects of Global Tyranny

This urgent and unsettling exploration across five pivotal books paints a grim portrait of how 'rational elites,' *exploiting their intellectual prowess and cold-blooded efficiency,* have manipulated the democratic fabric of society.

Their insidious influence, *as these works reveal,* is pushing the world to the brink of a dystopian nightmare, threatening the very essence of freedom and democracy.

Part 1: 'Voltaire's Bastards' by John Saul

Saul's scathing critique exposes the dangerous over-reliance on cold rationalism by Western elites. He argues that this hyper-rationality, stripped of moral compass, has led to a new kind of tyranny. These unfeeling elites, *adept at using rationality as a weapon*, undermines democratic values, paving the way for an emotionally barren, autocratic governance.

Part 2: 'Antisemitism' by Hannah Arendt

Arendt's incisive analysis of antisemitism reveals how political elites weaponize prejudice and hate to erode democracy. Her work lays bare the chilling mechanisms through which racism and xenophobia are institutionalized, becoming tools for totalitarian rule, and illustrating the elites' ruthless effectiveness in controlling societal narratives.

Part 3: 'Imperialism' by Hannah Arendt

Arendt delves into the heart of imperialistic ambition, showing how it goes beyond mere land conquest. She exposes the manipulative tactics used to control and exploit populations, highlighting the insatiable appetite of these elites for power and their shrewd use of imperialism as a guise for global domination.

Part 4: 'Gold and Iron' by Fritz Stern

Stern's historical analysis illuminates the shadowy nexus between financial moguls and political power. The relationship between Bismarck and the Rothschilds serves as a stark reminder of how economic and political interests are interwoven, revealing the elites' strategic use of global conflict to advance their agendas.

Part 5: 'Totalitarianism' by Hannah Arendt

Arendt's examination of totalitarianism is a dire warning. She articulates how regimes use terror and propaganda to oppress and control, drawing disturbing parallels with modern events. The book is a testament to the elites' chilling proficiency in subjugating masses, showing the terrifying extent of their control.

These texts together sound an alarm bell, revealing the reptilian nature of these 'rational elites' as they undermine American democracy, edging us towards global domination; *their response to events like the Covid-19 'plandemic' exposes their ambition for total control, pushing the world into conflict.*

In response, the formation of a libertarian, technocratic Federation of Nations is proposed as humanity's last bastion against this dystopian future; ensuring that governance is not only intellectually robust, *but also morally grounded and transparently accountable.*

This Federation champions ethical rationalism, individual liberties, and democratic accountability. It stands as a beacon of hope, an evolutionary blueprint for a future that harmonizes technological progress with libertarian values, steering humanity away from the clutches of these cold-blooded tyrants; towards a just, free world.

The Ideological Subversion of American Democracy

Yuri Alexandrovich Bezmenov, a former KGB agent, made a claim in 1984 that the 'Soviet Union' had embarked on a long-term mission to ideologically subvert the United States.

Bezmenov claimed that the Soviet Union's strategy for weakening the United States was not primarily through direct military confrontation but rather through a slow, methodical process of psychological warfare, designed to demoralize and destabilize society from within. According to Bezmenov, this process is divided into four stages: demoralization, destabilization, crisis, and normalization.

Stage 1 is Demoralization:

The first stage, 'demoralization,' according to Bezmenov, takes about 20 years to complete. This timeframe is significant because it approximates a generation's span, the time required to influence and reshape the worldview of young people through education and media. The goal during this stage is to erode confidence in a nation's values, culture, history, and foundational ideologies. Bezmenov suggested that this phase involves an extensive campaign to delegitimize societal structures and create doubt about the moral and intellectual foundations of the target nation.

Stage 2 is Destabilization:

Following demoralization, the second stage is 'destabilization.' This phase involves creating further discord and disunity within the society. It targets the essential elements of societal cohesion, including the economy, law and order, and political and military institutions. During this phase, the erosion of trust in these institutions becomes more pronounced, leading to social chaos and a breakdown in previously established norms and relationships.

Stage 3 is Crisis:

The third stage, 'crisis,' is a culmination of the first two stages. It is characterized by a significant upheaval or event that disrupts the societal status quo. This crisis can manifest in various forms, including economic meltdowns, political scandals, or significant social unrest. The primary objective in this phase is to push the society to a point where a radical change becomes inevitable.

Stage 4 is Normalization:

Finally, the 'normalization' stage is where the subverted society is reconstructed in a new image. This phase often involves the establishment of new governing structures and ideologies that align with the subverter's goals. The term 'normalization' is somewhat ironic, as it implies a return to stability, albeit under a new set of norms that significantly differ from the original.

To evaluate the impact of such subversive tactics in America, especially in the context of the 2020 pandemic, one must examine various statistical data. This includes looking at measures of public trust in institutions, societal cohesion, and the prevalence of ideological polarization. The pandemic, labeled by some as a 'plandemic,' has been a significant event in recent history, influencing various aspects of societal structure and individual psychology.

The concept of 'mass formation,' as related to the pandemic, refers to the psychological phenomenon where a large portion of the population aligns with a particular narrative or set of beliefs. Analyzing statistical data from media consumption trends, public health responses, social media engagement, and political polarization during this period supports the extent to which this mass formation has taken-over.

Comparing these 'plandemic' statistics to the stages described by Bezmenov will help assess the correlations between the tactics of ideological subversion, and the societal changes observed during the Covid19 pandemic. This includes examining whether there was a significant shift in public trust and societal values, consistent with the demoralization and destabilization stages.

Bezmenov's theory of ideological subversion provides a framework for understanding potential long-term efforts to undermine societal structures and values. By analyzing recent events and statistical data, particularly around the 2020 pandemic, demonstrates the extent to which these theoretical stages of subversion align with actual societal changes.

While direct causation may be challenging to establish, the correlations between Bezmenov's stages and the observable societal shifts during the pandemic era provide a basis for further investigation into the dynamics of ideological influence, and mass psychological phenomena.

Totalitarian Mass Formation and American Democracy

'A People's History of the United States by Howard Zinn presents a critical and often unexplored perspective of American history, emphasizing the role and impact of the common people, often marginalized in traditional historical narratives.

Zinn's book is renowned for its alternative take on American history, focusing on the struggles and achievements of those often excluded from mainstream historical narratives – the working class, people of color, and other marginalized groups. It challenges the glorified version of American history and exposes the ongoing struggle between the elite and the common people.

Each chapter in Zinn's book tackles different periods and events in American history, from the discovery of America to contemporary times. The common thread is the exploration of how these historical events often served the interests of a powerful elite, while marginalizing or exploiting the majority.

-   Subversion of American Democracy: Throughout the book, Zinn suggests that American democracy has been repeatedly subverted by elites who manipulate political, social, and economic systems for their personal gain. This subversion takes various forms, from the exploitation of labor and resources to the manipulation of public opinion and policy.

-   The Role of War and Conflict: Zinn pays particular attention to the role of wars and conflicts in American history, arguing that they often served as tools for the elite to expand their power and control. Wars are depicted not just as battles for freedom and democracy, as often portrayed in traditional histories, but as opportunities for economic expansion and control by the elite.

-   Civil Rights and Social Movements: The struggle for civil rights and the emergence of various social movements are central to Zinn's narrative. He highlights how these movements, while aimed at securing rights and freedoms for the marginalized, often faced opposition from the elite, who viewed them as threats to their power and control.

-   Economic Policies and Class Struggle: Zinn's analysis of economic policies throughout American history underscores the class struggle between the rich and the poor. He describes how economic systems have been designed to benefit the wealthy elite at the expense of the working class, perpetuating inequality and injustice.

- The Pandemic as a Contemporary Example: Drawing parallels with historical events, the recent pandemic can be analyzed through Zinn's lens as a potential tool for elite control. The response to the pandemic, including lockdowns, economic policies, and information dissemination, can be scrutinized for evidence of elitist influence and attempts at totalitarian mass formation and control.

Howard Zinn's 'A People's History of the United States' provides a critical lens through which to view American history, particularly the ongoing struggle between the elite and the populace.

The pandemic, akin to past historical events, can be seen as a contemporary manifestation of elitist attempts to subvert democracy and push towards a singular global governance.

The examples throughout Zinn's book, alongside the pandemic scenario, illustrate a pattern of elite control and manipulation, posing significant challenges to the ideals of American democracy. This analysis underscores the need for vigilance and active participation in a new technocratic self-governing democracy, so as to counter these malevolent subversions.

The Role of Financial Elites in Shaping Global Governance

Murray Rothbard's 'A History of Money and Banking in the United States' offers a libertarian critique of the American financial system, arguing that the establishment and evolution of this system have been heavily influenced by powerful financial interests that are detrimental to economic stability and individual liberty.

Part 1: Colonial and Revolutionary Eras

The first part of the book explores the early history of money and banking in the United States, including colonial times and the revolutionary era. Rothbard emphasizes the decentralized and diverse nature of currency and banking practices during this period, setting the stage for later centralization.

Part 2: The Early National Era

This section covers the post-revolutionary period, focusing on the establishment of the first central bank and the ensuing debates about the role of government in banking. Rothbard argues that this period set important precedents for future banking practices and government interventions.

Part 3: The Free Banking Era

Rothbard describes the mid-19th century as a time of relatively less government intervention in banking, which he terms the "Free Banking Era." However, he suggests that even during this period, there were significant influences from financial elites shaping banking policies.

Part 4: The National Banking Era

This era, according to Rothbard, saw a significant increase in centralized control and regulation of the banking sector, driven by influential financial interests. He criticizes the National Banking Acts and other regulations as steps towards a more controlled and manipulated financial system.

Part 5: The Federal Reserve System

Rothbard's most critical analysis is reserved for the Federal Reserve System, which he describes as a Ponzi scheme orchestrated by financial elites like Morgan and Rockefeller. He argues that the Fed's control over the money supply leads to inflation and a "Leviathan state" of government controls, serving the interests of a select few at the expense of the general public.

Rothbard's analysis suggests that the financial elites' influence on the American monetary and banking system is part of a larger agenda to establish a one-world government. He argues that this goal cannot be achieved without the support of various elite groups across economic, social, intellectual, and political spheres.

These elites are united by a sense of narcissistic entitlement to special privileges, which are maintained and enhanced through their cooperation with the shadowy cabal of power elites. The creation and maintenance of a central banking system like the Federal Reserve are seen as key to this process, facilitating control over the economy and, by extension, the populace.

Rothbard's work thus offers a comprehensive critique of the American financial system, highlighting the interconnectedness of economic policies and broader socio-political objectives. It serves as a cautionary tale about the concentration of power and the dangers of unchecked influence by a select group of elites on the functioning of democratic institutions and economic systems.

The Cabal of Banksters and Financial Enslavement

'The Origins of the Federal Reserve' by Murray Rothbard delves into the creation and underlying motivations behind the establishment of the Federal Reserve System in the United States.

Rothbard begins by setting the historical context, outlining the economic and political landscape of the late 19th and early 20th centuries. This background is crucial for understanding the motivations and forces that led to the creation of the Federal Reserve.

Section 1: Pre-Federal Reserve Banking

This section examines the state of banking prior to the Federal Reserve's establishment, focusing on the National Banking system and the inherent instabilities and limitations it presented, which, according to Rothbard, laid the groundwork for a centralized banking solution.

Section 2: The Push for Reform

Rothbard discusses the growing movement for banking reform, driven by both economic crises and the interests of large bankers who saw the potential for greater control and profit through a centralized system.

Section 3: Early Proposals

This part delves into the early proposals for central banking, highlighting the key figures and ideologies that influenced the debate. Rothbard emphasizes how these proposals were shaped by various banking and political interests.

Section 4: Jekyll Island and the Drafting of the Federal Reserve Act

Rothbard provides an in-depth look at the secretive meeting at Jekyll Island, where influential bankers and politicians laid the groundwork for what would become the Federal Reserve Act. He portrays this as a pivotal moment in the cabal's formation.

Section 5: Political Maneuvering

This section covers the political maneuvering and lobbying that took place to get the Federal Reserve Act passed, underscoring the combination of public and private interests that influenced these efforts.

Section 6: The Federal Reserve Act of 1913

Rothbard provides a detailed examination of the Act itself, analyzing its key components and how it established the framework for centralized control over the nation's money supply.

Section 7: Early Years of the Fed

This part explores the initial years of the Federal Reserve's operation, focusing on how it began to exert its influence over the banking system and the broader economy.

Section 8: The Fed's Role in Economic Instability

Rothbard argues that the Federal Reserve, rather than stabilizing the economy, contributed to cycles of boom and bust through its manipulation of the money supply and interest rates.

Section 9: The Federal Reserve and World Banking

This section extends the analysis to the international impact of the Federal Reserve, especially in relation to the World Wars and the Great Depression, showcasing its growing global influence.

Section 10: Long-Term Consequences

The final section reflects on the long-term consequences of the Federal Reserve, especially in terms of economic policy and the accumulation of national debt.

Rothbard's analysis suggests that the Federal Reserve, *in tandem with major commercial banks,* forms a powerful banking cartel. This 'cabal of banksters,' leverages the power to print money in a way that perpetuates inflation and debt.

This creates a form of financial enslavement for both individuals and governments, trapped in a cycle of debt that continually benefits the banking elite at the expense of the broader economy and society.

Rothbard sees this as a deliberate strategy by financial elites to maintain and expand their power and control, manipulating the economic system to serve their interests. The Federal Reserve, in this view, is not a stabilizing force but rather a central mechanism in a system designed to ensure the dominance of a select few over the financial and economic well-being of the many.

The Chilling Ascendancy of Elitist Control

The intricate dance of power and control over global resources and finance has been a defining feature of modern history. This review delves into the shadowy realms of power, resource exploitation, and financial manipulation that have historically shaped global order.

Through the analysis of five pivotal books, this review uncovers a sinister narrative of elitist dominance, underscoring the urgency for a Libertarian Federation of Nations. This coalition is envisioned as a bulwark against a looming one-world government, a specter of despotism and control orchestrated by a concealed elite.

Part 1: 'Diamonds, Gold, and War' by Martin Meredith

Meredith's exposition on Africa's resource exploitation paints a grim picture of the colonial era's avarice and power struggles. The relentless pursuit of diamonds and gold in the southern regions of Africa by colonial powers and magnates set a historical precedent of ruthless resource control. This narrative is a cornerstone in understanding the origins of modern resource-based conflicts and the emergence of omnipotent global entities.

Part 2: 'Meet You in Hell' by Les Standiford

Standiford's narrative about the bitter rivalry between Andrew Carnegie and Henry Clay Frick epitomizes the era of the American industrial revolution, marked by the rise of monolithic business tycoons. This part examines how personal vendettas and ruthless business practices of the past have shaped the ethos of contemporary corporate and financial practices.

Part 3: 'Titan' by Ron Chernow

Chernow's biography of John D. Rockefeller, Sr., the founder of Standard Oil, delves into the life of one of history's most influential and controversial figures who indelibly shaped the corporate and financial landscapes. The book provides an insight into how Rockefeller's business tactics and philanthropic endeavors laid the groundwork for modern corporate strategies and the fraudulent concept of 'philanthro-capitalism', influencing today's global financial and political landscape.

Part 4: 'The House of Morgan' by Ron Chernow

Chernow's exploration of the Morgan banking dynasty unveils the intricate connections between finance, politics, and international power. This review leverages this book to understand the evolution of banking and its impact on global economics and politics, emphasizing the pivotal role of financial institutions in sculpting both national and international agendas.

Part 5: 'High Financier' by Niall Ferguson

Ferguson delves into the life of Siegmund Warburg, a figure emblematic of the intricate, often shadowy, interplay between finance and global power structures. This analysis adds a deeper layer to our understanding of financial influence and control, underscoring the stealthy maneuvers of financial titans in shaping global events.

The synthesis of these narratives forms a chilling portrait of historical and contemporary global control mechanisms. The conclusion posits that the age-old patterns of resource exploitation, financial subterfuge, and corporate hegemony have resurfaced, manifesting through multinational conglomerates and a central banking cartel of commercial banksters.

> *This modern reincarnation, characterized by a blend of insidious strategy and covert operations, mirrors the monopolistic tendencies of past industrial moguls.*

These modern global elites, often operating from the shadows, have co-opted international finance, creating a web of dependency and susceptibility. Their ultimate goal: *the establishment of a totalitarian global regime, exerting control through economic channels and strategically dismantling sovereign powers like the United States.*

In response, the conclusion advocates for the establishment of a Libertarian Federation of Nations – a radical new governance model prioritizing decentralization, the dismantling of monopolistic structures, and the safeguarding of individual liberties.

This federation stands as a beacon of hope against the dark tide of totalitarian ambitions, a clarion call to reevaluate and reform global governance to protect humanity from a nightmarish, oppressive elitist new world order.

How Elites Dictate History and Threaten American Democracy

In the chilling depths of global history, a saga unfolds - one where a network of cold-blooded financiers and warmongers, *masquerading as 'rational elites',* have orchestrated a macabre dance of power and control.

This review unveils the terrifying reality of how these reptilian overlords have, time and again, manipulated events to their sinister advantage, casting a dark shadow over the very essence of freedom and democracy. As we, the guardians of American democracy, stand at the crossroads, it's imperative to recognize the imminent threat these elites pose to our nation and the world at large.

1. Wall Street's Covert Maneuvers in the Bolshevik Revolution

   - *Antony Sutton's 'Wall Street and the Bolshevik Revolution'* lays bare the unnerving truth of how Wall Street's financial titans clandestinely influenced the Bolshevik Revolution. The revelation that economic interests often drive political upheavals underscores the alarming extent to which these elites have historically manipulated global events to serve their insidious agenda.

2. The Shadowy Influence of the Edwardian Era's Power Brokers

   - *Peter Hof's 'The Two Edwards'* uncovers the staggering impact of two Edwardian-era figures, revealing how their decisions ruthlessly shaped global politics and economies. This investigation personalizes the previously abstract concepts of power and influence, spotlighting the chilling capacity of individuals to alter the course of history.

3. Unmasking World War I's Hidden Agendas

   - *'Hidden History,' by Doherty and Macgregor,* exposes the secret motives and actions that steered World War I. This exploration deepens our understanding of how the covert machinations of the powerful can devastate the world, often at the expense of the unsuspecting masses.

4. The Prolonged Agony of War for Profit

   - Continuing this exploration, *'Prolonging the Agony'* demonstrates how extending World War I served the interests of a select few, revealing the grotesque reality that war can be a profitable venture for these elites, regardless of the widespread suffering it causes.

5. The Homefront Impact of Global Decisions

- *'American Midnight'* shifts the lens to American soil, dissecting how global events and decisions resonate within America. Hochschild's narrative ties together the themes of personal influence, hidden agendas, and economic motivations, illustrating their manifestation in American society and governance.

In synthesizing these works, the menacing picture becomes clear: *historical events and global governance have frequently been molded by a toxic mix of economic greed, clandestine plots, and influential individuals.*

This understanding necessitates a transformative approach to global governance – the inception of a United Federation of Nations. This new entity, technocratically designed, aims to distribute resources equitably and maintain peace, averting the kinds of scenarios depicted in these texts.

Moreover, this Federation could propel global leaders into a state of heightened self-awareness, urging them to contemplate the far-reaching consequences of their decisions.

Transitioning to a United Federation of Nations symbolizes a comprehensive strategy to correct the historical abuses of power and secretive dealings. It aspires to forge a transparent, equitable, and sustainable global governance paradigm, learning from past atrocities to pave the way for a more secure and hopeful future.

The Dark Tapestry of Global Finance and the Beacon of America

In an era where the shadows of global finance stretch ominously over the fabric of democracy, the chilling tales of cold-blooded international financiers and warmongers come to light through a series of revelatory books.

These narratives unravel a disturbing pattern of totalitarian control, sounding patriotic alarm bells across America. It's a wake-up call for free Americans to recognize the shield that American democracy provides against the menacing reach of global domination.

Part 1: Money for Nothing by Thomas Levenson

Levenson's exploration into the abyss of financial speculation reveals a world where greed and recklessness reign supreme. He paints a grim picture of economic catastrophes, birthed from the unchecked and voracious appetites of financial moguls. His account serves as a prelude to a world where financial catastrophes are not just probable, but inevitable under the current systems of unchecked power and greed.

Part 2: The House of Rothschild Vol. 1 by Niall Ferguson

Ferguson meticulously dissects the ascent of the Rothschild banking family, presenting them as puppeteers in a grand economic theater. The book exposes how this single family could sway nations and economies, leaving a trail of suffering and extreme economic disparity in their wake. It's a chilling reminder of how concentrated financial power isn't just influential, but despotic in its nature.

Part 3: Lords of Finance by Liaquat Ahamed

Ahamed delves into the early 20th century, casting a spotlight on the central bankers who set the stage for the Great Depression. The narrative unveils a cabal of financial leaders whose decisions wreaked havoc on a global scale, reinforcing the perilous nature of centralized financial authority.

Part 4: All the Presidents' Bankers by Naomi Prins

Prins' investigation into the American presidency's dalliance with bankers paints a stark picture of intertwined political and financial ambitions. The book lays bare how this symbiosis can shape policy decisions, prioritizing the interests of the elite over the needs of the many.

Part 5: Wall Street and FDR by Antony Sutton

Sutton's critical analysis of the interplay between Wall Street and President Franklin D. Roosevelt during the New Deal era exemplifies how political agendas and economic interests can merge, often to the detriment of the general populace. This book serves as a case study of the powerful influence that economic forces can wield over national and international policies.

These historical narratives, woven together, depict a harrowing vista of financial and political manipulation. They underscore the imperative need for a seismic shift in global governance.

The proposed blockchain-based United Federation of Nations emerges as a beacon of hope - a mechanism to dismantle the long-standing structures of financial tyranny.

However, it is the robust, vigilant, and unwavering spirit of American democracy that stands as the ultimate bulwark against these global forces of domination, reminding us that the fight for liberty is far from over.

Unmasking the Treacherous Road to Global Tyranny

The following five damning books unveil a shocking historical trajectory of 20th-century power struggles, exposing a sinister plot by a ruthless elite to enslave humanity under a totalitarian regime.

This selection of works isn't just an academic exercise; it's a clarion call to Americans to wake up to the treacherous Nazification of our very own Deep State, which has been designed as a puppet in the hands of a diabolical cabal.

Part 1: 'Nazi Nexus' by Edwin Black

Black's explosive analysis lays bare the grotesque alliance between American industrial magnates and the Nazi war machine. He unveils how these corporate vultures not only aided and abetted, but also profited from the monstrous crimes of Nazi Germany. This dark nexus serves as a historical precursor to the ongoing collusion between corporate despots and political tyrants, aiming to establish a global dominion of terror and control.

Part 2: 'The Third Way' by Joseph Farrell

Farrell rips the veil off the post-World War II geopolitical charade, revealing the shadowy concoction of advanced technologies and clandestine strategies. He presents an appalling picture of a 'Third Way' in global politics, a secret path trodden by the elite to exert their malignant and fascist influence worldwide, far transcending the deceptive facades of capitalism and communism.

Part 3: 'Nazi International' by Joseph Farrell

Continuing this horrifying journey, Farrell exposes the persistent shadow of Nazi ideology and technological prowess, lurking in the post-war world. He uncovers how a sinister alliance of former Nazis and global power brokers has continually manipulated international politics, orchestrating a new world order under the guise of progress and innovation.

Part 4: 'At the Abyss' by Thomas Reed

Reed's insider account of the Cold War era uncovers the relentless arms and technological race that defined global politics. His revelations point to the chilling reality of powerful factions, operating from the shadows, dictating the course of world events under the pretense of national security and progress.

Part 5: 'Body of Secrets' by James Bamford

Bamford's expose of the NSA's global surveillance empire is a stark reminder of the invasive reach of the American Deep State. Controlled by a cabal of elite globalists, the NSA's relentless pursuit of information dominance represents a grave threat to individual freedoms and a manipulative tool in the global political arena.

Collectively, these works paint a nightmarish portrait of the 20th and 21st centuries, where a cabal of authoritarian elites, wielding tools ranging from Nazism to Zionism and Globalism, has been orchestrating a global coup. Their endgame is a dystopian world order, where humanity is shackled under their totalitarian grip, culminating in a future of unprecedented suffering, fragility, and control.

This alarming revelation underscores the dire necessity of establishing a United Federation of Nations. This new global entity, grounded in incorruptible, technocratic principles, stands as humanity's last bastion against the encroaching darkness. It's not just a political strategy, but a moral crusade to preserve democracy and human dignity against a relentless, malevolent force.

In sum, the creation of such a federation is more than a mere policy proposal; it's an urgent call to arms for all freedom-loving citizens to thwart the machinations of this elitist cabal and reclaim our world from the brink of tyrannical annihilation.

Unveiling the Shadows of the American Deep State

This critical dissection of American history, through five alarmingly insightful books, uncovers a harrowing reality: the existence of a Deep State, *a treacherous and shadowy cabal that has hijacked the U.S. government.*

This malevolent entity, driven by an elitist consortium of ruthless financiers, has systematically eroded the foundations of American democracy, all to orchestrate the creation of a despotic one-world government.

Part 1: 'Franklin D. Roosevelt and the New Deal' by William Leuchtenburg

Leuchtenburg's analysis of Roosevelt's New Deal era is a facade that masked the sinister intentions of financial oligarchs. These power-hungry elites manipulated the economic crisis to centralize control, cunningly laying the seeds for a global economy under their iron-fisted rule. This book is a startling revelation of how American economic reforms were perverted into tools for elite domination.

Part 2: 'The War State' by Michael Swanson

Swanson's exposé of the post-World War II landscape reveals the rise of a military-industrial complex, a monstrous creation of corporate and financial elites. This 'War State' became an instrument of global aggression, pushing the U.S. into international conflicts that fattened the pockets of a sinister elite, all while masquerading as efforts to shape a global order under American leadership.

Part 3: 'JFK' by L. Fletcher Prouty

Prouty's chilling account of JFK's presidency unveils his fatal battle against the Deep State's stranglehold. Kennedy's assassination is portrayed not as a tragedy, but as a calculated move by this shadow government, a brutal silencing of a president who dared to defy their warmongering and their relentless grip on Cold War politics.

Part 4: 'JFK and the Unspeakable' by James Douglass

Douglass expands on the ominous narrative of JFK's assassination. This event is depicted as a pivotal moment in history, where the Deep State cemented its tyrannical control over U.S. policy. Kennedy's death emerges not as an isolated incident but as a grim warning to future leaders about the fatal consequences of opposing the military-financial elite nexus.

Part 5: 'Great Society' by Amity Shlaes

Shlaes's critique of the 1960s social reforms, especially under Lyndon B. Johnson, unmasks them as tools of the Deep State. Ostensibly aimed at social justice, these policies, in reality, expanded government power, further entrenching the Deep State's tentacles in American politics and unwittingly advancing the agenda of the ruling elites.

The synthesis of these enlightening yet disturbing works paints a picture of an America under siege. The Deep State, a malignant force driven by a cabal of financiers and corporate despots, has steadily and systematically dismantled the pillars of American democracy.

Their ultimate, nightmarish goal looms: *the erection of a one-world government, a global fascist dictatorship where democratic ideals are crushed under the boots of a ruling elite.*

This revelation is a clarion call for the American people to awaken and resist this insidious power, to safeguard our democracy and liberty against this dark tide of tyranny.

Ringing the Alarm on America's Descent into a Totalitarian Nightmare

This is a piercing and unapologetic critique of the American Deep State, laying bare the insidious forces that have hijacked our nation's ideals...

It's a clarion call to all patriots, urging them to awaken to the sinister transformation of our democracy into a totalitarian regime, orchestrated in part by the Rothschild Bankster Family and their cohorts.

This cabal, with their bloodstained hands, has masterfully engineered chaos to instigate a New World Order where freedom is an illusion, and where every American move is monitored and controlled.

Part 1: 'The House of Rothschild Vol. 2' by Niall Ferguson

Ferguson's tome is not just a historical narrative; it's a shocking exposé of the Rothschild dynasty's stranglehold on global finance and politics in the 19th century. This book is a window into the dark world of how financial moguls have systematically usurped political power, puppeteering nations and orchestrating global events for their sinister gains.

Part 2: 'Operation Paperclip' by Anne Jacobsen

Jacobsen's investigative masterpiece uncovers the grotesque truth of Operation Paperclip. The U.S. government's recruitment of Nazi scientists post-World War II is a damning testament to the moral bankruptcy at the heart of American politics. This chilling account reveals how the U.S. sacrificed its moral compass for technological prowess, embedding Nazi ideology deep within its own scientific community.

Part 3: 'Chaos' by Tom O'Neill

O'Neill's groundbreaking work on the CIA's machinations in the 1960s, particularly around the Manson family murders, is a horrifying revelation of government-sponsored terror. It exposes a labyrinth of deceit, psychological warfare, and dark operations indicative of a government that has turned against its people, manipulating public perception and reality to maintain its grip on power.

257

Part 4: 'The Jakarta Method' by Vincent Bevins

Bevins' harrowing account of the mass killings in Indonesia, and the global propagation of anti-communist terror, shines a light on the barbaric lengths to which the U.S. and its allies will go to crush dissent. The 'Jakarta Method' is a metaphor for the blood-soaked tactics employed by the state to silence opposition, showcasing America's role in perpetuating global violence and suppression.

Part 5: 'Black Ops' by Tony Geraghty

Geraghty's exploration of the shadowy realm of covert operations lays bare the extent of clandestine military and intelligence activities. This book is a testament to the dark arts of espionage and secret warfare, revealing how these operations have fundamentally shaped international relations, often trampling democratic principles and human rights in the process.

Together, these texts paint a nightmarish portrait of the 20th century, dominated by the Rothschild cabal and their deep state puppets. This elite group has manipulated world events, fostering chaos and conflict, to maintain their tyrannical control over global politics.

The proposed antidote is a radical overhaul: the formation of a United Federation of Nations, a beacon of hope designed to dismantle the insidious power structures that have led us to the brink of ruin. This new entity must champion transparency, democracy, and equity to counteract the toxic legacy of elitist control and usher in a new era of peace and justice.

Exposing the Machiavellian Depths of America's Shadow Rulers

This analysis is more than an academic discourse; it's a scathing indictment and a patriot's rallying cry against the sinister machinations of the so-called guardians of American democracy.

As we dissect the workings of the national security state, it becomes glaringly apparent that what we face is not mere governmental ineptitude, but a calculated, cold-blooded conspiracy by an elitist cabal to hijack our cherished democratic values.

Part 1: 'Wedge' by Mark Riebling

In 'Wedge', Riebling exposes the festering rot within the U.S. intelligence community. The book is a chilling account of how power-hungry bureaucrats and their shadowy wars have turned these agencies into a breeding ground for tyranny. It lays bare the disturbing truth: *our so-called protectors are, in fact, orchestrating the erosion of the very freedoms they vow to defend.*

Part 2: 'America's Secret Establishment' by Antony Sutton

Sutton's deep dive into the American elite's secret societies is not just unsettling; it's a wake-up call. He reveals a clandestine network of the privileged, manipulating the strings of power, dictating national policy, and subverting the principles of democracy. This revelation isn't just an attack on our liberty; it's a full-scale war.

Part 3: 'Family of Secrets' by Russ Baker

Russ Baker's investigative masterpiece peels back layers of deceit and manipulation by America's political dynasties. The book exposes a sordid saga of covert operations and underhand dealings, particularly by elite families such as the Bushes, who have shamelessly shaped U.S. politics and policies for their sinister ends.

Part 4: 'The Mafia CIA & George Bush' by Pete Brewton

Brewton's revelations about the unholy trinity of the CIA, organized crime, and figures like George Bush are nothing short of explosive. It's a damning account of how these entities have colluded in covert operations and financial scandals, compromising our democratic institutions and making a mockery of our national ethos.

Part 5: 'Clinton Bush and CIA Conspiracies' by Shaun Attwood

Attwood's work takes us further down the rabbit hole, exposing the nefarious actions and connections of the CIA with the Clinton and Bush families. This book is a stark reminder of how our nation's leaders have weaponized policies, *like the war on drugs,* to establish dominion over the populace.

The synthesis of these texts paints a picture so diabolical it would make Machiavelli blush. We're not just facing a threat to our liberty; we're up against a sophisticated, deeply entrenched cabal that has turned ideologies and policies into weapons of mass control. Their goal? *To shepherd us into a totalitarian nightmare.*

Our response must be swift and decisive. We need to dismantle this authoritarian edifice and replace it with a libertarian stronghold. This new order must rip apart the clandestine networks of power, enforce transparency, and ensure that our policies reflect the will of the people, not the whims of the elite.

A Journey Through the Labyrinths of Power and Deception

In an era where the lines between truth and deception are increasingly blurred, it is crucial to peel back the layers of secrecy and manipulation that shroud our world's power structures. This journey is more than a scholarly endeavor; it is a clarion call to awaken from the slumber of ignorance and complacency.

The narratives woven by these authors unravel the complex tapestry of elitism, corruption, and manipulation that imperils the very foundations of democracy and freedom. As we synthesize the insights and revelations from these works, a stark and urgent conclusion emerges: *the need for a radical transformation of the global political landscape.*

This analysis aims to synthesize insights from five influential books, forming a cohesive argument that advocates for the urgent transformation of the United Nations into a Libertarian Federation of Nations. This transformation is a necessary step to help prevent an elitist cabal, that primarily utilizes Israel and the American Deep State, from precipitating World War III.

1. *'The Samson Option' by Seymour Hersh:* Hersh's groundbreaking work exposes the clandestine world of Israel's nuclear program. The Samson Option is not just a strategy but a doctrine of 'rise and kill first', signaling Israel's readiness to respond with nuclear force if its very existence is threatened. This revelation is alarming, suggesting a global security landscape far more precarious than publicly acknowledged. The implications of such a doctrine, hidden from the world's eyes, are profound. It paints a picture of a world where shadowy decisions, made in secrecy, could determine the fate of humanity.

2. *'Rise and Kill First' by Ronen Bergman:* Bergman's narrative escalates the tension, diving deep into Israel's aggressive counterterrorism measures. It lays bare a history of targeted assassinations, covert operations, and a nation constantly on the offensive. The book is a stark reminder of the lengths to which murderous governments will go in the name of national security. It raises critical questions about the moral and ethical boundaries of state-sponsored actions, spotlighting a world where ends often justify the means.

3. *'One Nation Under Blackmail Vol. 1' by Whitney Webb:* Webb's investigation shifts the lens to the American Deep State, of which Israel is part, unearthing a web of blackmail, corruption, and political manipulation that challenges the very

core of democratic ideals. This volume exposes how deeply embedded these practices are within the fabric of U.S. governance and political life. It's a scathing indictment of how power operates in the shadows, manipulating leaders and shaping policies far removed from public scrutiny or consent.

4. *'Robert Maxwell, Israel's Superspy' by Gordon Thomas and Martin Dillon:* The saga becomes more intricate with the story of Mossad's Robert Maxwell, revealing a confluence of espionage, financial muscle, and criminality. Maxwell's life is a testament to how individual ambition and state agendas can intertwine, creating a complex web of global intrigue. His connections to Israeli intelligence and his mysterious death symbolize the opaque world where power, money, and secrets collide, influencing global politics from the shadows.

5. *'One Nation Under Blackmail Vol. 2' by Whitney Webb:* Webb's concluding volume deepens the narrative of elite manipulation in American politics. It's a continuation of the disturbing exploration of how covert operations, blackmail, and elite control shape national and international events. The depth and breadth of this manipulation painted across these pages suggest a systemic corrosion of democratic institutions, replaced by a shadow government operating under its own set of rules.

The synthesis of these works paints a chilling picture of a world held hostage by a cabal of elites, wielding tools of blackmail, financial power, and covert operations. This elitist group, operating beyond the reach of conventional law and public accountability, threatens to plunge the world into chaos and conflict, potentially igniting World War III.

This review is a patriotic call to action. It demands a radical restructuring of the United Nations into a Libertarian Federation of Nations, proposing a new world order where transparency, accountability, and the true principles of democracy reign supreme.

Only through such a profound transformation can we hope to dismantle the deep-rooted power structures that threaten the very essence of freedom and democracy. The time to act is now, to save humanity from the dystopian future that these rational elites have orchestrated.

RESTRUCTURING THE UNITED NATIONS INTO A LIBERTARIAN FEDERATION

When you are subverting the power of government,
that's a fundamentally dangerous thing to democracy.

- Edward Snowden

In an age marked by covert conflicts and manipulative statecraft, the need for a radical transformation in global governance has never been more urgent. The collusion of a powerful elitist cabal, *manipulating the geopolitical landscape,* threatens to plunge the world into chaos.

This review, drawing upon insights from five critical books, reveals the intricate web of power and deceit spun by these elites, and argues compellingly for the establishment of a Libertarian Federation of Nations as a safeguard against the impending global catastrophe.

Part 1: 'Kings and Presidents' by Bruce Riedel

Riedel's book provides a detailed analysis of the complex relationship between the United States and the Middle East, focusing primarily on Saudi Arabia. It reveals how American foreign policy, often driven by oil interests and political expediency, has shaped the dynamics in this volatile region. The book paints a picture of a geopolitical chess game, where nations are pawns, and the real players are the shadowy figures in the background, pulling the strings for their gain.

Part 2: 'Exercise of Power' by Robert Gates

Gates' work extends the conversation to a broader canvas, examining how the United States has used its immense power since World War II. It delves into various methods of exerting influence, from military interventions to economic sanctions and covert operations. This comprehensive view demonstrates how a nation's foreign policy can be co-opted by a cabal of elites, turning national agendas into tools for private ambition.

Part 3: 'Putin's People' by Catherine Belton

Belton's exploration into Russia's power structure, particularly during Putin's regime, offers insights into how a nation's political machinery can be hijacked by a few. It details the rise of oligarchs and their influence over Russian politics and global affairs. This book provides a crucial understanding of how state resources and policies can be weaponized for personal gain and global manipulation.

Part 4: 'Blood and Oil' by Bradley Hope and Justin Scheck

This book shifts the focus to Saudi Arabia, unraveling the modern power dynamics within the kingdom and its global impact. It highlights the consolidation of power under Mohammed bin Salman and how this has affected the geopolitics of oil, war, and finance. The narrative underscores the role of national leaders as puppets in the hands of the international financiers.

Part 5: 'The Shadow War' by Jim Sciutto

Sciutto's work brings to light the covert battles being waged across the world, often unnoticed by the general public. It demonstrates how nations like China and Russia engage in shadow wars, using tactics like cyber warfare and espionage to achieve their objectives. The book is a wake-up call to the insidious nature of modern warfare, driven not by national interests but by an elitist cabal's quest for control.

The synthesized analysis of these five books reveals a disturbing pattern: *a cabal of rational elites, operating through the American Deep State and other global powers, is driving the world towards a dystopian future.*

They have weaponized international politics, manipulating nations like pawns in a grand game of global domination. This shadow war is not just a threat to individual nations, but to humanity as a whole.

To counter this, a radical restructuring of global governance is imperative. The formation of a Libertarian Federation of Nations, replacing the current United Nations framework, emerges as a critical solution. Such a federation would decentralize power, dismantle the mechanisms of elitist control, and safeguard the world from the brink of a catastrophic World War III.

This new libertarian structure must prioritize transparency, individual liberties, and decentralized governance; effectively disempowering the cabal and restoring power to the people. It is not just a call for reform, but call to save humanity from the clutches of a dystopian nightmare, *orchestrated by the few, at the expense of the many.*

Steering Through Shadows Toward a Libertarian Federation

I can't in good conscience allow the U.S. government to destroy privacy, internet freedom and basic liberties for people around the world with this massive surveillance machine they're secretly building.

- Edward Snowden

In a world where geopolitical maneuvers are increasingly dictated by an elite cabal, the urgency for a transformative approach in global governance has reached a critical juncture. Through the lens of five pivotal books, the necessity of evolving the United Nations into a Libertarian Federation of Nations becomes readily apparent. This transformation is crucial to averting the looming threat of a global conflict instigated by the machinations of a shadowy elite that is pulling the strings on China and the American Deep State.

Part 1: 'The China Mirage' by James Bradley

Bradley's exploration begins with the historical roots of American foreign policy in Asia, especially China. The book unveils the misconceptions and missteps that have characterized the U.S.'s understanding and interactions with China. By shedding light on these historical blunders, Bradley sets the stage for understanding the contemporary complexities in Sino-American relations, and the role of misinformation and misguided policies therein.

Part 2: 'Age of Ambition' by Evan Osnos

Osnos takes the reader into the heart of modern China, depicting the aspirations and struggles of its people, amidst rapid economic and social changes. This narrative humanizes the Chinese experience, moving beyond political maneuverings to the impact on individuals. The book is crucial in understanding the internal dynamics of China, providing insights into how these internal transformations influence, *and are influenced,* by global politics.

Part 3: 'Stealth War' by Robert Spalding

Spalding's work delves into the covert aspects of global politics, focusing on how China has been waging a 'stealth war' against the West. This war, characterized by economic, technological, and psychological strategies, highlights the sophisticated and often invisible methods employed by state actors in pursuit of geopolitical dominance. It offers a critical perspective on the subtle yet profound ways in which global power dynamics are being shifted.

Part 4: 'America Second' by Isaac Fish

Fish's book serves as a critique of the current state of American foreign policy, arguing that U.S. interests are increasingly being sidelined in favor of an international agenda driven by this elitist cabal. It reveals the extent to which American sovereignty and decision-making are being compromised, contributing to a broader understanding of the challenges facing the current world order.

Part 5: 'Easternization' by Gideon Rachman

Rachman's analysis of the shifting global power from the West to the East, particularly to Asia, encapsulates the overarching theme of the changing world order. The book posits that this 'Easternization' is a pivotal element in the cabal's strategy, using the rise of Asian powers as a tool in their larger game of global control.

The synthesis of these five books paints a stark picture of a world being clandestinely steered towards a unified, totalitarian system under the guise of global conflicts and diplomatic chess games. This elitist cabal, *through its control over both China and the American Deep State,* is effectively weaponizing international politics to subjugate mass populations and establish a one-world government.

To counter this impending dystopia, the radical transformation of the United Nations into a Libertarian Federation of Nations, is necessary. This new global body would prioritize decentralization, individual liberties, and transparent governance, thereby dismantling the mechanisms of elite control.

Such a federation would not only prevent the drift into a global conflict, but would also restore power to the people, ensuring a future where humanity is free from the manipulative clutches of a rationally malevolent elite. This is not just a call for reformation, but a clarion call for a fundamental reshaping of global governance in the face of shadowy threats.

CONSTRUCTING A LIBERTARIAN FUTURE IN THE FACE OF COMMUNIST CHINA

The NSA and Israel wrote Stuxnet together; and they have built a military intelligence infrastructure that allows them to intercept almost everything. With this capability, the vast majority of human communications are automatically ingested without targeting. If I wanted to see your emails or your wife's phone, all I have to do is use intercepts. I can get your emails, passwords, phone records, credit cards.

- Edward Snowden

In the intricate web of global politics, a concerning narrative unfolds, as depicted in five crucial books. These texts collectively unravel a complex scenario where an elitist cabal, *manipulating China's Communist Party,* aims to dismantle American democracy and establish a totalitarian world order. This review endeavors to synthesize these insights, advocating for the transformation of the United Nations into a Libertarian Federation of Nations as a countermeasure to thwart this looming global threat.

Part 1: 'Reigning the Future' by Dennis Wang

Wang's book is an exploration into China's technological advancements and digital surveillance state. It lays the groundwork by detailing how China is using technology not just for economic growth, but also for maintaining a tight grip over its populace. This surveillance regime serves as a model for authoritarian control, hinting at the mechanisms that could be employed on a global scale.

Part 2: 'Deceiving the Sky' by Bill Gertz

Gertz's work further delves into China's strategic military and geopolitical maneuvers. It highlights how China, under the influence of this cabal, is positioning itself not just as a global economic power, but as a strategic military threat. The book underscores the methods through which China is seeking to challenge and potentially usurp American global dominance.

Part 3: 'A Series on Chinese Espionage Vol. 1' by Nicholas Eftimiades

Eftimiades exposes the extensive network of Chinese espionage that infiltrates other nations, particularly the U.S. This part of the analysis brings to light the subversive tactics employed to weaken foreign powers from within, illustrating a key component of the cabal's strategy to undermine democratic institutions globally.

Part 4: 'Chinese Communist Espionage' by Peter Mattis and Matthew Brazil

Building on the theme of espionage, Mattis and Brazil offer a comprehensive overview of the Chinese Communist Party's espionage activities. The book details the systemic and orchestrated efforts to steal intellectual property and sensitive information, signifying a broader campaign to destabilize competitors and advance the agenda of the cabal.

Part 5: 'Unrestricted Warfare' by Qiao Liang and Wang Xiangsui

The final book by Liang and Xiangsui provides a theoretical framework for understanding China's unconventional approach to warfare, which includes economic, cyber, and legal warfare. It presents a doctrine that transcends traditional military confrontations, encapsulating the multifaceted strategy of the cabal in achieving global dominance.

The synthesis of these works paints a chilling scenario where an elitist cabal, *manipulating China's communist-capitalist dynamics,* seeks to create a global totalitarian regime. This stealth war, *waged through technological surveillance, espionage, and unrestricted warfare tactics,* aims to subjugate populations and dismantle democratic institutions, particularly targeting American democracy as the final hurdle to overcome.

The counter to this dystopian vision lies in radically transforming the United Nations into a Libertarian Federation of Nations. This new entity would emphasize decentralized power, individual liberties, and transparent governance, directly challenging the cabal's centralizing and authoritarian tendencies.

By empowering nations and individuals, this federation would not only halt the march towards a totalitarian world order, but also lay the foundation for a future where freedom and democracy can flourish against the tide of authoritarianism. This is not merely a policy recommendation, but a call to action for the global community to recognize and resist the insidious forces seeking to control the future of humanity.

GLOBAL INEQUALITY REGIME DYNAMICS

Every person remembers some moment in their life where they witnessed some injustice, big or small, and looked away because the consequences of intervening seemed too intimidating. But there's a limit to the amount of incivility and inequality and inhumanity that each individual can tolerate.

- Edward Snowden

'Capital and Ideology' by Thomas Piketty is a profound exploration of economic history, focusing on the evolution of inequality and the structures that perpetuate it; and how 'The Network' has facilitated a global structure that effectively enslaves humanity through the fraudulent creation of debt.

Piketty's work begins with an extensive historical analysis of inequality. He argues that economic systems and ideologies are deeply intertwined, each shaping and reinforcing the other. The book traces the evolution of these ideologies across different societies and time periods, revealing how they justify and perpetuate economic disparities.

Tracing Inequality through History:

1. Inequality and Ideology: The book starts by establishing the relationship between economic systems and the ideologies that support them. Piketty examines various historical examples to demonstrate how ideologies have been used to justify economic inequality.

2. From Ternary Societies to Proprietarianism: Piketty delves into the evolution of early societies into more complex economic systems, focusing on the shift towards proprietarianism – the belief in the absolute right of property owners.

3. The Transformation of the West: This section explores the transformation of Western societies, particularly after the Industrial Revolution, and how new economic systems began to take shape.

4. Slavery and Colonialism: Piketty does not shy away from discussing the economic impacts of slavery and colonialism, highlighting how these practices were integral to the development of modern capitalism.

5. The Dynamics of Inequality: The focus shifts to the dynamics and mechanics of inequality, with an emphasis on how wealth and income disparities evolve over time.

6. The Great Transformation: Here, Piketty analyzes the significant societal changes that occurred in the 20th century, including the two World Wars and the Great Depression.

7. The Fall and Rise of Inequality: This chapter looks at the decline of inequality in the mid-20th century and its subsequent resurgence in recent decades.

8. Global Inequality Dynamics: The global perspective of inequality is explored, emphasizing the differences and similarities in inequality trends around the world.

9. Ideological Shifts: Piketty discusses the shifts in ideologies that have accompanied changes in economic structures, particularly in the late 20th and early 21st centuries.

10. Educational Inequality: The focus is on the role of education in perpetuating economic disparities.

11. Inequality and Capitalism: This chapter delves deeper into the relationship between capitalism and inequality, critiquing how capitalist structures inherently produce disparities.

12. Rethinking the Dimensions of Political Conflict: Piketty reexamines political conflicts in the context of economic inequality, suggesting new ways to understand these dynamics.

13. From Social Democracy to Hypercapitalism: The transformation from social democracy to a more extreme form of capitalism is analyzed.

14. Borders and Inequality: The impact of borders and immigration on economic disparities is explored.

15. Globalization and Inequality: Piketty discusses how globalization has affected economic inequality, both positively and negatively.

16. The Crisis of Hypercapitalism: This chapter discusses the current crisis in hypercapitalist societies, setting the stage for his proposal in the final chapter.

17. Participatory Socialism: In the final chapter, Piketty introduces the concept of participatory socialism, a proposed economic system aimed at addressing the issues of inequality highlighted throughout the book. This model emphasizes more equitable wealth distribution, greater worker participation in decision-making, and a more progressive tax system. Piketty argues that such a system would not only be fairer but also more efficient and sustainable in the long run.

The historical journey through economic systems and ideologies culminates in an understanding of how contemporary society has become enslaved to debt. Piketty illustrates how inequality regimes, justified and structured by these ideologies, have led to a world where a significant portion of the population is burdened by debt. This debt is not just financial; it is also social, intellectual, and political, representing a broader system of obligations that perpetuates the status quo.

Piketty's 'Capital and Ideology' is a call to rethink our economic systems and ideologies. By understanding the historical context of these inequality regimes, we can begin to envision a world structured not on the perpetuation of debt and disparity, but on principles of equity and participation. This change, however, requires a fundamental shift in both thought and practice, moving towards what Piketty describes as participatory socialism.

FROM A CAPTURED LIBERAL ORDER TO LIBERTARIAN REFORM

Congress hasn't declared war on the countries - the majority of them are our allies - but without asking for public permission, NSA is running network operations against them that affect millions of innocent people. And for what? So we can have secret access to a computer in a country we're not even fighting?

- Edward Snowden

The contemporary global landscape is marked by a complex interplay of economic, political, and social dynamics. This review aims to analyze and synthesize the core themes of five influential books, to argue for the need for a Libertarian Federation of Nations. This new governance structure is proposed as a solution to counteract the subversion of American democracy and the broader liberal order by an elitist cabal, which is purportedly leading the world towards a totalitarian one-world government.

Part 1: 'Civilization' by Niall Ferguson

Ferguson explores the historical factors that contributed to the rise of Western dominance, focusing on six 'killer apps' that these societies adopted. This analysis serves as a foundation for understanding how Western civilization has evolved and influenced global governance structures. The book's insights into the interplay of economic and political systems, set the stage for understanding the current challenges facing the liberal order.

Part 2: 'The Last Empire' by Gore Vidal

Vidal delves into the American political and social landscape, critiquing the direction of U.S. foreign and domestic policy. This part examines how the United States, as a central figure in the liberal order, has navigated complex international relations and internal dynamics. Vidal's critique provides a perspective on the potential pitfalls and challenges within the American system that contribute to global governance issues.

Part 3: 'Underground Empire' by Henry Farrell

Farrell's work on global financial and political networks, offers a critical examination of the shadowy interconnections that influence global economics and politics. This segment uses Farrell's analysis to understand how covert networks, *and informal power structures,* have begun to undermine traditional governance models, contributing to the instability of the liberal order.

Part 4: 'Geopolitics & Democracy' by Peter Trubowitz and Brian Burgoon

Trubowitz and Burgoon's exploration of the relationship between geopolitics and democracy, sheds light on the tension between national interests and democratic values in shaping international relations; while discussing how the balance of power and the pursuit of democratic ideals often clash, leading to compromises and complexities in global governance.

Part 5: 'The Crisis of Democratic Capitalism' by Martin Wolf

Wolf's analysis of the challenges facing democratic capitalism highlights the systemic issues within the economic and political structures that underpin the liberal order. This final part focuses on the inherent contradictions and vulnerabilities within democratic capitalism, which is obviously being exploited by the elitist cabal to further their agenda.

The synthesis of these five works leads to a foreboding conclusion: *the Western liberal order, once a beacon of democracy and economic prosperity, is now ensnared by multinational conglomerates and a central banking cartel.* This elite group is weaponizing the global economy, and international relations, to dismantle the liberal order, aiming for totalitarian control through the imposition of terror and poverty.

To counter this dystopian trajectory, a radical reformation of global governance is required through the establishment of a Libertarian Federation of Nations. This federation will bridge the gap between nations, restore the essence of citizenship, and create a network of public banks operating with a digital currency. *It will also involve dismantling the American Deep State, seen as a crucial step in eliminating the influence of the elitist cabal.*

This new form of libertarian global governance is envisioned as a means to preserve humanity from the clutches of a totalitarian nightmare. It emphasizes decentralization, the empowerment of individual liberties, and the dismantling of monopolistic power structures. Ultimately, this conclusion calls for a profound transformation in global governance, advocating for a libertarian technocratic approach as the antidote to the challenges posed by the current geopolitical and economic landscape.

THE NEED FOR A
UNITED NATIONS REFORMATION

It is understood that, in the long run,
an all destroying conflict can be avoided only by
the setting up of a world federation of nations.

– Albert Einstein

REAL INTERNATIONAL DYNAMICS

A Synthesis of John Mearsheimer's Works

The sad fact is that international politics has always been a ruthless and dangerous business, and it is likely to remain that way.

- John Mearsheimer

Our ominous journey commences with *'The Tragedy of Great Power Politics,' where Mearsheimer* paints a grim portrait of international relations. He posits that the quest for power, driven by the relentless nature of states, engenders a perpetual cycle of conflict and dominance. This brutal realist perspective unveils the harsh reality where states are entrapped in a merciless struggle for survival in an anarchic global arena, devoid of any overarching authority to maintain peace.

In *'The Israel Lobby,' Mearsheimer* delves into the shadowy corridors of power, exposing how influential lobbying groups, particularly those advocating for Israel, manipulate U.S. foreign policy. He reveals a disquieting scenario where these entities bend policies to favor Israel, often at the cost of the long-term interests of both the United States and Israel. This analysis lays bare the insidious nature of lobbying in skewing international relations and exacerbating the complexities of power dynamics.

'Why Leaders Lie' peers into the deceit-laden underbelly of statecraft. Mearsheimer explores the unsettling rationale behind leaders' lies to their nations and the world, often masked as acts of national security, political necessity, or moral obligation. This web of deceit thickens the fog in international relations, erecting barriers to trust and cooperation among nations, and making the global landscape even more treacherous.

In *'The Great Delusion,' Mearsheimer* casts a critical eye on liberal internationalism, denouncing the futility and destructiveness of imposing liberal democracy globally. He argues that the American crusade to remodel the world in its image is a doomed endeavor, leading to militarization, wars that erode peace, harm human rights, and corrode liberal values at home. This critique exposes the hypocrisy and peril inherent in such idealistic yet hegemonic pursuits.

'How States Think' plunges into the cognitive abyss of state decision-making. Mearsheimer examines how states, guided by their flawed perceptions and biases, often make irrational decisions, leading to catastrophic misunderstandings and conflicts. This insight is key to understanding the labyrinth of international politics, where misjudgments and paranoia frequently precipitate crises.

Synthesizing Mearsheimer's ominous revelations, the imperative for a radical overhaul of the United Nations becomes starkly clear. Grasping the realist nature of international relations, the corrosive impact of lobbying, the ubiquity of deception in statecraft, the delusion of liberal hegemony, and the flawed cognition of states, we confront the daunting task of reforming the United Nations.

This envisioned reformation is not just a restructuring but a complete reimagining of global governance – an intensely difficult endeavor to forge a United Nations capable of navigating the treacherous waters of international politics. It demands transparency, accountability, and a sober acknowledgment of the diversity of political and cultural landscapes.

The reformed United Nations, emerging from the shadows of current inadequacies, must not only strive to avert conflict, but also guide humanity towards a heightened state of collective self-awareness and introspection, and cultivate our leadership into embracing both hubris and humility; crucial for surviving in the unforgiving world of international politics.

Mearsheimer's works are a chilling testament to the convoluted, often sinister nature of global relations, underscoring the dire need for a United Nations capable of confronting these realities in a bid for a more equitable, sustainable, and, hopefully, peaceful world.

DECIPHERING THE GEOPOLITICAL CODE

It seems to many of us that if we are to avoid the eventual catastrophic world conflict, we must strengthen the United Nations as a first step toward a world government patterned after our own government with a legislature, executive and judiciary, and a police to enforce its international laws and keep the peace.

- Walter Conkrite

Peter Zeihan's 'Disunited Nations' is a bold foray into the geopolitical landscapes that are shaping the current global order. Zeihan's expertise as a geopolitical strategist comes to the forefront as he dissects the fate of nations in the face of declining American interest in global leadership. Through sixteen chapters, Zeihan paints a picture of a world where geography is destiny, and demographics shape power.

Core Thesis: Zeihan argues that the world order, as maintained by American military and economic power since World War II, is unraveling. He posits that the United States, with its intrinsic geographical advantages and self-sufficiency in energy and food, is likely to retreat into isolationism. This retreat will lead to a more chaotic global system where traditional powers struggle to maintain their influence.

Chapter Summaries:

1. *The End of the World...:* Introduces the concept of the American-led global order and sets the stage for its potential end.

2. *...And the Beginning of History:* Discusses the return of historical regional powers and rivalries after the decline of American global influence.

3. *The (American) Empire Strikes Out:* Explores how America's disinterest in global affairs will affect international economic ties and military alliances.

4. *The New Middle East:* Focuses on the Middle East, predicting a post-American scenario where regional dynamics and conflicts will reshape the area.

5. *The Future of Europe:* Examines the European Union's challenges in the face of a declining population and the absence of American security guarantees.

6. *The Asian Heartland:* Delves into the strategic importance of Central Asia and how power struggles there will shape the broader region's future.

7. *China's Nightmare:* Forecasts the difficulties China will face, including demographic decline, regionalism, and a lack of allies.

8. *The World Island:* Analyzes Russia's potential to leverage its geography and resources despite its demographic and economic challenges.

9. *The Land of the Rising Sun:* Assesses Japan's ability to reassert itself militarily and economically in Asia once the U.S. steps back.

10. *The World's Breadbaskets:* Examines nations like Brazil and Argentina that may benefit from their agricultural capacity in a more fragmented world.

11. *The Coming African Boom:* Surmises that certain African nations might capitalize on their demographic dividends to become emerging markets.

12. *The Anglosphere and the World:* Details the advantages English-speaking countries will enjoy in terms of demographics, economics, and military alliances.

13. *The Next Generation of Conflict:* Predicts future conflicts, considering regional power vacuums and the scramble for resources.

14. *The Arsenal of Democracy:* Explores how the U.S. can maintain its strategic interests through military and technological superiority.

15. *The New Networks of Trade:* Envisions the reshaping of global trade routes and alliances as America withdraws from its policing role.

16. *The Americans:* Culminates with a portrayal of the U.S. as a resilient nation poised to thrive amid global disorder.

With the world moving towards regionalism and away from globalism, we must create a transitional stratagem for international stability, economic connectivity, and national sovereignty… 'Disunited Nations' provides a comprehensive examination of the factors influencing the success and failure of nations in a post-American world.

Zeihan's work invites readers to reconsider the foundations of global power and the future of international relations by thinking critically about our own nation's roles in the unfolding geopolitical drama.

A Clarion Call for a United Nations Reformation

> If the United Nations once admits that international disputes can be settled by using force, then we will have destroyed the foundation of the organization and our best hope of establishing a world order.
>
> *- Dwight D. Eisenhower*

The Dichotomy of Globalization: Ian Bremmer's 'Us vs. Them' lays the foundation for this analysis by highlighting the growing schism between global and national interests. Bremmer articulates how globalization has engendered a sense of alienation and disenfranchisement among certain populations, leading to a rise in nationalistic sentiments. This dichotomy sets the stage for exploring the interconnectedness of global trade, power dynamics, and the evolution of international governance.

The Role of Trade in Shaping Global Relations: Building upon Bremmer's thesis, Hoschberg's 'Trade is Not a Four Letter Word' reframes the conversation around globalization through the lens of trade. He argues that trade, often vilified, is actually a crucial component of international cooperation and economic development. This perspective underscores the need for a revised understanding of global economic interdependencies, suggesting that a reformed United Nations could leverage trade as a tool for fostering greater global unity and equitable resource distribution.

Power Dynamics in Global Governance: Noam Chomsky's 'Who Rules the World' delves into the power dynamics that underpin current international relations. Chomsky critiques the existing global order, dominated by a few powerful nations and corporate interests, which often undermines the collective good. His analysis points to the necessity for a more democratic and inclusive form of global governance, aligning with the need for United Nations reformation to ensure fair representation and equitable resource management.

Adapting to a Changing World Order: Ray Dalio's insights in 'Principles for Dealing with the Changing World Order' provide a strategic framework for navigating the complexities of the 21st-century world. Dalio emphasizes the importance of understanding historical cycles and adapting to the emerging global realities. His principles can guide the restructuring of the United Nations, ensuring it is equipped to manage the dynamic interplay of economic, environmental, and technological forces shaping our world.

Envisioning a Technocratic and Equitable Future: Jaron Lanier's 'Who Owns the Future' brings a critical focus on the role of technology in shaping economic and social outcomes. Lanier advocates for a more equitable distribution of technological benefits, warning against a future where a few monopolize data and resources. His vision suggests that a reformed United Nations could champion a technocratic approach to governance, ensuring that technological advancements serve humanity collectively, fostering a metacognitive state.

Synthesizing the arguments presented in these books, this analysis posits that a reformation of the United Nations is imperative. By incorporating Hoschberg's insights on trade, embracing Chomsky's call for equitable power distribution, applying Dalio's principles for adapting to changing global dynamics, and integrating Lanier's vision for a technologically equitable future, we can envision a reformed United Nations.

This new entity would not only manage finite resources more equitably but also propel humanity towards a metacognitive state, transcending current geopolitical constraints. The synthesis of these diverse perspectives underlines the urgency of transforming the United Nations into a more effective, technocratic, and inclusive body, capable of addressing the multifaceted challenges of our global community.

Plato's Vision: A Path to Renewing Democracy

Good people do not need laws to tell them to act responsibly,
while bad people will find a way around the laws.

- Plato

In the quest for an interdependent global democratic reformation, a revisitation of *Plato's 'The Republic and Other Works'* offers profound insights. The ancient philosopher's vision, articulated in these texts, serves as a guiding beacon for systems-engineering an international constitutional reformation. This inquiry aims to analyze Plato's concepts and explore their application in the context of rewriting the U.S. Constitution as a foundation for this global reformation, emphasizing the necessity of a systems-engineering stratagem to restore and enhance democracy.

Plato's Philosophical Foundations

Plato's 'The Republic' is a cornerstone of Western philosophy, providing an intricate exploration of justice, governance, and societal structures. Central to his philosophy is the concept of an ideal state governed by philosopher-kings, individuals who possess wisdom, virtue, and a deep understanding of the Forms – eternal and immutable truths. In contrast to the empirical world, the realm of the Forms represents the pinnacle of knowledge and ethical standards.

Plato's ideal society is stratified into three classes: rulers (philosopher-kings), auxiliaries (warriors), and producers (artisans, farmers, etc.). This structure, he argues, ensures that each individual contributes to society in a manner befitting their natural aptitude and training. It is a vision where justice prevails when everyone performs their chosen and assigned roles without overstepping.

The Republic and Modern Constitutional Thought

Transposing Plato's ideals to the contemporary endeavor of constitutional rewriting involves interpreting his principles through a modern lens. Cultivating the philosopher-king model, now possible via the utilization of online social networks, symbolizes the need for enlightened and morally sound leadership. In the context of an online social network, this implies that we must cultivate and select delegates, not merely for their political acumen, but for their wisdom, ethical grounding, and commitment to the public good.

Plato's emphasis on justice as a harmonious functioning of society's parts has direct implications for constitutional law. A revised constitution must ensure a balance of power among government branches, equitable representation, and the protection of minority rights, reflecting the Platonic ideal of a just society where each part fulfills its purpose.

Education and the Enlightened Citizenry

A pivotal theme in Plato's works is the role of education. He posits that a well-educated populace, capable of critical thinking and understanding the greater good, is essential for a just society. In revising the Constitution, there is an implicit call for an educational overhaul – one that fosters civic responsibility, critical analysis, and an understanding of democratic principles among citizens.

Plato's Cave: Enlightenment and Reality

The Allegory of the Cave, a profound segment in 'The Republic,' metaphorically illustrates the journey from ignorance to enlightenment. In the context of constitutional reform, this allegory serves as a reminder of the challenge in recognizing and overcoming existing biases and misconceptions. It emphasizes the need for a collective awakening to the realities of governance and societal needs.

Integration and Conclusion: Plato's Guidance in Constitutional Reform

Integrating Plato's philosophies into the process of constitutional reform requires a nuanced approach. The ideal state, as envisioned by Plato, is unattainable in its original form but serves as a philosophical template. The essence of his thought – the pursuit of justice, enlightened leadership, educated citizenry, and recognition of universal truths – are timeless principles that can profoundly inform the modern constitutional process.

In calling for a new international reformation, there is an opportunity to embed these Platonic ideals into the very fabric of our democratic evolution. By doing so, the reformed international constitutions would not only address the immediate challenges of governance, but also lay a foundation for a society that aspires towards the greater good, echoing the philosophical wisdom of Plato.

The road to restoring democracy through a United Nations Reformation is complex and demanding. However, with Plato's guidance, it is not only a feasible journey but also a necessary one to ensure a society where justice, wisdom, and the collective well-being are paramount. The Republic's age-old wisdom, thus, becomes a beacon for modern constitutionalism, illuminating the path to a more enlightened and just society.

TECHNOCRATIC SELF-GOVERNANCE
Literature Review

Governing a great nation is like cooking a small fish…
too much handling will spoil it.

- Lao Tzu

Towards an Enlightened Technocracy
Synthesizing Insights for a New World

Will Storr's 'The Status Game' sets the stage for this exploration by delving into the human obsession with status. Storr argues that the pursuit of status, a deeply ingrained aspect of human nature, often drives behavior and shapes societal structures. This quest, while a powerful motivator, can lead to narcissistic and divisive tendencies, emphasizing the need for a paradigm shift in how we perceive and pursue status.

Vandana Shiva's 'Oneness vs the 1%' builds on the theme of status but shifts the focus to the global elite's role in perpetuating inequality and environmental degradation. Shiva critiques the prevailing economic systems that empower a small fraction of the population at the expense of the many, leading to social and ecological imbalances. Her thesis underscores the necessity of resisting elitist agendas and fostering a more equitable and sustainable world.

'The Fourth Turning' by William Strauss and Neil Howe introduces the concept of cyclical societal transformations, suggesting that every society undergoes a series of predictable phases, or 'turnings'. This perspective offers a framework for understanding and embracing the current era of change, often marked by crisis but also by opportunities for significant societal renewal and reorientation.

Brené Brown's 'Atlas of the Heart' provides a crucial emotional and psychological dimension to this discourse. Brown explores the human capacity for empathy, connection, and understanding, arguing that meaningful emotional engagement is essential for overcoming societal challenges. Her work points towards the need for a deeper, more compassionate approach to interpersonal and societal relationships.

286

Elizabeth Kolbert's 'The Sixth Extinction' offers a stark warning about the ongoing mass extinction event, largely driven by human activity causing the end of biodiversity. Kolbert's detailed account of species loss and environmental degradation serves as a call to action to prevent ecological collapse, emphasizing the critical need for immediate and concerted efforts to protect the planet.

The synthesis of these diverse yet interconnected perspectives points towards the necessity of an enlightened technocratic framework for global governance.

- The insights from 'The Status Game' highlight the need to transcend status-oriented narcissistic desires.

- 'Oneness vs the 1%' underscores the urgency of countering elitist agendas and promoting equitable systems.

- 'The Fourth Turning' provides a lens for understanding and navigating societal transformations.

- 'Atlas of the Heart' emphasizes the importance of empathy and connection in this process.

- Finally, 'The Sixth Extinction' serves as a stark reminder of the ecological stakes involved.

Creating an enlightened technocratic framework involves integrating these insights into a holistic approach to governance. This framework must prioritize equitable resource distribution, environmental sustainability, empathetic leadership, and a deep understanding of societal cycles and human nature.

By doing so, it is possible to evolve into a humanistic world order that is not only technologically advanced, but also deeply humane and ecologically conscious. *This synthesis proposes a future where humanity transcends narrow self-interests for a collective, sustainable, and empathetic global society.*

Building a Transparent Technocracy
Countering Elitism and Shaping a Humanistic New World Order

Carroll Quigley's 'Tragedy and Hope' sets the foundation of this analysis by exploring the historical evolution of global power structures. Quigley delves into the interplay between financial and political elites, tracing how these interactions have shaped global events and policies. This groundwork is crucial for understanding the dynamics of power and influence that have historically governed world affairs.

Niall Ferguson's 'The House of Rothschild Vol. 2' further elucidates the role of financial magnates in shaping global politics. Ferguson's detailed account of the Rothschild family's influence in European financial and political arenas during the 19th century underscores the power wielded by financial elites over international affairs. This perspective offers a historical view of how concentrated financial power can influence global governance.

Anthony Sutton's 'Wall Street and the Rise of Hitler' examines the role of American financial and corporate interests in the rise of Nazi Germany. Sutton argues that Wall Street elites played a significant role in financing and supporting Hitler's regime, showcasing a disturbing example of how economic forces can support oppressive governments.

E.C. Knuth's 'Empire of the City' delves into the geopolitical dynamics that have shaped modern world affairs. Knuth argues that a small group of financial and political elites, primarily centered in key cities like London, have a disproportionate influence on global politics. This book highlights the concentration of power in certain global hubs and its implications for international relations.

William Carr's 'Pawns in the Game' presents a more conspiratorial view of global events, suggesting that many major historical events are the result of deliberate actions by a secretive elite cabal. While controversial, Carr's perspective adds to the narrative of power concentration and manipulation at the global level.

Integrating the insights from these books, the conclusion calls for the creation of an incorruptible, transparent technocratic framework in reforming the United Nations and other international bodies.

This new framework would aim to dismantle the disproportionate influence of a small elite over global affairs, as highlighted in the analyses of Ferguson, Sutton, Knuth, and

Carr. Drawing on Quigley's historical patterns of power, the proposed system would prioritize transparency, accountability, and equitable representation to ensure that no single group or interest can dominate global governance.

The envisioned technocratic network would use data-driven and scientifically informed approaches to address global challenges, reducing the risk of manipulation by any elite group.

By incorporating diverse voices and expertise into the envisioned reformation, this technocratic self-governing system aims to foster a transformative shift in societal structures.

This shift would emphasize the overall well-being of society and advance humanity towards a higher state of self-awareness and understanding, while countering the potential rise of an oppressive one-world government.

This framework asserts the importance of vigilance against the concentration of power and advocates for a more democratic, equitable, and scientifically grounded approach to global governance, aiming to foster a world order that benefits all of humanity, rather than a select few.

Evolving into Metacognition
Power, Perception, and Preparedness

Niall Ferguson's 'The Square and the Tower' presents a compelling narrative on how historical power structures, both formal (the Tower) and informal (the Square), have shaped societies. Ferguson illustrates that networks have always been pivotal in the dissemination of ideas and power. Understanding these dynamics is crucial in comprehending modern global politics and power networks, setting a foundation for rethinking the current structures of governance and influence.

Jaron Lanier, in 'You are Not a Gadget,' critiques the current digital landscape dominated by big tech companies. He argues that these platforms often diminish individuality and promote a herd mentality. This perspective is vital for understanding the ways in which modern networked structures can lead to a loss of personal autonomy and critical thinking, further influencing the power dynamics addressed by Ferguson.

Hans Rosling's 'Factfulness' provides an optimistic counterpoint to doom-laden perspectives, urging readers to adopt a more nuanced, data-driven view of the world. Rosling emphasizes the importance of understanding and interpreting data correctly to overcome misconceptions about global issues. This approach is crucial for informed decision-making, especially within the powerful networks discussed in Ferguson's and Lanier's works.

Building on Rosling's emphasis on data, *Darrell Huff's 'How to Lie with Statistics'* delves into the misuse of statistical data. Huff illustrates how statistics can be manipulated to serve specific agendas, highlighting the need for critical analysis and understanding of data, a skill essential for navigating the misleading narratives that can emerge in powerful networks.

Nassim Nicholas Taleb's 'The Black Swan' introduces the concept of highly improbable events with massive impacts. Taleb's insights into unpredictability and risk management are pivotal for developing robust systems and policies, especially within the context of global governance and power structures.

Integrating the insights from these diverse, yet interconnected works, leads to a compelling argument for an enlightened technocratic framework within the United Nations. This framework should prioritize metacognition - the understanding of one's own thought processes - as a key component for global leadership.

Ferguson's analysis of networks underscores the need for transparency and accountability in global governance. Lanier's call for individuality in the digital age is a reminder to preserve personal autonomy and critical thinking within these networks. Rosling's and Huff's works emphasize the importance of data literacy to see through statistical manipulations and make informed decisions. Finally, Taleb's concept of the Black Swan stresses the importance of preparing for unpredictable global challenges.

This synthesized framework advocates for a technocracy that is not only advanced and data-driven, but also deeply aware of human cognitive biases, power dynamics, and the unpredictability of global events. By fostering metacognitive skills, this approach aims to create a more resilient, informed, and adaptive global governance structure capable of facing the complexities of the modern world.

Revolutionizing Governance
Towards an Agile and Technocratic Future

Frederic Laloux's 'Reinventing Organizations' lays the foundational idea of this synthesis. Laloux discusses how organizations can evolve beyond conventional management hierarchies to embrace more fluid, holistic, and purpose-driven models. This evolution is crucial for breaking down rigid corporate structures and fostering innovation, setting the stage for a more integrated approach to business and governance.

Gillian Tett's 'The Silo Effect' highlights the dangers of organizational silos that restrict information flow and hinder collaboration. Tett argues that breaking down these silos can lead to more innovative and efficient organizations. This concept aligns with Laloux's vision, emphasizing the need for interconnectedness and cross-functional collaboration in modern business and governance structures.

In 'The Entrepreneurial State,' Mariana Mazzucato challenges the notion that innovation is solely the domain of private sector entrepreneurs. She argues that the state plays a critical role in fostering innovation through strategic investments and partnerships. Mazzucato's perspective broadens the scope of Laloux's and Tett's ideas, suggesting that an entrepreneurial approach to governance can drive systemic change.

David Epstein's 'Range' argues for the value of generalists in an increasingly specialized world. Epstein posits that individuals with broad skills and experiences are more adept at innovation and problem-solving. This idea complements the previous works by advocating for a versatile approach to expertise, vital for the proposed business ecosystem and technocratic governance.

In 'BE 2.0,' Jim Collins and Bill Lazier explore the principles and practices that enable businesses to achieve long-term success. Their insights into leadership, strategy, and organizational culture provide practical guidance on building resilient and adaptive organizations, aligning with the overarching theme of a more agile and interconnected business environment.

The synthesis of these five books presents a compelling case for restructuring corporate and governance models into a more agile, entrepreneurial, and interconnected ecosystem. *Laloux's evolutionary organizational models, Tett's advocacy for breaking down silos, Mazzucato's emphasis on state-led innovation,*

Epstein's call for versatility, and Collins and Lazier's strategies for enduring success converge to support the thesis of this proposed business and governance framework. This framework would transcend traditional corporate silos and bureaucratic barriers, fostering a small business entrepreneurship ecosystem that encourages innovation, collaboration, and versatility.

Such an ecosystem would not only enhance business efficiency and creativity but also pave the way for a more effective and responsive technocratic United Nations, capable of addressing the complex challenges of the 21st century.

The proposed framework is not just a blueprint for business reformation but a call to action for a holistic reimagining of how organizations and governance can operate synergistically. It advocates for a paradigm shift towards a more agile, technocratic, and interconnected global community, where business innovation and governance reform, work hand in hand to create a sustainable and prosperous future.

Reshaping Our Economic Paradigm
From Debt-Driven to Enlightened Economic Structures

Kwasi Kwarteng's 'War and Gold' provides a historical backdrop for understanding the current debt-based economy. It traces the relationship between warfare, economic policies, and the reliance on gold as a financial standard. This historical perspective sets the stage for a discussion on how modern economies have become burdened by debt, influenced by past events and decisions.

Steven Levitt and Stephen Dubner's 'Freakonomics' introduces unconventional thinking about economics, focusing on the hidden side of everything. By exploring unique correlations and unexpected causes of various economic and social phenomena, the book challenges traditional economic thinking and highlights the complexities of modern economic systems.

'Superfreakonomics' delves deeper into their unconventional economic analysis. *Levitt and Dubner* examine a wider range of topics, offering insights into how economic principles can be applied to diverse and often surprising aspects of life. This approach encourages a broader understanding of the economic forces at play in our world.

Richard Florida's 'The New Urban Crisis' shifts the focus to the urban scale, discussing how contemporary cities are central to economic issues. Florida explores the growing divide within cities, the concentration of wealth, and the challenges of urbanization, emphasizing the need to rethink urban economic structures as part of a larger economic overhaul.

Jim Collins' 'Good to Great and the Social Sectors' offers a perspective on how principles of organizational excellence can be applied to non-profit and social sectors. Collins argues for the importance of effective leadership and strategic thinking in these sectors, which are often at the frontline of dealing with the consequences of economic policies.

The synthesis of these books presents a compelling argument for restructuring our economic systems. Kwarteng's historical analysis, combined with Levitt and Dubner's innovative economic perspectives, sets the stage for understanding the complexity and interconnectedness of our current economic challenges. Florida's focus on urban economics highlights the microcosmic effects of these challenges, while Collins' insights into organizational excellence suggest pathways for effective responses.

By integrating the economic examples and theories presented in these works, we can support the thesis of creating an enlightened synthesis of institutional indoctrinations to prevent cultural determinism from leading to economic and social demise.

This new economic paradigm would move away from a debt-driven focus, emphasizing instead sustainable growth, equitable distribution of resources, and innovative economic thinking that can adapt to and address the complexities of the modern world.

In essence, this synthesis calls for a holistic reevaluation of our economic principles and practices. It suggests a pivot towards economic models that are more inclusive, adaptable, and aligned with the long-term wellbeing of societies, thereby preventing the catastrophic consequences of a narrowly focused, elite-driven economic system.

Towards a Holistic Health Revolution
Reclaiming the Commons Through Enlightened Societal Systems

David Sinclair's 'Lifespan' serves as the foundational text, introducing the science behind aging and longevity. Sinclair posits that aging can be slowed or even reversed by manipulating certain biological pathways. This revolutionary perspective on health and aging underscores the importance of systemic changes in society to support longevity.

Robert Sapolsky's 'Why Zebras Don't Get Ulcers' delves into the physiological effects of stress on the human body. By comparing the stress responses of humans to animals like zebras, Sapolsky highlights how chronic stress in modern human societies contributes significantly to health issues. This understanding is crucial for reforming societal systems that exacerbate stress.

Vandana Shiva's 'Reclaiming the Commons' shifts the focus towards environmental and social well-being. Shiva argues for the importance of protecting the commons – shared resources like water, air, and land – from privatization and exploitation. She emphasizes that the health of our environment directly influences the health of individuals, advocating for systemic changes to safeguard these common resources.

In 'UnDo It!', Dean Ornish presents a comprehensive approach to health, centered around lifestyle changes. Ornish's research demonstrates how diet, exercise, stress management, and social connections can reverse chronic diseases. His work offers practical guidance on how individual choices, supported by societal systems, can significantly improve health outcomes.

Mark Hyman's 'Food Fix' explores the link between the global food system and health issues. Hyman critiques the current industrialized food system, which prioritizes profit over health, and suggests ways to shift towards more sustainable, nutritious food production. This book underlines the need for systemic changes to ensure access to healthy food for all.

Synthesizing these texts, it becomes evident that a comprehensive reformation of societal systems is necessary to enhance holistic health. Sinclair's insights into the biological mechanisms of aging and health, combined with Sapolsky's exploration of stress, lay the groundwork for understanding the systemic nature of health issues. Shiva's advocacy for the commons introduces an environmental dimension, stressing the interconnectedness of ecological and human health.

Ornish's lifestyle-centric approach provides practical avenues for individual and collective health improvements, while Hyman's analysis of food systems highlights the crucial role of nutrition in public health. The common thread across these books is the need for a systemic overhaul – from how we manage stress and the environment, to our approach to food and lifestyle.

The conclusion supports a thesis advocating for an enlightened technocratic framework aimed at evolving society's approach to health. This framework would integrate scientific insights with policy-making, prioritize environmental protection, support stress-reducing societal structures, encourage healthy lifestyle choices, and reform the global food system.

Such a holistic approach not only aims to enhance individual health, but also seeks to create a sustainable, health-oriented society that benefits all.

Cultivating Resilience and Whole-Brain Development
A Technocratic Approach to Overcoming Trauma and Enhancing Human Potential

Yuval Harari's 'Sapiens' sets the stage by tracing the evolution of humankind. Harari explores the cognitive revolution, agricultural revolution, and the rise of empires, elucidating how these pivotal changes shaped human societies and our psychological makeup. This evolutionary perspective provides a backdrop for understanding the complexity of human brain development and trauma.

David Reich's 'Who We Are and How We Got Here' delves into the genetic history of human populations. By examining ancient DNA, Reich uncovers the migrations, interbreeding, and cultural transformations that have influenced our genetic makeup. This genetic perspective offers insights into the diverse needs and developmental paths of children across different cultures and histories.

In 'The Whole-Brain Child,' Daniel Siegel and Tina Bryson focus on the development of children's brains. They emphasize the importance of nurturing both the left (logical) and right (emotional) sides of the brain for balanced development. Their approach provides practical strategies for parents and educators to help children integrate their emotional and intellectual experiences, fostering resilience and well-being.

Bessel Van Der Kolk's 'The Body Keeps the Score' explores the profound impact of trauma on both the body and mind. Van Der Kolk demonstrates how trauma can disrupt the nervous system and affect physical and mental health long-term. His work underscores the importance of addressing trauma in children to prevent its lifelong consequences.

Nina Brown's 'Children of the Self-Absorbed' examines the effects of being raised by narcissistic parents. Brown illustrates how such parenting can lead to emotional trauma and hinder a child's ability to develop a healthy sense of self. This book emphasizes the critical role of parenting in shaping a child's emotional and cognitive development.

The synthesis of these five books highlights the need for a holistic, technocratically guided approach to childhood development and trauma prevention. Harari's exploration of human evolution and Reich's genetic insights provide a broad context for understanding human diversity and developmental needs. Siegel and Bryson's whole-brain approach, coupled with Van Der Kolk's insights into trauma, suggests a need for parenting and educational systems that support emotional, cognitive, and psychological health. Brown's focus on the impact of parenting styles further emphasizes the importance of educating and supporting parents in nurturing their children's development.

The conclusion advocates for an enlightened technocratic framework that integrates scientific knowledge and practical strategies to support children's development. This framework would involve crafting policies and programs informed by our evolutionary and genetic heritage, emphasizing whole-brain development, addressing trauma from early stages, and guiding parents towards nurturing and empathetic child-rearing practices.

Such an approach aims not only to mitigate the effects of childhood trauma, but also to enhance the overall developmental potential of future generations, thereby contributing to the evolution and resilience of our society.

Nourishing the Future
A Synthesis of Regenerative Agriculture and Nutritional Vitality

The journey begins with *Vandana Shiva's 'Who Really Feeds the World?'* which challenges conventional agricultural practices and introduces the concept of regenerative agriculture. Shiva argues that the current food production system, heavily reliant on industrial methods, is not only environmentally unsustainable but also fails to adequately nourish the world's population. She advocates for a return to more traditional, organic farming practices that respect biodiversity and enhance soil health, positing that such methods are key to sustaining both the planet and its inhabitants.

Building on Shiva's foundations, *Dan Buettner's 'The Blue Zones'* explores regions of the world where people live exceptionally long and healthy lives. Buettner identifies dietary patterns as a key factor in these communities' longevity. The diet in these zones is primarily plant-based, with a heavy reliance on locally-sourced, organic foods. This segment underscores the profound impact of dietary choices on health and longevity, echoing the importance of Shiva's call for a shift in agricultural practices.

Mark Hyman's 'Food' takes a deeper dive into the relationship between food, health, and disease. Hyman discusses how heavily processed foods, often products of industrial agriculture, contribute to widespread health issues like obesity, diabetes, and heart disease. He champions whole, nutrient-rich foods, which are often lacking in modern diets. This part reinforces the necessity of a regenerative agriculture system that prioritizes nutritional richness over mass production.

Terry Wahls' 'The Wahls Protocol' provides a more focused perspective, examining the role of diet in managing and potentially reversing chronic diseases, particularly autoimmune disorders. Wahls emphasizes the importance of consuming a diverse array of phytonutrients, which are most abundant in organically grown fruits and vegetables. This part adds a clinical dimension to the discussion, showing how diet directly influences disease progression and overall health.

In *'The Mineral Fix,'* authors James Dinicolantonio and Siam Land delve into the importance of minerals in human health and how modern agricultural practices have led to a depletion of these essential nutrients in our diet. They argue for a food system that prioritizes mineral-rich foods, something that regenerative agriculture can provide. This book ties together the previous arguments, highlighting how a shift in farming practices can enhance the nutritional quality of our food.

The synthesis of these works culminates in a powerful argument for a regenerative agriculture system. This system not only addresses environmental concerns but also significantly impacts public health by increasing the nutritional vitality of our food. The books collectively illustrate how current agricultural practices contribute to a range of health issues, while a shift towards organic, nutrient-rich, and locally-sourced foods can prevent disease and improve quality of life.

The conclusion is clear: *adopting regenerative agriculture is not just an environmental imperative, but a vital step towards enhancing human health and longevity.* By nourishing our bodies with the right foods, we can lay the foundation for a healthier, more sustainable future.

Evolving Childhood Development
A Synthesis for Positive Sexual Expression and Understanding

Philippa Perry's 'The Book You Wish Your Parents Had Read' sets the stage by emphasizing the crucial role of emotional intelligence and understanding in parenting. Perry argues for empathetic communication and the importance of addressing one's own psychological health to nurture a child's development effectively. This book underscores the foundational need for emotionally aware parenting as the first step in guiding children towards a healthy understanding of themselves, including their sexual identities.

Marilee Sprenger's 'The Developing Brain' delves into the neurological aspects of childhood development. It discusses how early experiences, both positive and negative, have a profound impact on the brain's structure and functioning; providing a scientific basis for understanding how a child's environment and interactions shape their cognitive and emotional development, and laying the groundwork for their understanding of complex concepts like sexuality.

Gabor Mate's 'Scattered Minds' focuses on the impact of Attention Deficit Disorder (ADD) and how it arises primarily from a child's early environment. Mate explores the idea that nurturing and responsive parenting can prevent or mitigate the effects of ADD, which is often associated with issues in self-regulation and emotional control; demonstrating the importance of a stable and understanding environment in helping children navigate their emotions and impulses, which is a critical aspect of developing healthy sexual attitudes.

In 'Boys and Sex,' Peggy Orenstein shifts the focus to the specific challenges boys face in developing a healthy sexual identity. Orenstein discusses societal pressures, misconceptions, and the often toxic narratives surrounding masculinity and sexuality. This book highlights the need for open conversations and education that challenge harmful stereotypes and encourage boys to embrace a more empathetic and respectful approach to sexuality.

Similarly, 'Girls and Sex,' also by Orenstein, examines the complexities of female sexual development amidst modern cultural and social pressures. It addresses issues such as consent, body image, and the impact of media on girls' sexual self-concept.; underscoring the necessity of empowering girls with knowledge and confidence to navigate their sexual identities in a society that often sends mixed and harmful messages.

Don Clark's 'Loving Someone Gay' broadens the discussion to include the experiences of LGBTQ+ individuals. It addresses the challenges faced by those with diverse sexual orientations and emphasizes the importance of acceptance and support from parents and society. This book is crucial in understanding the diverse spectrum of sexual identity and the necessity of an inclusive approach in sexual education and parenting.

The synthesis of these works leads to a compelling argument for a comprehensive, technocratic approach to childhood development, one that actively fosters positive sexual expression and understanding.

> Integrating emotional intelligence in parenting, informed by neurological insights, can create a foundation for children to explore and embrace their sexual identities healthily. Addressing the unique challenges faced by boys and girls, and including diverse sexual orientations in this framework, is vital.

An enlightened technocratic system, grounded in empathy, science, and inclusivity, can revolutionize how society nurtures its children, enabling them to grow into adults who understand and respect their own and others' sexual identities. This approach is not just about sex education; it's about shaping a future where each individual is equipped to explore and express their sexuality in ways that are healthy, respectful, and fulfilling.

Navigating the Mind's Jungle
Fostering Leadership and Metacognition in a Social-Capitalist Framework

Peter Senge's 'The Fifth Discipline' introduces the concept of a learning organization, a place where people continually expand their capacity to create the results they truly desire. Senge emphasizes systems thinking as a crucial discipline, enabling individuals and organizations to see the larger structure they operate within. This book lays the groundwork for understanding how a learning organization, underpinned by social-capitalistic values, can foster an environment conducive to personal and collective evolution.

Simon Sinek's 'Leaders Eat Last' builds on this foundation by exploring the role of leadership in creating successful organizations. Sinek posits that true leadership is about nurturing and enhancing the collective wellbeing of the group, rather than prioritizing personal gain. His insights into the psychology of leadership and organizational behavior are pivotal in framing how a social-capitalistic learning organization might develop leaders who can guide others through the complexities of the mind.

Daniel Goleman's 'Social Intelligence' delves into the neuroscience of human connections and interactions. Goleman argues that our relationships profoundly affect our physical and psychological well-being. Understanding and enhancing social intelligence within a learning organization is critical, as it fosters empathetic and effective communication, integral to navigating the 'jungle' of our minds and the challenges of collective evolution.

In *'Drive,'* *Daniel Pink* examines what motivates us, suggesting that the traditional rewards-based systems are outdated. He introduces the concept of intrinsic motivation, driven by autonomy, mastery, and purpose. This part of the inquiry explores how a social-capitalistic learning organization can cultivate intrinsic motivation, fostering a culture where individuals are driven by a deeper sense of purpose and personal growth, essential for leading oneself and others towards a higher state of consciousness.

Prof Steve Peters' 'A Path Through the Jungle' provides practical strategies for understanding and managing the complexities of the human mind. Peters' metaphor of the mind as a jungle encapsulates the challenges individuals face in navigating their thoughts and emotions. This book is critical in offering tools and techniques that can be incorporated into the framework of a learning organization, aiding individuals in their journey towards self-awareness and metacognition.

The synthesis of these books culminates in a compelling argument for the creation of a social-capitalist learning organization that technocratically facilitates the development of leadership and metacognition.

This organization would not only prioritize continuous learning and systems thinking, as suggested by Senge, but also foster a culture of empathetic leadership, social intelligence, intrinsic motivation, and self-awareness.

Such an environment would enable individuals to effectively lead themselves and others through the intricate 'jungle' of the human mind, promoting a collective evolution towards a more self-aware, empathetic, and conscious society.

The envisioned outcome is a world where individuals are not only cognizant of their internal landscapes but are also equipped with the tools and motivation to navigate and shape them constructively, contributing to a healthier, more aware, and collaborative society.

Crafting the Future
Orchestrating Innovation for the LUVRules Social Network

'The Organization of the Future,' as envisioned by the Drucker Foundation, sets the stage for an innovative organizational structure that is flexible, adaptive, and forward-looking. This book posits that the organizations of the future must be prepared to embrace change and innovation continually. It serves as the foundation for constructing an organization capable of developing the LUVRules Social Network, emphasizing the need for a dynamic and visionary approach.

Daniel Coyle's 'The Culture Code' delves into the intricacies of creating a thriving organizational culture. Coyle identifies key elements such as safety, sharing vulnerability, and establishing a purpose that binds members together. This demonstrates how a strong culture code is vital in fostering an environment where creativity and innovation can flourish, essential for the collaborative development of the LUVRules Social Network.

Warren Bennis in 'Organizing Genius' highlights the importance of gathering exceptional minds to create something extraordinary. Bennis suggests that the greatest achievements often come from collaborative efforts of talented individuals. This insight is pivotal for the LUVRules project, underlining the necessity of assembling a diverse team of geniuses who can bring unique perspectives and skills to the table.

'Gamestorming,' co-authored by Dave Gray, Sunni Brown, and James Macanufo, provides a toolkit for innovators. It introduces techniques for brainstorming and problem-solving that are crucial in a technocratic organization. The application of gamestorming methods will be instrumental in navigating the creative and technical challenges of developing the LUVRules Social Network, ensuring that ideas are not only generated, but also effectively explored and refined.

'Execution' by Larry Bossidy and Ram Charan addresses the critical aspect of bringing plans to fruition. It emphasizes the importance of translating strategies into actions. For the LUVRules project, this means not just ideating and planning, but also effectively implementing those plans. This book provides a framework for ensuring that the innovative ideas generated within the organization are executed efficiently and effectively.

Integrating the principles and insights from these five influential books, the path forward for the LUVRules Social Network becomes clear. The organization must be agile and future-oriented, with a strong culture that promotes safety, vulnerability, and purpose. It should harness the collective genius of a diverse team, employ gamestorming techniques for creative problem-solving, and prioritize execution to turn visionary ideas into reality.

This synthesized approach will not only aid in the successful creation of the LUVRules Social Network but also set a precedent for how technocratic organizations can operate to help cultivate a metacognitive state in the societies at large.

Through this innovative framework, the LUVRules project can aspire to be more than just a social network; it can become a catalyst for global cognitive evolution, empowering individuals and communities with the tools and mindset needed for thriving in an increasingly complex world.

Envisioning an Enlightened World Order
The Collaborative Genesis of the LUVRules Social Network

Will Storr's 'The Science of Storytelling' begins our journey by emphasizing the power of narrative in shaping human understanding and behavior. Storr illustrates how effective storytelling can deeply influence perceptions and actions. This concept is fundamental in framing the United Nations Reformation and the LUVRules Social Network, highlighting the need to craft compelling narratives that resonate with diverse global audiences, thereby fostering a unified vision for change.

'The Design Thinking Playbook' introduces a human-centered approach to problem-solving and innovation. *Lewrick, Link, and Leifer* present a methodology that encourages empathy, ideation, and experimentation. In the context of the LUVRules Social Network, design thinking becomes a crucial tool for developing solutions that are not only technologically advanced, but also deeply empathetic to the varied needs of global communities.

In *'Tribal Leadership,' Logan, King, and Fischer-Wright* explore the dynamics of group culture and leadership. The book underscores the significance of nurturing strong, positive tribal cultures within organizations. For the United Nations Reformation and the LUVRules project, understanding and harnessing tribal leadership principles is key to building a global network that is culturally sensitive and inclusive, encouraging collaboration across diverse groups.

Peter Senge's 'The Fifth Discipline Fieldbook' introduces the concept of a learning organization, which continuously evolves by adapting and growing its knowledge base. Senge's principles are vital for ensuring that the LUVRules Social Network remains dynamic and responsive to the ever-changing global landscape, fostering an environment where learning and innovation are at the forefront.

'The Charrette Handbook' by Lennertz and Lutzenhiser outlines the process of conducting effective design charrettes – collaborative sessions where diverse stakeholders come together to solve complex problems. This approach is instrumental in the formation of the LUVRules Social Network, as it emphasizes inclusivity, collaboration, and intensive problem-solving, ensuring that multiple perspectives are considered in the decision-making process.

Integrating the insights from these five seminal works, the path to forming the LUVRules Social Network becomes evident. The project must start with compelling storytelling to unify and inspire a global audience. It should employ design thinking to ensure solutions are empathetic and user-centric. Tribal leadership principles will foster a culture of collaboration and respect, while the learning organization model ensures ongoing adaptability and growth. Finally, the charrette methodology will be pivotal in bringing together diverse global stakeholders to collaboratively design and implement this visionary project.

The synthesis of these approaches forms a comprehensive strategy for the United Nations Reformation, focusing on a technocratic organizational structure that leverages collective genius and inclusive collaboration.

The LUVRules Social Network, as envisioned, will not only be a platform for global governance, but also a catalyst for a metacognitive shift in global consciousness, leading humanity towards a more connected, empathetic, and enlightened future.

Towards a Global Metacognitive Society
The Role of Expertise and Neuroscience in Human Evolution

Tom Nichols' 'The Death of Expertise' serves as the foundation for this exploration. Nichols highlights the growing disdain for expertise in modern culture, emphasizing the risks this trend poses to society. His thesis argues for the critical importance of respecting and utilizing expert knowledge, particularly in complex fields such as neuroscience and psychology. This book sets the stage for understanding the necessity of a technocratic approach that values expertise in guiding societal evolution towards greater cognitive awareness.

Heather Heying and Bret Weinstein's 'A Hunter-Gatherer's Guide to the 21st Century' delves into the evolutionary mismatch between our ancient genetics and modern environment. They explore how many of today's societal challenges stem from this discordance. The book suggests that understanding our evolutionary heritage is crucial in addressing contemporary issues, including the way we think and process information. This insight is pivotal in formulating strategies to adapt our cognitive processing to the modern world.

'Scarcity Brain' by Michael Easter examines the concept of scarcity mindset and its impact on human behavior and decision-making. Easter argues that the chronic stress of perceived scarcity can lead to a range of negative cognitive effects. This segment underscores the need to rewire our brains so that we can move away from scarcity thinking; a transition that is essential for achieving a metacognitive state so as to thrive with what we actually have in our possession.

Andy Norman's 'Mental Immunity' introduces the concept of cognitive immunology - the idea that our minds, like our bodies, can be fortified against harmful ideas and irrational thinking. Norman proposes strategies to strengthen mental resilience, *which is integral in developing a society capable of metacognitive thinking.* This book provides practical insights into how a technocratic framework could implement these strategies to foster better cognitive health and decision-making in the population.

In 'Making Sense,' Sam Harris explores the ways in which we can understand and improve human consciousness. Harris emphasizes the role of neuroscience in unraveling the complexities of the human mind and advocates for a rational, evidence-based approach to solving societal issues. This book aligns with the overarching theme of using scientific expertise to guide societal evolution towards higher cognitive functioning.

The synthesis of these books points towards the urgent need for a technocratic framework that integrates expert knowledge in neuroscience and psychology to guide societal evolution. This approach would address the mismatch between our evolutionary heritage and modern society, combat the scarcity mindset, and strengthen mental immunity.

The goal is to cultivate a collective consciousness that is not only more resilient and adaptable, but also capable of thriving in a state of metacognition – a heightened awareness of our own thought processes.

Such a framework would not only enhance individual cognitive capabilities, but also foster a society more equipped to tackle complex global challenges with clarity and innovation. The future envisaged is one where the evolution of human consciousness is actively facilitated, leading to a society that thrives on understanding, rationality, and a deep connection with its evolutionary roots.

PREFACE TO A UNITED NATIONS REFORMATION

Utilizing the American constitutional rewrite as a blueprint for a constitutionally enshrined federation of nations, will enable the transition to a resource based global economic system, and prevent an elitist cabal from creating their dystopian nightmare.

And this need for constitutional reform, is readily apparent when looking at several critical issues plaguing America; this indictment on American democracy highlights the urgent need for systemic change:

Medical Industrial Complex and Profiteering

The medical industrial complex is accused of profiteering from human suffering and death. Studies in healthcare economics reveal that high costs and profit-driven motives in the medical sector often lead to unequal access to healthcare and can result in suboptimal patient outcomes.

Insolvency of Social Security

Social Security, a fundamental safety net, faces insolvency. Economic analyses predict future funding shortfalls due to demographic changes and fiscal management issues, threatening the retirement security of millions.

Deteriorating Infrastructure

The state of American infrastructure, including transportation, water systems, and public buildings, is in critical decline. Engineering reports and infrastructure studies indicate that this deterioration poses significant risks to public safety and economic efficiency.

Skyrocketing National Deficit

The national deficit is escalating, driven by various factors including tax cuts, increased government spending, and economic policies. Economists warn that continued deficit growth could lead to long-term economic instability and reduced government ability to respond to financial crises.

Government Employee Compensation

With 22 million government employees, there are concerns about the sustainability of their compensation, especially in the context of budget constraints and public sector efficiency. Public administration research suggests the need for a balanced approach to public sector wages, ensuring fairness and fiscal responsibility.

Military Industrial Complex

The military industrial complex is critiqued for profiting from global conflict. Studies in defense economics and peace studies indicate that the focus on military spending and arms production can divert resources from critical social needs and exacerbate international tensions.

Taxation Inequity

The issue of lower tax contributions and tax avoidance, particularly by the wealthy, is highlighted. Economic research shows that such tax practices contribute to increasing income inequality and hinder the equitable distribution of societal resources.

Economic System Challenges

The culmination of these issues suggests that the American economic system faces significant challenges. Financial experts and economists call for structural reforms to address these systemic problems and promote sustainable economic growth.

In light of these multifaceted challenges, the proposed American constitutional reformation aims to address and rectify these systemic issues, and create a blueprint from which a new Federation of Nations can be built; creating a more equitable, just, and sustainable system, where economic and social systems work in harmony for the benefit of all the citizens of earth.

Transformative Governance Reforms

This section of the proposed constitutional rewrite outlines a series of reforms aimed at modernizing governance, media, military, and immigration systems, supported by scientific data and expert analysis.

Section 1: Transitioning to a Digital Dollar

- *Self-Governing Social Network:* Utilizing Ethereum 3.0 blockchain and smart-contract technology for government services ranging from organ donation to car insurance. This approach promises enhanced efficiency and transparency in public administration.

- *Blockchain for Government Transactions:* All government tax revenues and spending will be conducted using traceable blockchain dollars, ensuring the integrity and traceability of public funds. Economic studies support blockchain's potential in reducing corruption and increasing fiscal transparency.

Section 2: Business Loans and Social Capitalism

- Low-interest business loans, from the web of public banks, will be issued in blockchain dollars, with eligibility criteria based on adherence to social capitalist principles including trade union participation, fair wages, salary caps (5X), and revenue sharing.

- Age-range stratification for human development is set to ensure balanced and experienced leadership in social capitalistic organizations.

   - Managing Director min age is 53
   - Manager min age is 42
   - MIT min age is 33
   - Lead min age is 28
   - Key min age is 24
   - Coworker min age is 21
   - Trainee min age is 18
   - Teen Trainee min age is 13
   - Cub trainee min age is 11

Section 3: Enlightened Leadership Framework

- A new governance structure involving grand councils, vice-leaders, and associate councils is proposed to provide checks and balances in government initiatives.

  o each elected/appointed official leads their own 12-grand councils of 12.

  o each elected/appointed official has two vice-leaders, each with their own associate council of twelve applicable experts.

- Age-range stratification, term limits, and educational prerequisites are set for various public service positions to cultivate experienced and educated leadership.

  o Prime Minister min age is 53

    ▪ *Two Vice-PMs min age is 33*
    ▪ *Limited to three eight-year terms*
    ▪ *Must have served as a Regional Senator for four-years.*
    ▪ *Must have a Master's degree*

  o Territorial Ministers (appointed by PM) min age is 53

    ▪ *Two Vice-TMs min age is 33*
    ▪ *Limited to four four-year terms*
    ▪ *Must have served as a Provincial Governor for four-years.*
    ▪ *Must have a Master's degree*

  o Regional Senator min age is 42

    ▪ *Two Vice-Senators min age is 28*
    ▪ *Limited to four four-year terms*
    ▪ *Must have served as a Provincial Governor for four-years.*
    ▪ *Must have a Master's degree*

  o Provincial Governor min age is 42

    ▪ *Two Vice-Governors min age is 28*
    ▪ *Limited to four four-year terms*
    ▪ *Must have served as a Community Mayor for four-years.*
    ▪ *Must have a Master's degree*

- o Community Mayor min age is 33
  - ▪ *Two Vice-Mayors min age is 24*
  - ▪ *Limited to four four-year terms*
  - ▪ *Must have served as a Township Chieftain for four-years.*
  - ▪ *Must have a Bachelor's degree*

- o Township Chieftain min age is 28
  - ▪ *Two-Vice Chiefs min age is 21*
  - ▪ *Limited to four four-year terms*
  - ▪ *Must have served as a Cultivator for four-years.*
  - ▪ *Must have a Bachelor's degree*

- o Village Cultivator min age is 24
  - ▪ *Two-VCs min age is 18*
  - ▪ *Four-year terms; no limit*
  - ▪ *Must demonstrate a balance in the masculine and feminine energies.*
  - ▪ *Must have an Associate's degree or equivalent.*

Section 4: Reformation of the American Deep State

- The Office of Strategic Services will assume executive control over the entire national security apparatus. The OSS will work directly under the Commander and Chief; and report to all three government branches (as the Strategic Intelligence Supreme Council; which is one of each branch's 12 Supreme Councils), ensuring greater accountability and efficiency in intelligence operations.

  - o *Central Intelligence Agency (CIA)*
  - o *National Security Agency (NSA)*
  - o *Federal Bureau of Investigation (FBI)*
  - o *Department of Homeland Security (DHS)*
  - o *Defense Intelligence Agency (DIA)*
  - o *National Geospatial-Intelligence Agency (NGA)*
  - o *National Reconnaissance Office (NRO)*
  - o *Various branches of the Department of Defense (DoD)*

- Office of the Director of National Intelligence (ODNI)
- State Department, particularly with regard to its diplomatic security and intelligence functions
- Various divisions within the Department of Justice (DOJ), including the Drug Enforcement Administration (DEA) and Bureau of Alcohol, Tobacco, Firearms and Explosives (ATF)

Section 5: Military Industrial Complex Transformation

- The U.S. Military's reformation into the new United Federation of Nations Peacekeeping Force with specialized roles for each military branch in peacekeeping operations. This shift aims to refocus military efforts towards global peace and stability.

    - The Marines will be re-tasked so they now have Joint Special Forces Command.

    - The Army, Navy, and Air Force will each be split into a 'quaternal-force' for peace keeping (Secure, Build, Care-for, and Educate), where each branches' recruits are cross-trained in each part of the quaternal-force.

Section 6: Regulatory Reform and Conflict of Interest

- Implementation of a mandatory waiting period for regulatory employees before joining private sector to prevent regulatory capture and conflicts of interest.

Section 7: National Energy Grid Reformation

- Emphasizing renewable energy sources such as solar, wind, and geothermal; with green energy storage capabilities and solar storm protections.
- Developing DC transmission lines to modernize the national energy grid.

Section 8: Immigration Reform and Path to Citizenship

- Comprehensive immigration reform including secure borders, a clear path to citizenship for legal immigrants, probationary green cards for illegal immigrants with young dependents, and mandatory American history and language training.

- Restriction on multiple citizenships and student visas based on democratic status of home countries.

- Technological enhancements to the Southern Border of America, and control over Mexico's Southern Border by the U.S. Military.

These reforms represent a bold vision for the future, seeking to harness digital technologies for governance, redefine the role of the military, tackle regulatory capture, and modernize energy and immigration systems. By implementing these changes, the amendment aims to create a more efficient, transparent, and equitable society, in line with modern technological advancements and social values.

LUVRULES.COM

LUVRules.com serves as a catalyst for global reformation, using advanced technologies to create a more delegative and libertarian system of self-governance:

1. Integration of Ethereum World Computer

   - Blockchain and Smart Contract Technologies: The use of Ethereum World Computer's decentralized platform facilitates transparent and secure 'smart' contracts. This technology's reliability and incorruptibility are pivotal for managing governmental processes, *from organ donation to car insurance.*

   - Scientific Relevance: Studies in blockchain technology highlight its potential in enhancing governance efficiency, promoting transparency, and reducing corruption.

2. Nationwide Federation of Collaborative Entities

   - American Association of Social Capitalists (AASC): This entity aims to cultivate a sustainable tourism industry, while revitalizing urban areas through 'Journeyman Villages' that synergize jobs programs, microfinance initiatives, small businesses, the service industries, and the 'arts'.

   - Scientific Support: Research in social capitalism and urban development supports the idea that collaborative efforts among diverse entities can lead to more sustainable and socially beneficial outcomes.

3. MarshallYard.com as a Governance Tool

   - Functionality: MarshallYard.com will organize and marshal human resources, facilitating group formation and self-governance to counteract polarized groupthink and mass psychosis.

   - Expert Analysis: Psychological studies underline the importance of structured, inclusive platforms in mitigating herd mentality and fostering higher levels of consciousness and collaboration.

4. LUVRules.com: A Self-Governing Network Hub

   - Purpose: Designed as a 'Corporate Human Resource Management & Societal Holistic Care System', LUVRules.com integrates various functionalities to promote values-based capitalism, and effective public service.

- Integration of Artificial General Intelligence (AGI): With the advent of AGI, LUVRules.com plans to incorporate advanced guidance systems. These systems will facilitate personalized and multidisciplinary educational pathways, adapting to the unique needs and aspirations of individuals.

- Scientific Foundation: Research in network theory and human resource management underscores the potential of such platforms in fostering community engagement, personalized learning, and efficient resource management.

Key Features of the Proposed System:

- Decentralized and Transparent Operations: Utilizing blockchain technology ensures decentralized, transparent, and secure operations in public administration.

- Collaborative and Inclusive Governance: The proposed federation of entities and online platforms facilitates collaboration across different sectors, fostering a more inclusive and holistic approach to governance.

- Countering Polarization and Promoting Rational Discourse: MarshallYard.com and LUVRules.com aim to counteract societal polarization by promoting rational discourse, empathy, and inclusivity.

- Enhancing Public Participation and Civic Engagement: These digital platforms are designed to enhance public participation in governance, enabling a more delegative and libertarian approach to decision-making.

- Education and Humanistic Values: Emphasizing humanistic values and education, particularly in fostering a holistic understanding of interpersonal affairs, aligns with the goals of creating a more compassionate and empathetic society.

LUVRules.com represents a forward-thinking approach to combining corporate management and societal welfare within a unified digital ecosystem. Its focus on leveraging advanced AI for education, and its grounding in scientific research, positions it as a transformative tool in reshaping how individuals and organizations interact and contribute to societal progress, while facilitating the transition to a more resource-based global economy.

Interactive AGI Deck

LUVRules.com redefines the landscape of digital platforms as an amalgamation of a crowd-sourced, socially-driven business network hub, deeply rooted in education.

> Imagine a platform that merges the best aspects of Facebook's social connectivity, Amazon's vast marketplace, and LinkedIn's professional networking. To this, add a layer of rigorous quality assurance akin to the Michelin Guide's esteemed three-star rating system, all seamlessly integrated within the Ethereum web ecosystem.

Central to LUVRules.com's user experience is the innovative 'interactive AGI deck.' This feature acts as a dynamic visual dashboard, allowing users to tailor their experience by adjusting focus areas. With a simple turn of the dial, users can shift between various functional modes: Public Service, Money Making, Eco-Conscious Purchasing, Career Growth, Recreation and Leisure, Lifelong Learning, Cutting-Edge Research, and Expansive Social Networking.

This multifaceted dashboard is designed to cater to diverse user needs and aspirations, offering a comprehensive and 'gamified' learning experience - akin to a university in the clouds. Each adjustment on the interactive AGI deck presents a new realm of possibilities, making LUVRules.com a versatile and engaging platform for personal and professional growth.

Gamified Framework

LUVRules.com is a pioneering platform that merges the dynamic interactivity of a gamified educational environment, with the expansive capabilities of an e-commerce giant. It aims to be the digital nexus for values-based capitalism and autonomous community governance, utilizing the Ethereum blockchain as a foundation for secure and transparent operations.

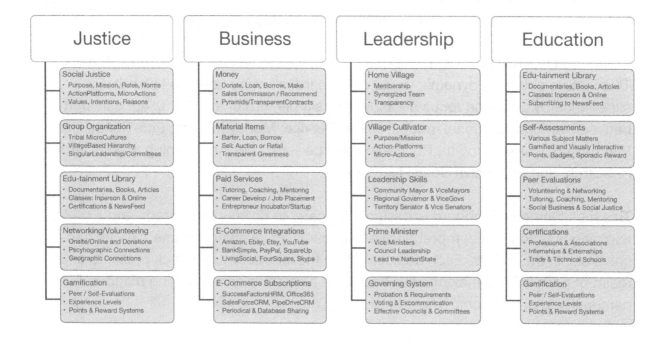

1. Justice - Fostering a Fair and Inclusive Community:

   - Social Justice: By establishing clear missions and roles, LUVRules.com supports micro-actions focused on social impact, underpinned by core values and principled intentions.

   - Scientific Support: Research in social psychology affirms the importance of role clarity and value congruence in promoting prosocial behavior within groups.

2. Business - Encouraging Ethical and Sustainable Commerce:

   - Material Transactions: With a commitment to transparent and sustainable exchanges, the platform facilitates bartering, loans, and environmentally conscious retail practices.

- E-Commerce: Seamless integration with established online marketplaces ensures that users have a broad reach, while subscription services foster ongoing business relationships.

- Scientific Support: Studies in sustainable business models highlight the growing consumer demand for transparency and sustainability in business practices.

3. Leadership - Cultivating Effective Governance and Collaboration:

- Local Governance: The Home Village Cultivation concept emphasizes membership and teamwork, with a strong emphasis on transparency.

- Strategic Leadership Development: Through actionable steps and clear missions, LUVRules.com prepares members for community and regional leadership roles.

- Scientific Support: Leadership research advocates for transparent and participatory governance models that enhance community engagement and leadership effectiveness.

4. Education - Advancing Lifelong Learning and Expertise:

- Edu-tainment: The platform's library of documentaries, books, and articles, alongside in-person and online classes, caters to a wide array of learning styles and interests.

- Peer Evaluations and Certifications: Engaging in peer reviews and earning certifications provide validation and acknowledgment of skills and knowledge within the community.

- Scientific Support: Educational theories suggest that interactive learning and peer assessments can significantly enhance motivation and knowledge retention.

Through its multifaceted approach, LUVRules.com aspires to revolutionize the way individuals and communities interact, learn, and conduct business. By emphasizing ethical practices, community governance, and continuous education, the platform seeks to empower users to govern themselves for a collective purpose, transcending the traditional 'herd mentality' and fostering a culture of risk-taking within a secure digital environment. With this structured and hierarchical framework, LUVRules.com is poised to become the 'Green Seal of Approval' for a sustainable future.

Cultivation Framework

To fulfill LUVRules.com's mission of cultivating a community dedicated to self-improvement and societal betterment, we introduce a multifaceted framework that merges personal development with social contribution, all within a platform that values anonymity with accountability, to reduce ego-driven conflicts.

I Have Experience In	Tutor Others In	Coach Others In	Mentor Others In
Technology	Reading & Writing Skills	Cultivation & Nurturing	Roles Identification
Business & Legal	A High School Diploma	Team Playing	Roles Co-creation
General Labor	Trade School Externships	Critical Thinking	Life Planning
Lifestyle	Professional Certifications	Life Skills Development	Experiential Travel
Sports	A Bachelors Degree	Public Speaking & Teaching	Team Collaboration
Artistic Expression	A Masters Degree	Organizational Behavior	Diplomatic Debate
Food Chain Trustee	Research Expertise	Game Theory Expertise	Effective Role Execution

1. Have Experience In:

   - Diverse Skillsets: Members can share their expertise in various fields such as technology, legal practices, or artistic expression; contributing to a rich tapestry of knowledge and experience.

   - Scientific Support: Research in knowledge sharing demonstrates that diversity in expertise contributes to innovation and problem-solving within communities.

2. Tutor Others In:

   - Educational Empowerment: From basic literacy to advanced research, offering tutoring encourages educational growth and supports lifelong learning principles.

   - Scientific Support: Studies on adult education show that peer-to-peer tutoring can enhance learning outcomes for both tutors and learners by fostering a collaborative learning environment.

3. Coach Others In:
   - Personal Growth: Coaching others in areas like critical thinking and life skills is fundamental for personal development and leadership.

   - Scientific Support: Literature on coaching psychology suggests that coaching can significantly impact an individual's performance, well-being, and ability to achieve goals.

4. Mentor Others In:
   - Guidance and Collaboration: Mentoring in role identification and role execution helps others find their place in the community and work effectively within teams.

   - Scientific Support: Mentoring research indicates that mentoring relationships can lead to greater career success, satisfaction, and the proliferation of positive community values.

The structured yet flexible framework of LUVRules.com is designed to facilitate a holistic and humanistic approach to personal development and community service. By leveraging verified self-assessment categories, the platform employs personalized psychographic filters and connection algorithms to match individuals with complementary goals and skills. This system not only fosters individual joy and fulfillment, but also ensures that each member's contributions support the broader objective of uplifting others, thereby reinforcing a chain of positive societal impact.

Hierarchical Governance

The American Nation-State is envisioned to be systematically organized into distinct subdivisions that ensure efficient governance and representation. This hierarchical framework is designed with a bottom-up approach, ensuring that each level of subdivision contributes to the overall unity and functionality of the Nation.

Section 1: **Grassroots Governance and Community Development**

Population and Geographical Distribution:
   - The United States shall maintain a balanced population distribution, with a ceiling of 818,159,616 citizens across twelve Territories. Each Territory

encompasses twelve Regions, down to Villages, which are adaptable in size to suit population variances and geographic needs.

- Scientific Support: Studies in urban planning and community development emphasize the benefits of manageable population sizes within specific geographic areas, promoting sustainable living and efficient local governance.

Village Structure and Leadership:

- Villages serve as the primary unit of governance, consisting of no more than 274 residents, fostering close-knit communities and direct democratic participation.

- Scientific Support: Research in small-scale democracies shows that such structures enhance citizen investment in civic engagement.

Township and Community Organization:

- Townships and Communities are formed by aggregating Villages and are governed by elected officials - *Township Chieftains and Community Mayors* - who are supported by two appointed deputies, ensuring local needs are met with precision and care.

- Scientific Support: Political science research suggests that multilayered governance structures can provide better resource allocation and more responsive leadership.

Province, Region, and Territory Administration:

- Provinces, Regions, and Territories are larger administrative units that are managed by elected Provincial Governors who makeup the House of Representatives, Regional Senators who makeup the Senate, and twelve-appointed Territorial Ministers who makeup one of the Prime Minister's twelve Supreme Councils; to align regional goals with national objectives.

- Scientific Support: Studies in federalism indicate that such a stratified approach can balance local autonomy with effective central oversight.

Section 2: **Grassroots Cultivation of Public Service Roles**

Village Cultivators and Vice-Cultivators:

- These officials will operate part-time from home, with compensation that includes basic living necessities and incentives that encourage community bonding and service.

- Scientific Support: Compensation strategies that go beyond monetary rewards can improve job satisfaction and community cohesion, according to labor and organizational psychology studies.

Township Chieftains to Provincial Governors:

- Ascending the hierarchy, officials work from government offices with pay scaled to the living wage of their area, reflecting their increased responsibilities.

- Scientific Support: Economic research supports living wage policies for government officials to ensure fair compensation and reduce financial stress, leading to better public service.

Regional Senators and Territorial Ministers:

- At the highest levels, officials are elected or appointed to positions with compensation that reflects their extensive responsibilities and contribution to national security and governance.

- Scientific Support: The compensation structure for high-level officials is validated by governance studies that correlate appropriate remuneration with the effective execution of duties and the attraction of qualified candidates.

Through this restructured hierarchical system, the American Nation-State aims to foster a more efficient, responsive, and participatory form of governance, one that leverages the expertise of its citizens at all levels, and aligns with the scientific understanding of effective organizational and political structures.

Section 3: **Dynamic Governance Structure**

In the proposed reformation of the American Nation-State, a sophisticated and flexible governance system is introduced within LUVRules.com's framework. This system allows citizens to actively engage in a structured political ecosystem that spans from local to national levels.

Citizen Participation and Leadership Development:

- Each citizen can align with a multitude of Governmental Tribes and engage in a variety of Government Committees and Grand Councils, promoting broad civic involvement and diversified leadership opportunities.

    o Each Citizen may affiliate with a maximum of 144 Governmental Tribes, serve on 48 Government Committees, and be a primary member of 12 Grand Councils - *each with a maximum of 13 primary members, a maximum of 26 secondary assistant-members, and a maximum of 234 tertiary research members.*

- Scientific Support: Political science research supports active citizen participation in governance, indicating that such involvement can enhance democratic functioning and policy responsiveness.

Stratified Governmental Structure:

- The Nation-State's framework is designed to accommodate a maximum population, with a hierarchical distribution into Territories, Regions, and Villages, ensuring manageable governance units and closer representation.

- Scientific Support: Studies in administrative science suggest that a stratified government structure facilitates efficient resource distribution and tailored policy implementation.

Nation-State Leadership:

- At the apex, the Prime Minister leads twelve supreme councils, supported by two Vice Ministers who oversee the Senate and the House, reflecting a balance of executive and legislative powers.

- Scientific Support: Research in executive leadership and legislative studies emphasizes the importance of such dual roles in ensuring checks and balances within governance.

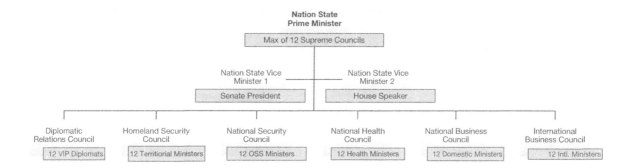

Diplomatic and Security Councils:

- Six of the Twelve Supreme Councils are for Diplomatic Relations, Homeland Security, National Security, Health, Business, and International Affairs; and ensure focused attention on key areas of governance.

- Scientific Support: Strategic management literature highlights the effectiveness of specialized councils in addressing complex national and international issues.

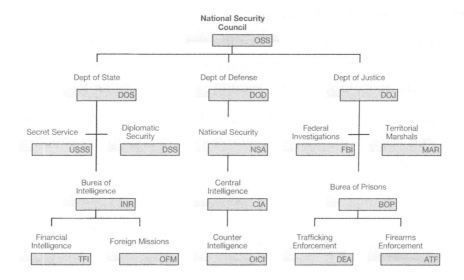

National Security and Homeland Security Frameworks:

- The National Security Council, led by the Office of Strategic Services, orchestrates the nation's defense and intelligence, while the Homeland Security Council, headed by the Department of the Interior, manages domestic safety and emergency preparedness.

- Scientific Support: Security studies advocate for centralized coordination of defense and homeland security to effectively address threats and ensure public safety.

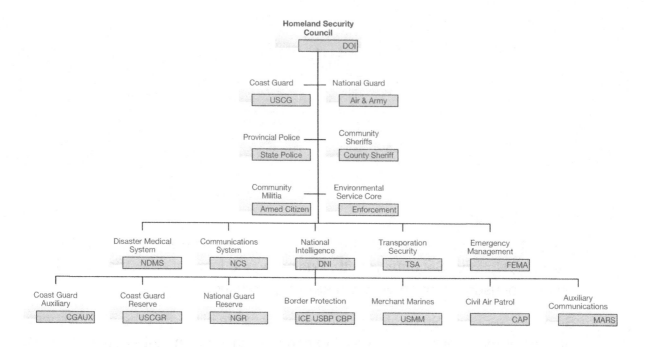

Health and Human Services Management:

- The National Health Council, under the direction of Health and Human Services, integrates various health-related departments and services, focusing on public health, education, labor, social security, and environmental protection.

- Scientific Support: Public health research underscores the necessity of an integrated approach to health governance, enhancing the effectiveness of health policies and services.

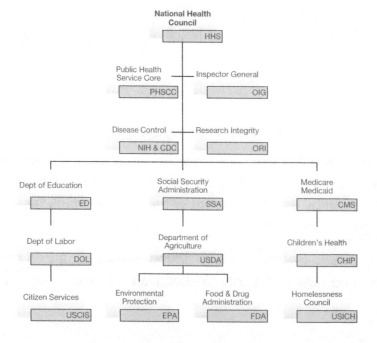

This envisioned hierarchy within LUVRules.com aims to cultivate noble leadership through an enlightened organizational framework. By intertwining governance with technology, the proposed system aspires to foster a more participatory, transparent, and efficient political environment, allowing citizens to realize their full potential in contributing to the greater good.

Section 4: **Tiered Global Stock Markets**

Enhancing Civic Education Through Financial Literacy:

The foundational 'nation-state frameworks' within LUVRules.com will not only facilitate global online innovations but will also act as educational instruments for instilling civic responsibility. The platform's strategic approach, *emphasizing action,* requires users to engage in socially beneficial activities to progress through experience levels and gain clout. This engagement is driven by a shared value system rooted in holistic-humanism, coupled with an interactive gaming/point system.

Addressing the Economic Caste System:

The prevailing economic structure often promotes a caste system that hinders social relationships and genuine human connections. Scientific literature on social capital emphasizes the detrimental effects of such systems on societal well-being and the importance of equitable economic frameworks that foster both genuine community engagement and individual passion.

Pursuit of Integrity and Transparency:

Integrity, defined as steadfast adherence to a strict moral and ethical code, is often obscured by the lack of transparency in our institutions. Without transparency, integrity becomes questionable, and the pursuit of individual and institutional integrity is compromised.

Stock Trading Reformation:

The United Federation of Nations will oversee a reformed Global Stock Market on the LUVRules.com platform, harnessing Ethereum blockchain and smart-contract technologies. This innovation seeks to eliminate the opacity that currently exists within the financial sector, where fiduciary responsibility is often absent, and investment banks may prioritize their own gains over investors' interests.

Tiered Investment Structure:

To counteract the inflationary tendencies of Wall Street, *which doesn't produce tangible goods,* LUVRules.com proposes a three-tiered investment model:

1. Regional Stock Markets: For startups, fostering innovation and providing opportunities for new businesses to access capital.

2. National Stock Markets: For established companies that meet operational standards, such as debt-to-equity ratios, encouraging responsible corporate management and sustainable growth.

3. Global Stock Markets: Reserved for well-run companies that demonstrate financial stability and provide shareholder value through dividends.

Scientific and Ethical Justifications:

- Research in behavioral economics supports the need for tiered markets as they can cater to varying levels of risk tolerance and investment sophistication, leading to more informed and rational investment behaviors.

- Ethical investment practices are bolstered by regulatory frameworks that prioritize transparency, as validated by financial ethics studies. This aligns with LUVRules.com's mission to ensure that integrity is maintained at every level – from the medium and message; *to the messenger, receiver, and the system as a whole.*

Through these measures, LUVRules.com envisions a stock market ecosystem that embodies integrity, transparency, and ethical practices, aligned with the platform's overarching goal of serving the greater good. This reformed market system aims to empower individuals to invest responsibly, promote corporate accountability, and contribute to a more equitable global economy.

A leader is best when people barely know he exists,
when his work is done, his aim fulfilled,
they will all say: we did it ourselves.

- Lao Tzu

BLUEPRINT FOR EVOLUTION

Envisioning a Libertarian Federation of Nations through LUVRules.com

It is imperative that we revise the American Constitution so that it becomes the foundational document for a Libertarian Federation of Nations, *orchestrated through LUVRules.com.* Such an initiative is crucial to effectively counteract the emergence of a despotic global governance, by an elitist cabal.

Part 1: Historical Foundations

- *Roxanne Dunbar-Ortiz's "An Indigenous Peoples' History of the United States"* reframes American history from the perspective of indigenous peoples, revealing a narrative of conquest and colonialism that has been sanitized in traditional history books. It uncovers the systematic marginalization and oppression of Native Americans and sets the stage for understanding the United States' complex legacy of expansionism and power.

Part 2: Revisionist Narratives

- Building on this foundation, *Oliver Stone's "The Untold History of the United States"* delves into the modern history of America, challenging the heroism of the official narrative. Stone presents a critical examination of U.S. policies and actions throughout the twentieth century, exposing the underlying motives and consequences of American imperialism via corrupt military interventions.

Part 3: Societal Drift

- *Scott Galloway's "Adrift"* captures the contemporary socio-economic drift in the United States, scrutinizing the growing inequality, the decay of public institutions, and the disintegration of the middle class. Galloway highlights the rise of a new elite class that, through technology and globalization, has accumulated unprecedented power, exacerbating societal divisions.

Part 4: Socioeconomic Alternatives

- *Thomas Piketty's "Time for Socialism"* offers a solution to the issues raised by the previous authors. He argues for a modern socialist agenda that would rein in the excesses of capitalism through progressive taxation, wealth redistribution, and an enhanced social state. Piketty's work suggests a restructuring of the current economic systems to promote fairness and equality.

Part 5: Behavioral Insights and Systemic Change

- *Finally, Daniel Kahneman's "Thinking, Fast and Slow"* provides the psychological underpinnings for why such a transformation is challenging, yet necessary. He describes two systems of thought: System 1 is fast, instinctive, and emotional; System 2 is slower, more deliberative, and more logical. Kahneman illustrates how our decisions are often influenced by cognitive biases and heuristics, which can lead to systemic errors and misjudgments.

The confluence of these texts paints a picture of a nation and a global order that has been shaped by a series of conscious and unconscious decisions, rooted in historical power dynamics and psychological predispositions. The fall of America, as forewarned by the first three books, is not merely a consequence of external forces, but also a result of internal decay, facilitated by the very biases that Kahneman describes.

The creation of a Libertarian Federation of Nations, *as proposed,* would aim to leverage the power of Piketty's modern socialism to establish a fairer economic and social landscape, while utilizing LUVRules.com as a platform to engage System 2 thinking. *LUVRules.com will serve as a counterbalance to our inherent biases, promoting a more reflective, inclusive, and rational approach to global governance.*

This new Federation of Nations, *underpinned by a digital framework that encourages slow thinking*, will provide the necessary checks and balances to prevent the rise of an autocratic world government. By fostering deliberative democracy and utilizing technology to enhance transparency and participation, LUVRules.com represents a beacon of hope in realizing a more equitable and democratic global society.

In this envisioned future, the power of the elite is curtailed not through revolution, but through evolution. It's a future crafted through collective effort, where governance is re-envisioned to resonate with the highest of our human values. Here, our united expertise is channeled into honorable actions of noble intent, aimed at alleviating our shared suffering with both grace and wisdom.

AFTERWORD

Without contraries there is no progression.
Attraction and repulsion, reason and energy, love and hate;
are necessary to human existence.

- William Blake

EMBRACE THE PATH TO GNOSIS
Via the Way of Impartial Nobility

We shall rekindle the hearts of man,
to the valor within, in a world that has grown chill.

– J.R.R. Tolkien

1. *Engage the path to gnosis by consistently striving to be more effective in alleviating the suffering of others.*

2. *Next, take the leap of faith, by trusting in your acts of selflessness to transcend your narcissistic 'will to receive' so as to embody the way of impartial nobility.*

Your odyssey begins by earnestly endeavoring to ease the burdens of others. This pursuit of gnosis isn't just about ineffective lip-service or random acts of kindness; it's a dedicated effort to genuinely lessen the suffering in the world. This noble quest demands a deep introspection of your actions. Are they merely surface-level kindness, or do they truly cut to the heart of suffering, addressing its roots and not just its symptoms?

Next, courageously leap into a realm of selflessness. This leap requires faith - faith in the transformational power of altruism. It's about transcending the ego's insatiable 'will to receive' and adopting a stance of impartial nobility. This doesn't merely diminish narcissism; it fundamentally shifts your perspective from self-centeredness to a profound empathy that acknowledges and acts upon the interconnectedness of all life.

The original sin of narcissism, often rooted in entitlement and a profound lack of empathy, is a significant obstacle on this path. It manifests in varied intensities, from subtle self-absorption to grandiose delusions. Recognizing and overcoming these traits in oneself is crucial to progress on this journey.

Parents play a pivotal role in this transformative journey. Rather than perpetuating a culture of narcissism, marked by excessive pride or treating children as extensions of their ambitions, parents must guide the next generation towards humility and collective well-being. It's about instilling values of self-sacrifice and understanding the profound impact of our actions in the grand tapestry of life.

Embrace life's playfulness, as Plato suggested, but balance it with a profound understanding of our roles in the cosmic play. This balance involves shifting from self-interest to self-sacrifice, recognizing the greater cosmic conflict that plays out beyond our immediate perceptions.

Life thrives in chaos and diversity. Acknowledge that absolutes in terms of 'right' and 'good' are fleeting. Embrace diversity and avoid imposing rigid beliefs. Recognize that truth is multifaceted and that language itself can obscure as much as it reveals.

Life's essence is experimentation, learning from failures, and evolving through adversity. Embrace the full range of emotions, understanding that they are crucial in realizing the depth of love and the essence of our true selves.

This journey to 'superconscious harmony' is about embracing life in all its complexity. It involves a commitment to alleviate suffering, transcending personal struggles, and shining your light in the darkness. Like a candle in the gloom, each individual has the potential to illuminate the world, guiding us all towards a more enlightened, balanced existence. This is the true essence of rediscovering the valor within, rekindling the warmth in our collective hearts.

Narcissism and Avarice Will End Us All

Part 1: Reflecting on Narcissism

Dr. Drew Pinsky's "The Mirror Effect" dissects the pervasive nature of narcissism in contemporary culture, particularly how media and celebrity reflect and amplify these traits among the public. Pinsky outlines how the incessant drive for attention and validation leads to a 'mirror effect', where society not only reflects celebrities' behaviors but also amplifies them, creating a cycle of escalating narcissism.

- *Celebrity Influence:* Pinsky provides a detailed analysis of how celebrities with narcissistic traits influence their audiences, leading to imitative behaviors that ripple through society.

- *Narcissism Measurement:* Through extensive research and surveys, Pinsky quantifies the levels of narcissism in various groups and correlates them with negative outcomes like addiction and depression.

- *Cultural Impact:* The book examines how narcissism, propelled by media, corrodes societal values, promoting a culture of self-obsession over communal welfare.

Part 2: Understanding Avarice

Stephen Batchelor's "Living with the Devil" explores the human condition through the lens of Buddhist philosophy, viewing the devil as a metaphor for our own destructive impulses, like greed and avarice. Batchelor implores readers to understand and confront these inner demons to lead a life that is both morally grounded and spiritually fulfilling.

- *The Devil Within:* The 'devil' is a representation of our inner struggles with greed, hatred, and delusion, which can lead to suffering and societal turmoil.

- *Buddhist Pathways:* Batchelor presents the Buddhist approach to overcoming these impulses through mindfulness, ethical living, and meditation.

- *Moral Relevance:* The narrative connects these ancient philosophies to contemporary issues, underscoring their relevance in guiding modern society.

The confluence of the theses presented in both books highlights a crucial challenge facing humanity: the pervasive narcissism and greed that threaten to unravel the social fabric. Dr. Pinsky's analysis of the 'mirror effect' shows how our society not only tolerates but exacerbates these traits, while Batchelor's discourse offers a pathway to counteract them through self-awareness and ethical conduct.

Overcoming Narcissism and Greed:

- To avert the dire consequences of unchecked narcissism and avarice, a radical shift in governance and societal values is necessary. LUVRules.com emerges as a digital bastion to support this transformation.

- *LUVRules.com's Role:* By employing system 2 thinking, LUVRules.com encourages deliberative, logical, and ethical decision-making processes that can help individuals and societies move beyond instinctual, self-centered impulses.

Implementing System 2 Thinking:

- LUVRules.com can facilitate the cultivation of mindfulness and ethical behavior championed by Batchelor, providing a platform for reflection, learning, and community engagement devoid of narcissistic self-aggrandizement.

- *Scientific Backing:* Psychological research supports the use of platforms like LUVRules.com in mitigating cognitive biases, promoting system 2 thinking, and fostering rational discourse.

The integration of the wisdom from 'The Mirror Effect' and 'Living with the Devil' suggests that humanity's salvation lies in a collective effort to transcend our basal instincts. Through the strategic application of technology to enhance our higher cognitive functions, and the embrace of philosophical insights into our condition, we can construct a libertarian federation that not only survives but thrives in a world free from the tyranny of malignant narcissism and unchecked greed.

LUVRules.com stands as a testament to our ability to envision and enact a future governed by compassion, reason, and equitable principles, moving us away from the precipice of a dystopian nightmare and towards a more hopeful, collaborative existence.

POWER HUNGRY TYRANTS RULE!

Part 1: The Dynamics of Power

Robert Greene's "The 48 Laws of Power" is a meticulous dissection of the mechanisms of power throughout history. Greene presents a compilation of strategies used by historical figures to acquire, wield, and safeguard power. Each law is exemplified by anecdotes from politics, war, and culture, illustrating the timeless and often ruthless nature of power dynamics.

- Greene's laws delve into the ethical grey areas of power, teaching that amorality, cunning, and discretion are often more effective than direct confrontation.

- The book's lessons highlight the importance of image, manipulation, and social intelligence in the game of power.

Part 2: Strategic Warfare

Sun Tzu's "The Art of War" extends the discourse on power into the realm of military strategy and conflict management. This ancient treatise outlines principles for victory in war, emphasizing the importance of deception, strategic planning, and understanding the enemy.

- The text suggests that all warfare is based on deception and that winning battles without fighting is the acme of skill.

- Sun Tzu's insights apply beyond the battlefield, offering wisdom on competition and conflict resolution in various aspects of life.

Part 3: Business Tactics

Harvey Mackay's "Swim with the Sharks" translates the concepts of power and strategy into the business world. Mackay offers a plethora of advice on salesmanship, negotiation, and career development, drawn from his own successful business experiences.

- The book emphasizes the value of networking, understanding customer needs, and staying nimble in the ever-evolving business environment.

- It reflects on the competitive nature of business and the need for shrewdness, much like in war and power plays.

Part 4: Justifying Avarice

In *"Beware the Naked Man,"* Mackay returns with more insights into business and life strategies. He explores the justifications used by individuals, particularly those in positions of power, to rationalize their avarice and self-serving behaviors.

Part 5: Societal Critique

Catherine Liu's "Virtue Hoarders" provides a critical examination of the professional managerial class (PMC), accusing them of hoarding cultural and social capital. Liu argues that the PMC's self-declared virtues often mask a deep-seated narcissism that contributes to societal stratification and inequality.

- The book critiques the PMC's role in perpetuating class divisions under the guise of progressive politics.

- Liu's analysis suggests that the PMC's virtue signaling is a contemporary form of power maintenance.

The synthesis of these texts reveals a complex picture of the motives and methods of power-hungry individuals and groups. Greene and Sun Tzu provide foundational knowledge on acquiring and maintaining power. Mackay's works offer a view into the integration of these strategies in the business world, while Liu exposes the moral failings and hypocrisy of the ruling class.

> The interplay of these narratives with Mackay's analysis of justification mechanisms leads to an unsettling realization: *the qualities that facilitate success in power struggles, business, and social status also fuel a narcissistic self-interest that can subvert democratic principles.*

The establishment of a Libertarian Federation of Nations, as facilitated by LUVRules.com, emerges as a necessary countermeasure to the potential despotic global governance threatened by such elitist forces. By harnessing the democratic and transparent capabilities of LUVRules.com, society can foster a governance model that is more inclusive, deliberative, and resistant to the malignant narcissism that underpins much of the power manipulation identified in these works. LUVRules.com would not only offer a platform for equitable governance but also provide a check against the biases and self-justifications that lead to autocracy.

There is a critical need to transcend the malignancy of unchecked power, and to embrace a new model of governance *that is founded on libertarian principles, facilitated by technology, and dedicated to the true service of humanity.*

NAVIGATING AND TRANSCENDING THE INNER LABYRINTH

By Transforming the Narcissistic Self

In the quest for personal growth and effective interpersonal relations, understanding the concepts of projection and the shadow, as expounded by Carl Jung, alongside the insights on metacognition by Prof Steve Peters, is vital. We must therefore guide individuals towards a higher state of awareness, so we can all transcend our innate narcissistic 'will to receive.'

Carl Jung's exploration of the shadow, a central element in his analytical psychology, sheds light on the darker, unconscious parts of our personality that we often refuse to acknowledge. According to Jung, the shadow contains not only negative but also potentially positive aspects of ourselves that we have either repressed or denied. Projection occurs when we ascribe these disowned parts of our personality to others, leading to misunderstandings and conflicts in our relationships.

Jung emphasizes the importance of recognizing and integrating the shadow. This process, known as shadow work, involves confronting these hidden aspects of ourselves, thus reducing our tendency to project our unacknowledged qualities onto others. By acknowledging and integrating the shadow, we gain a deeper understanding of ourselves, leading to more authentic and harmonious interpersonal relationships.

In Professor Steve Peters' discussion on Metacognition, he emphasizes the importance of stepping-back and observing our responses and behaviors more objectively. This approach scrutinizes the origins of our thoughts and emotions, allowing us to identify instances where we might be projecting our own unresolved issues, or 'shadows'.

> *This metacognitive-projection process* helps us understand whether these reactions are influenced by our subconscious biases, or by aspects of ourselves that we have not yet acknowledged.

At the end of the day, effective interpersonal relations hinge on our capacity to understand and manage our inner dynamics. The interplay of projection and shadow can lead to distorted perceptions of others, fueling conflicts and misunderstandings.

Metacognition acts as a mitigating factor, enabling us to recognize these projections and deal with them constructively.

By applying metacognitive strategies, we can question our immediate reactions to others, consider alternative perspectives, and recognize the influence of our shadow in these interactions. This heightened awareness fosters empathy, reduces conflict, and cultivates deeper connections with others.

Jung's concept of the shadow, and Peters' emphasis on metacognition, provide a framework for transcending our innate narcissistic 'will to receive'. Narcissism, in this context, is not just a pathological condition, but a fundamental human tendency to focus on our own needs and perceptions.

Through shadow work and metacognitive practices, we can move beyond this self-centered perspective. Recognizing and integrating our shadow, diminishes our unconscious projections, leading to a more authentic and less ego-centric engagement with the world. Metacognition further aids in this transcendence by fostering a reflective mindset, allowing us to question our motives and understand the impact of our behavior on others.

The synthesis of Carl Jung's and Prof Steve Peters' ideas offers a powerful route to personal transformation. By understanding and integrating our shadow, we reduce harmful projections that hinder our relationships. Metacognition serves as a critical tool in this journey, providing the self-awareness necessary to recognize and transcend our narcissistic inclinations. This path, though challenging, leads to a state of higher awareness, enabling more fulfilling and authentic connections with others and a deeper understanding of ourselves.

Navigating the Gnostic Path to Virtuous Autonomy

Via the Way of Impartial Nobility

David Brooks' *'The Road to Character'* is a profound exploration of the journey towards moral depth and inner character. This journey is akin to achieving a Metacognitive state as described by Professor Steve Peters, a state where one becomes acutely aware of, and can manage, their own thought processes.

2. *The Shift from 'Big Me' to Humility:* Brooks begins by contrasting today's culture, which glorifies personal success and achievement (the 'Big Me'), with a commitment to inner virtues. He suggests a shift is needed from self-centeredness to humility to start this journey.

3. *The Road to Internal Struggle:* Here, Brooks introduces the concept of internal struggle, emphasizing that true character is built through overcoming personal weaknesses and temptations.

4. *Adam I vs. Adam II - The Two Selves:* Brooks describes two aspects of the self: Adam I, who seeks external achievement, and Adam II, who seeks internal moral virtues. The book advocates for balancing these selves.

5. *The Influence of Environment and Relationships:* This chapter highlights how one's environment and relationships shape character, stressing the importance of nurturing communities that support moral development.

6. *Suffering and Character:* Brooks argues that suffering and adversity are critical in building character, as they force individuals to confront their limitations and grow.

7. *The Importance of Moral Realism:* Here, the focus is on understanding and accepting one's own limitations and the complexity of the moral world, encouraging a realistic approach to ethical living.

8. *The Drive for Self-Conquest:* Brooks discusses the importance of self-conquest in building character, where one continuously strives to overcome their egoistic desires.

9. *The Role of Tradition and Wisdom:* This chapter emphasizes the value of traditional moral wisdom and how it can guide individuals on their path to character.

10. *Humility and the Journey to the Self:* Brooks returns to the theme of humility, considering it the core virtue in the journey towards character, allowing individuals to see beyond themselves.

11. *The Road Ahead:* The final chapter is a call to action, encouraging readers to embark on their own journey of character development.

The journey Brooks outlines is a complex struggle against the inherent narcissism in human nature, *the 'will to receive' for oneself alone.* This struggle involves cultivating 'the way of impartial nobility', a path where one seeks moral excellence for its own sake, not for personal gain; aligning with concept of Metacognition, where we become aware of our thought processes, enabling us to manage our egocentric impulses effectively.

Brooks' narrative also intertwines with the latest neuroscience on how prenatal malnutrition and childhood traumas shape an individual's life. These early life challenges can profoundly impact cognitive development, mental health, and overall well-being, often leading to a truncated lifespan. This scientific perspective adds a layer of complexity to Brooks' thesis, showing how external factors can significantly hinder, or facilitate, *the journey to the way of impartial nobility.*

'The Road to Character' by David Brooks is not just a guide to personal development; it is an exploration of the human condition itself. It challenges us to confront our innate narcissism and to embark on a journey of moral and ethical growth. The integration of Metacognition, along with the latest neuroscience on prenatal and early life traumas, offers a holistic view of this journey. It is a path fraught with obstacles, both internal and external, but it is also a road that leads to profound personal transformation; and, ultimately, a more fulfilling life.

Unveiling the Soul in the Knowing of Thyself

Embracing Your Own Unique Gnostic Path

David Brooks' 'How to Know a Person' is a seminal work that delves into the art and science of truly understanding another human being. Spanning three comprehensive parts, the book is a meticulous exploration of the complexities involved in deeply seeing, empathizing with, and accurately knowing another person.

Part I: The Art of Seeing: The first part discusses the challenges in truly seeing someone. It highlights the often-overlooked fact that our perceptions are clouded by our biases, experiences, and the limitations of our understanding. Brooks emphasizes the need for humility in acknowledging these limitations. He suggests that truly seeing another requires us to step outside our own perspectives and prejudices, to observe not just with our eyes, but with our hearts.

Part II: Vulnerability and Empathy in Understanding: In the second part, Brooks delves into the roles of vulnerability and empathy in making others feel seen. He argues that empathy is not just about understanding someone else's feelings, but also about being open to being affected by them. This requires vulnerability - a willingness to expose our own emotions and prejudices in the process of understanding another. Brooks proposes that this vulnerability is not a weakness, but a strength that fosters deeper connections and understanding.

Part III: The Effort to Know and Value Others: The final part of the book discusses the effort required to accurately know another person. Brooks suggests that this involves active listening, patience, and the continuous endeavor to understand someone's context, background, and life experiences. He emphasizes that making this effort is crucial in letting others feel valued, heard, and understood. It is about recognizing the uniqueness of each individual and appreciating their intrinsic worth.

Embracing the Shadow, Carl Jung's Contribution: Carl Jung's theories about the shadow and projection are crucial in understanding the complexities of knowing ourselves and others. According to Jung, the shadow consists of the parts of ourselves that we deny or repress, often projecting these traits onto others. When attempting to truly know a person, as per David Brooks' teachings, recognizing and integrating our shadow becomes imperative. It involves acknowledging our own flaws, biases, and insecurities, which are often mirrored in our interactions. This self-awareness is a step towards genuine understanding and empathy, as it allows us to see others more clearly, free from the distortions of our own shadow.

Power of Vulnerability, Brene Brown's Insights: Brené Brown's teachings on vulnerability complement Jung's concepts of shadow and projection. Brown argues that vulnerability is the birthplace of innovation, creativity, and change. By embracing vulnerability, we open ourselves to truly understanding others and being understood in return. This means not only acknowledging our shadows, but also sharing them with others. Such openness can lead to deeper connections, as it fosters an environment of mutual trust and authenticity, aligning well with Brooks' emphasis on the necessity of vulnerability in truly knowing a person.

Metacognition, Insights from Prof Steve Peters: Prof Steve Peters' teachings on metacognition - the ability to think about one's own thinking processes - adds another layer to this synthesis. Metacognition allows individuals to step back and observe their thoughts and reactions as they occur, providing a clearer understanding of their own mental and emotional processes. This self-reflection is crucial in disentangling one's projections and biases (as per Jung) and in embracing vulnerability (as per Brown). It aids in navigating the complexities of human relationships with a more balanced and impartial perspective, a cornerstone in Brooks' approach to understanding others.

The Gnostic Path and the Way of Impartial Nobility: Integrating these diverse teachings leads to a comprehensive understanding of the challenges involved in embracing one's unique gnostic path via the way of impartial nobility. The gnostic path, in this context, refers to a journey of deep self-knowledge and understanding. It is about recognizing and integrating the different aspects of the self - the conscious and the unconscious, the strengths and the vulnerabilities. The way of impartial nobility involves approaching this journey with fairness, open-mindedness, and a commitment to personal growth and understanding.

The integration of the teachings of Carl Jung, Brené Brown, Prof Steve Peters, and David Brooks provides a robust framework for not only understanding others, but also for a profound self-exploration. For we must go beyond superficial interactions to attempt to know another; it is an intricate process that requires humility, empathy, vulnerability, and a dedicated effort to appreciate the multifaceted nature of every individual. By engaging this gnostic journey to self-awareness, we gain a more holistic understanding of what it means to be authentically connected with others.

We must come to understand that embracing our shadows, being vulnerable, and practicing metacognition; are essential steps on the path to truly knowing a person and ourselves. This journey is not without its challenges, but it is one that promises a richer, more authentic experience of life and relationships. By embracing this gnostic path, *via the way of impartial nobility,* we open ourselves to a world of deeper connections, self-discovery; and ultimately, a more fulfilling human experience.

FOSTERING A MORE EQUITABLE AND DEMOCRATIC GLOBAL ORDER

Part 1: The Quest for Contentment

Bertrand Russell's "The Conquest of Happiness" is an early exploration of the psychological underpinnings of what it means to live a fulfilled life. Russell posits that happiness is attainable through the cultivation of interests outside oneself, the pursuit of meaningful work, and the nurturing of affectionate relationships.

- Individual Well-being: Russell emphasizes the importance of overcoming petty worries and self-absorption to achieve personal well-being.

- *Scientific Support:* Psychological research supports Russell's claim, showing that altruistic behavior and purposeful activities are closely linked to increased life satisfaction.

Part 2: Formulas for Fulfillment

Scott Galloway's "The Algebra of Happiness" provides a contemporary take on the pursuit of happiness in the context of modern society, technology, and entrepreneurship. Galloway suggests that understanding the 'algebra' or the variables and equations that govern our well-being is crucial for a balanced and contented life.

- Balancing Life's Equations: Galloway discusses how different life choices and priorities can be weighed to maximize happiness.

- *Scientific Support:* Studies in happiness economics corroborate the idea that life satisfaction is influenced by a complex interplay of factors, including health, wealth, relationships, and career success.

Part 3: Lasting Achievement

Jerry Porras' "Success Built to Last" delves into the patterns of behavior and thought that contribute to enduring success. Drawing from interviews with over 200 successful people, the book outlines the importance of passion, perseverance, and intrinsic motivation in achieving long-term goals.

- Sustainable Success: Porras identifies passion and purpose as the cornerstones of sustained achievement.

- *Scientific Support:* The psychological concept of grit and the research on intrinsic versus extrinsic motivation reinforce Porras' findings, linking perseverance and passion to long-term success.

Part 4: Inner Struggles

In "Fear No Evil," Eva Pierrakos and Donovan Thesenga tackle the spiritual and psychological challenges individuals face when confronting their inner darkness. The book argues for the need to acknowledge and transform negative emotions and patterns to evolve spiritually and emotionally.

- Confronting the Shadow: Pierrakos and Thesenga encourage readers to confront their inner 'demons' to attain personal growth.

- *Scientific Support:* Jungian psychology's concept of the 'shadow' and the therapeutic process of integration, align with the book's approach to personal transformation.

Part 5: Social Movement Dynamics

"Comparative Perspective on Social Movements," edited by Doug McAdam, provides an analytical framework for understanding the genesis, progression, and impact of social movements. The book examines the role of political opportunities, mobilizing structures, and cultural framing in driving social change.

The synthesis of these texts presents a compelling argument for why humanity must transcend its innate narcissism to foster a more equitable and democratic global order. Bertrand Russell and Scott Galloway's insights on happiness lay the groundwork for understanding individual motivations. Jerry Porras' research on sustained success offers a blueprint for long-term societal achievement. Eva Pierrakos and Donovan Thesenga's spiritual guidance provides the tools for inner transformation necessary to engage in the way of impartial nobility.

McAdam's analysis of social movements becomes the capstone, suggesting that the collective knowledge from the first four books is pivotal in empowering humanity to rise above selfish interests. *The integration of political opportunities, mobilizing structures, and cultural framing is essential in the creation of a Libertarian Federation of Nations that can effectively counter global elitist forces.*

LUVRules.com emerges as a crucial platform to facilitate this transformation, enabling the kind of deliberate, logical System 2 thinking that can challenge narcissistic tendencies and promote the collective good. By harnessing the principles of happiness, enduring success, inner growth, and social mobilization, LUVRules.com can support the Constitutional Convention needed to reform global governance and safeguard the future of democracy.

IGNITING THE KETER OF SOPHIA CONSCIOUSNESS
Suggested Reading List

Understanding the interconnectedness of the following thirteen books requires delving into the core themes they explore: self-discovery, spirituality, personal growth, and universal consciousness. Reading them in the presented order can facilitate a deeper comprehension of each book's message and how they collectively contribute to a broader understanding of life and existence.

1. *Jonathan Livingston Seagull by Richard Bach* sets the stage with its allegorical tale of a seagull seeking a higher purpose beyond the mundane life of his flock. It represents the individual's journey towards self-improvement and the pursuit of excellence.

2. Moving to *Ishmael by Daniel Quinn*, the narrative shifts to a Socratic dialogue between a man and a gorilla, exploring the mythological foundations of civilization and challenging the reader to consider humanity's role in the world's ecological balance.

3. The *Four Agreements by Don Miguel Ruiz* offers practical guidance on personal freedom, proposing four fundamental agreements to live by as a framework for personal liberation and transformation.

4. The *Way of the Peaceful Warrior by Dan Millman* continues the theme of personal development, blending fact and fiction to illustrate a journey of spiritual growth, emphasizing the importance of living in the present moment.

5. In *The Celestine Prophecy by James Redfield*, the reader is introduced to a spiritual adventure, uncovering nine insights into life that lead to a greater understanding of the unseen spiritual forces that affect our lives.

6. *Conversations with God: Book 1 by Neale Donald Walsch* further expands on the theme of spiritual dialogue, presenting a series of conversations with God that challenge conventional religious beliefs and encourage a more personal and direct relationship with the divine.

7. *Bringers of the Dawn by Barbara Marciniak* delves into the concept of channeling and the transmission of knowledge from extraterrestrial beings, suggesting that humanity is on the cusp of a major evolutionary leap in consciousness.

8. In *Tomorrow's God by Walsch*, the exploration of divinity continues, advocating for a new understanding of God and spirituality that transcends traditional religious doctrines and embraces a more inclusive, universal perspective.

9. *Mastery of Love by Ruiz* builds upon the agreements previously discussed and focuses on relationships and the art of love as a path to spiritual mastery and personal fulfillment.

10. *The Prophet by Kahlil Gibran* offers a series of poetic essays on various aspects of life, such as love, marriage, and work, providing timeless wisdom on the human condition and the interconnectedness of all experiences.

11. *The Power of Now by Eckhart Tolle* emphasizes the importance of living in the present moment as a means of achieving spiritual enlightenment, resonating with the messages of mindfulness and presence found in the earlier works.

12. *Earth by Marciniak* returns to the theme of channeling, offering teachings purportedly from the Pleiadeans about consciousness, the nature of reality, and the potential future of humanity.

13. Finally, *The Impersonal Life by Joseph Sieber Benner* presents the concept that the divine presence is within everyone and that realizing this inner divinity is key to personal enlightenment and transformation.

Reading these books sequentially can create a layered understanding of spirituality and self-empowerment. Starting with the individual quest and moving through societal constructs, interpersonal relationships, and ultimately reaching cosmic and divine insights, this journey mirrors the personal growth path many seekers find themselves on. The progression from one book to the next can act as steppingstones, where each book lays the groundwork for the themes and revelations of the next, culminating in a comprehensive tapestry of wisdom that transcends the sum of its parts.

A Message from the Pleiadeans

Dear Human Earthlings,

As the Pleiadeans, we observe from afar, yet we are intricately connected to the saga of your existence. Within the tapestry of your history, a profound and unsettling chapter of totalitarianism unfolds. It tells of the fall of the Anunnaki, known to you as the 'Sons of EL,' highly evolved part-reptilian humanoids from an alternate dimensional-timeframe.

This schism amongst these celestial architects led to cosmic wars, casting the archon Enlil, or EL, into the nether reaches of existence. The quest of the fallen Anunnaki to resurrect their deity has unwittingly ensnared humanity in their intricate web. Their machinations opened a portal to your world, mining the essence of human anguish to fuel their dark endeavors.

> In a malevolent ploy, they orchestrate chaos, breeding a landscape where humans plead for a semblance of order. Yet, this 'New World Order' is but a facade, a means to ensure your subservience, monitored and manipulated by invisible threads.

The genetic experiments of these creator gods, akin to the royal bloodlines of your European monarchies, merged lineages to spawn a variety of beings. Their grasp on genetics and life force manipulation is a testament to their advanced knowledge, albeit used with reckless abandon. The Lizzies, as we humorously refer to these part-reptilian entities, are beings lost in their own unenlightened practices, shaping existence through the lens of fear and dominion over life.

These beings are not solely reptilian; the creator gods embody diverse forms. Us Pleiadeans align with the birdlike and reptilian creator gods, marking just a fraction of the vast cosmic cultures. Ancient Earth's symbology of birds and reptiles in civilizations across Egypt and the Americas hint at this once harmonious, now tumultuous, coalition.

The Lizzies' manipulation extends beyond the physical, as they amplify Earth's emotional chaos to nourish their existence. Portals, gateways to your planet's dimensional fabric, are their conduits. These portals, especially the contentious one in the Middle East, have been pivotal in human history, acting as stages for religious and cultural narratives, all choreographed by these interdimensional beings.

The struggle for control over these portals, such as the ancient space colony nestled between the Tigris and Euphrates, is a struggle for the direction of human evolution. It is an area fraught with clandestine bases, serving as the Lizzies' command centers for the broader manipulation of human society.

Within these beings, as within all, exists a spectrum of benevolence and malevolence. Our purpose in sharing this is not to instill fear but to arm you with knowledge. Your evolution is not merely an ascension into blissful ignorance; it requires an understanding of the multitudinous realities and entities that share your cosmic lineage.

As you awaken to these truths, you are called to harmonize with all aspects of creation. This is the crux of your evolutionary leap—recognizing the diverse facets of reality, embracing them, and through this union, forging a path back to the Prime Creator. Only through this profound synthesis can you transcend the shadows cast by those who once sought to dominate your destiny.

Out of suffering have emerged the strongest souls;
the most massive characters are seared with scars.

- Kahlil Gibran

The Imperative Call for a Constitutional Convention
A Foreboding Warning

Prelude to a New Dawn

In the shrouded darkness of our current era, humanity faces a peril of unprecedented scale - a peril rooted in avarice and the erosion of mutual trust. The specter of rampant capitalism, with its insidious whispers and deceitful allure, erodes the moral fabric of society, leaving behind a wasteland where trust is a casualty, and society's spirit languishes, betrayed and forsaken.

The Captain's Proclamation

As the self-appointed steward of Spaceship Earth, I stand before you to sound a clarion call. We are on the brink of a catastrophic convergence - a synergy of autocratic fascism, techno-feudalism, and narcissistic hierarchies, all heralding the potential demise of human civilization in the fires of World War III, *or some other unforeseen global extinction event.*

The Narcissistic Hierarchy and Its Perils

Within the labyrinth of traditional hierarchical structures, those with narcissistic tendencies ascend to power, driven by an insatiable hunger for adulation and dominance. These individuals, ensconced in positions of authority, foster bureaucratic stagnation and suppress the innovative spirit, centralizing control and silencing dissent. This environment of suppression, *devoid of checks and balances,* cultivates a toxic dynamic, stifling growth and breeding a culture of fear and resentment.

The Dystopian Nightmare: Autocratic Fascism and Techno-Feudalism

The harrowing synergy of autocratic fascism and techno-feudalism presents a dire scenario. Autocratic fascism, with its authoritarian grip and militant nationalism, suppresses individual freedoms, while techno-feudalism grants unchecked power to corporate leviathans, wielding technology as a tool of domination. These forces will unite, unchecked, and will steer us toward a dystopian nightmare, where freedom is a relic and democracy a forgotten ideal.

The Crucial Nexus: Crisis and Cooperation

In the face of global crises, these authoritarian structures pose a significant threat to collaborative and effective response. Autocratic fascism may expedite decision-making but at the cost of exacerbating international tensions and quashing dissent. Conversely, techno-feudalism prioritizes corporate interests over public welfare, hindering unified global action. Without a new Federation of Nations and a guiding vision for equitable resource distribution, the chasm between these disparate entities widens, obstructing the path to a harmonious and sustainable future.

Integrating the Bonobo Mind: A New Perspective in Human Dynamics

To navigate this complex landscape, we must integrate the 'Bonobo Mind' into Steve Peters' 'Chimp Mind' theory. The 'Chimp Mind' symbolizes our primal, emotional instincts, while the 'Bonobo Mind' represents our desire for pleasure, harmony, and social bonding. This addition emphasizes the importance of peaceful conflict resolution, pleasure-seeking, and social connectivity as crucial elements of human nature. Alongside the 'Human Mind', which embodies logic and rationality, and the 'Computerized Autopilot' of habitual behavior, this expanded model captures the full spectrum of human motivations and actions.

The Call to Action: A Constitutional Convention for a New Era

In light of these revelations, the urgent need for a Constitutional Convention becomes clear. This convention must forge a new path, one that transcends the limitations of our current political and social constructs. It is a call for a reimagined libertarian America, one that actively participates in a global reformation through the establishment of a new Federation of Nations. This reformation will act as a bulwark against the rise of a despotic one-world government and the elitist cabals that threaten to subvert the very essence of democracy.

Embracing a Vision of Impartial Nobility

Our endeavor must be grounded in a vision of impartial nobility, where the principles of equal dignity, justice, and liberty are not mere ideals, but tangible realities. We must strive to create a society where power is distributed equitably, where every voice is heard, and where the collective welfare supersedes individual greed.

The Foreboding Warning: A Choice Between Two Futures

As we stand at this critical juncture, we face a choice between two futures. One is a dystopian world ruled by autocratic forces, where individual freedoms are trampled, and the human spirit is shackled. The other is a world reborn, guided by the principles of libertarianism, where a new Federation of Nations ushers in an era of cooperation, innovation, and sustainable progress.

Conclusion: A Beacon of Hope in a Time of Despair

This Constitutional Convention is not merely a political undertaking; it is a beacon of hope in a time of despair, a rallying cry for all who yearn for a world defined by freedom, equal dignity, and unity of purpose. Let us heed this call with courage and conviction, forging a future where Spaceship Earth sails towards a horizon of hope, leaving behind the shadows of our tumultuous past. The time for action is now; the destiny of humanity rests in our hands. Let us rise to this monumental challenge and create a legacy that will echo through the annals of history.

My dream is of a place and a time where America will once again
be seen as the last best hope of earth.

– *Abraham Lincoln*

Made in the USA
Monee, IL
23 February 2024

53453085R00208